COMPUTATIONAL INTELLIGENCE APPLICATIONS FOR TEXT AND SENTIMENT DATA ANALYSIS

Hybrid Computational Intelligence for Pattern Analysis and Understanding

COMPUTATIONAL INTELLIGENCE APPLICATIONS FOR TEXT AND SENTIMENT DATA ANALYSIS

Series Editors

SIDDHARTHA BHATTACHARYYA
NILANJAN DEY

Edited by

DIPANKAR DAS
ANUP KUMAR KOLYA
ABHISHEK BASU
SOHAM SARKAR

ACADEMIC PRESS
An imprint of Elsevier

ISBN: 978-0-323-90535-0

For information on all Academic Press publications
visit our website at https://www.elsevier.com/books-and-journals

Publisher: Mara Conner
Editorial Project Manager: Zsereena Rose Mampusti
Production Project Manager: Swapna Srinivasan
Cover Designer: Greg Harris

Typeset by VTeX

Working together
to grow libraries in
developing countries

www.elsevier.com • www.bookaid.org

Contents

List of contributors

Abhishek Basu
Department of Computer Science & Engineering, RCC Institute of Information Technology, Kolkata, India

Subhayan Bhattacharya
Department of Computer Science and Engineering, Jadavpur University, Kolkata, West Bengal, India

Pushpak Bhattacharyya
Department of Computer Science & Engineering, Indian Institute of Technology Bombay, Powai, India

Erik Cambria
Nanyang Technological University, Singapore, Singapore

Arunava Kumar Chakraborty
Department of Computer Science & Engineering, RCC Institute of Information Technology, Kolkata, India

A. Chatterjee
Techno College Hooghly, Kolkata, West Bengal, India

Chitrita Chaudhuri
Department of Computer Science and Engineering, Jadavpur University, Kolkata, India

Chandrayee Chowdhury
Department of Computer Science and Engineering, Jadavpur University, Kolkata, West Bengal, India

A. Das
RCCIIT, Kolkata, West Bengal, India

B. Das
Techno College Hooghly, Kolkata, West Bengal, India

Dipankar Das
Dept. of Computer Science & Engineering, Jadavpur University, Kolkata, India

Sourav Das

Maulana Abul Kalam Azad University of Technology, Kolkata, India

Monalisa Dey

Institute of Engineering and Management, Kolkata, India

Paramita Dey

Department of Computer Science and Engineering, Jadavpur University, Kolkata, West Bengal, India

Rishi Dey

Indian Statistical Institute, Kolkata, India

Rounak Dutta

Livpure Smart Homes Pvt. Ltd., Bengaluru, India

Asif Ekbal

Department of Computer Science & Engineering, Indian Institute of Technology Patna, Patna, India

Soumitra Ghosh

Department of Computer Science & Engineering, Indian Institute of Technology Patna, Patna, India

Souvick Ghosh

School of Information, San José State University, San José, CA, United States

Aditya Joshi

SEEK, Melbourne, VIC, Australia

Diptesh Kanojia

Surrey Institute for People-centred AI, Guildford, United Kingdom

Anup Kumar Kolya

Department of Computer Science & Engineering, RCC Institute of Information Technology, Kolkata, India

Radhika Mamidi

IIIT Hyderabad, LTRC, Hyderabad, India

Mounika Marreddy

IIIT Hyderabad, LTRC, Hyderabad, India

Anupam Mondal

Institute of Engineering and Management, Kolkata, India

Sarbani Roy

Department of Computer Science and Engineering, Jadavpur University, Kolkata, West Bengal, India

Anindita Saha

Department of Computer Science and Engineering, Jadavpur University, Kolkata, West Bengal, India

Soham Sarkar

Department of Computer Science & Engineering, RCC Institute of Information Technology, Kolkata, India

Sankhamita Sinha

Department of Computer Science and Engineering, Jadavpur University, Kolkata, West Bengal, India

About the editors

Dipankar Das, PhD, Assistant Professor, Department of Computer Science & Engineering, Jadavpur University, Kolkata, India

Dr. Dipankar Das is an Assistant Professor in the Computer Science and Engineering Department, Jadavpur University, Kolkata, India and the Visveswaraya Young Faculty, Ministry of Electronics and Information Technology (MeitY), Government of India. Before that, he served as an Assistant Professor in the Computer Science and Engineering Department, National Institute of Technology (NIT), Meghalaya, and the Government of India from 2012 to 2014. His research interests are in the area of Natural Language and Speech Processing, especially in Emotion and Sentiment Analysis, Machine Translation, Social-Texts Analytics, Information Extraction, Machine Learning, Data Science, HCI, etc. He leads several research projects such as "Sevak – An Intelligent Indian Language Chatbot" under the IMPRINT II research scheme, funded by the Science & Engineering Research Board (SERB), DST, Government of India, "Claim Detection and Verification using Deep NLP: an Indian Perspective" funded by the Defence Research and Development Organisation (DRDO), "Detect Behavioral Maladjustments of Students through Sentiment Analysis from Social Media", funded by UGC RUSA 2.0 and "Preparing annotated corpus of three lesser known languages of West Bengal," funded by UGC RUSA 2.0, respectively. He has more than 200 publications in top journals, conferences, and workshops.

Anup Kumar Kolya, PhD, Assistant Professor, Department of Computer Science & Engineering, RCC Institute of Information Technology, Kolkata, India

Dr. Anup Kumar Kolya received his Ph.D. (Engg) from Jadavpur University, India in 2015. He is currently an Assistant Professor at the RCC Institute of Information Technology, Kolkata, India. He served as a postgraduate Program Coordinator in the Computer Science and Engineering Department from 4/4/2018 to 5/1/2020. Prior to this, he was a senior research engineer at Jadavpur University, from 2/1/2009 to 1/5/2014. Before that, he served as a lecturer in the Computer Science and Engineering Department of the Mallabhum Institute of Technology Bishnupur, India from 2005 to 2006. He is the co-editor of one book. Moreover, he has more than 40 research publications in international journals, conference proceedings, and edited volumes to his credit. He has been a program committee member, organizing committee member, publication chair, and reviewer of various international journals, book chapters, and conferences. His research interests include natural language processing, social-media data analysis, the Internet of things, and text-image data analysis.

Abhishek Basu, PhD, Associate Professor, Department of Electronics and Communication & Engineering, RCC Institute of Information Technology, Kolkata, India

Dr. Abhishek Basu received his PhD (Engg) from Jadavpur University, India in 2015. He is currently an Associate Professor and Faculty in Charge (Academics) at the RCC Institute of Information Technology, Kolkata, India. He served as an Undergraduate Program Coordinator and Head of Department in the Electronics and Communication Engineering Department (30/03/16–01/01/17 and 01/01/17–31/12/18, respectively). Prior to this, he was a lecturer of Electronics and Communication Engineering at the Guru Nanak Institute of Technology, Kolkata, India from 2008 to 2009. Before that, he served as a lecturer of Electronics and Communication Engineering at the Mallabhum Institute of Technology Bishnupur, India from 2005 to 2007. He is co-author of a book and co-editor of two books. Moreover, he has more than 50 research publications in international journals, conference proceedings and edited volumes to his credit. He has also filed three Indian patents to date. His research interests include digital image processing, visual-information hiding, IP-protection techniques, FPGA-based system design, low-power VLSI Design, and embedded system design. He is a lifetime member of the Indian Association for Productivity, Quality & Reliability, India and the Institute of Engineers (India). He is also a member of the IEEE and the International Association of Engineers.

Soham Sarkar, PhD, Associate Professor, Department of Electronics and Communication & Engineering, RCC Institute of Information Technology, Kolkata, India

Dr. Soham Sarkar received his PhD in Electronics and Telecommunication Engineering in 2016 from Jadavpur University, Kolkata. He is currently serving as an Associate Professor in the Department of Electronics and Communication Engineering, the RCC Institute of Information Technology, Kolkata, India. He has more than 12 years of teaching experience in academia. His research interests include Evolutionary Algorithms,

Soft-Computing Techniques, Pattern Recognition, and Digital-Image Processing. He has published his works in leading international journals and conference proceedings. He has 400+ Google Scholar citations to date. He has been associated with the program committees and organizing committees of several renowned regular international conferences including ISSIP, FUZZ-IEEE, SEMCCO, ICAPR, ICRCICN, etc. He is also co-editor of one book.

Preface

Sentiment-data analysis is a rapidly growing field of research that has become increasingly important in recent years as more and more data is being generated on social-media platforms and other online sources. With the escalation of social media and the profusion of online reviews and feedback, understanding and analyzing sentiment has become vital for commerce, administrations, and individuals.

This edited volume offers a wide-ranging overview of the state-of-the-art advancements in computational-intelligence applications for sentiment-data analysis. The volume brings together leading researchers and practitioners from academia to share their insights on the use of computational-intelligence techniques for analyzing and extracting sentiment information from large-scale datasets. This volume covers a wide range of topics and we anticipate that this volume will serve as a valuable resource for researchers and practitioners.

The book is organized into 11 chapters, covering various aspects of sentiment analysis, including Emotion Recognition, Social-Network Sensing, the Human–Computer Interface, Medical Corpus Annotation System Learning Sentiment Analysis, etc. Each chapter presents a particular aspect of sentiment analysis, providing readers with a comprehensive understanding of the state-of-the-art techniques and tools in the field.

Foreword

The ability to analyze and understand sentiment has become increasingly important in today's digital age. Sentiment analysis is one of the most rapidly growing research areas in artificial intelligence and machine learning, motivated by the explosion of online social-media platforms and other digital sources of information. The application of computational intelligence in sentiment-data analysis has opened up new possibilities for extracting insights and understanding sentiment at scale.

This edited volume brings together leading researchers and practitioners to share their expertise and insights in this rapidly evolving field. The chapters in this volume cover a wide range of topics, from machine-learning algorithms to natural language-processing techniques, providing a comprehensive overview of the latest developments in sentiment-data analysis. As the field of sentiment-data analysis continues to evolve, this volume will serve as a valuable resource for anyone interested in applying computational intelligence to this important area.

This edited volume on computational–intelligence applications for sentiment–data analysis is a timely and much–needed contribution to the field. It brings together some of the most talented researchers and practitioners to share their knowledge and expertise on the latest advances in this exciting area of research. The volume covers a wide range of topics related to sentiment analysis.

We are confident that this volume will serve as an excellent resource for researchers, academics, and practitioners working in the field of sentiment analysis, and we strongly recommend it to anyone interested in this exciting area of research.

Editors

CHAPTER 1

Sentiment analysis and computational intelligence

Dipankar Das[a], Anup Kumar Kolya[b], Soham Sarkar[b], and Abhishek Basu[b]

[a]Dept. of Computer Science & Engineering, Jadavpur University, Kolkata, India
[b]Department of Computer Science & Engineering, RCC Institute of Information Technology, Kolkata, India

1.1 Introduction

The task of obtaining and analyzing people's attitudes toward particular things from text texts is known as Sentiment Analysis (SA) [1]. In the literature, sentiment analysis is often referred to as opinion mining. However, there is a difference between "sentiments" and "opinions." In other words, whereas sentiment denotes a person's feelings towards something, opinions represent a person's perspectives on a certain subject. Nevertheless, the two ideas are closely equivalent, and opinion terms can frequently be employed to infer feelings [2,3].

Activities in the areas of opinion, sentiment, and/or emotion in natural language texts and other media are gaining ground under the umbrella of subjectivity analysis and affect computing [44]. Although sentiment-analysis research was started long ago and recently it is one of the hottest research topics, the question "What is subjectivity/sentiment/emotion?" still remains unanswered. It is very difficult to define sentiment and to identify its regulating or controlling factors. To date, moreover, no concise set of psychological and cognitive forces has been yet defined that really affects how writers' sentiment, i.e., broadly human sentiment, is expressed, perceived, recognized, processed, and interpreted in natural languages. In addition to being important for the advancement of Artificial Intelligence (AI), detecting and interpreting emotional information are key in multiple areas of computer science, e.g., human–computer interaction, e-learning, e-health, automotive, security, user profiling, and personalization. Thus this chapter highlights the impacts of such controlling factors for assessing sentiments expressed in natural languages with the help of recently developed intelligent techniques.

Computational Intelligence Applications for Text and Sentiment Data Analysis
https://doi.org/10.1016/B978-0-32-390535-0.00006-9
1

Computational Intelligence (CI) is defined as the theory, design, application, and development of biologically and linguistically motivated computational paradigms.[1] Currently, various large companies are using several computational-intelligence algorithms to understand customer's attitudes towards a product to successfully run their business. In that way, SA emerges as the current area in decision making. Amazon and Uber, providing services to more than 500 cities across the world, are two giant companies worldwide. These companies collect many suggestions, feedback, and complaints from customers. Often, social media (Facebook, Twitter, news) is used as the most favorable medium to record such issues.

Computational-Intelligence (CI) techniques play important roles here to solve the inherent problems of sentiment-analysis applications. For example, CI can be employed to forecast future market direction after sentiment analysis on a huge number of social-media datasets via feature selection and extraction, outlier detection, and de-noising, and time-series segmentation. Many state-of-the-art CI techniques exist, like Convolutional Neural Network, Fuzzy and Rough Set, Global Optimizers, and hybrid techniques. Several machine-learning and deep-learning tools are currently widely used to detect the sentiments of users more accurately.

Sentiment analysis can be applied as a new research method for mass opinion estimation (e.g., reliability, validity, and sample bias), psychiatric treatment, corporate-reputation measurement, political-orientation categorization, stock-market prediction, customer-preference study, public-opinion study, and so on. However, the challenges are also really huge, while coping with its fine-grained aspects. Thus this chapter illuminates the industrial aspects of sentiment analysis with its real-life challenging factors.

The remainder of this chapter lists themes and challenges followed by some common goals of sentiment-data analysis with the help of computational intelligence. The chapter also presents various contributions from the industrial and academic perspectives, after which some concluding remarks are made.

1.2 Themes and challenges

Human–machine interface technology has been investigated for several decades. Scientists have identified that emotion technology may be consid-

---

[1] https://cis.ieee.org/about/what-is-ci.

ered as an important component in artificial intelligence. Recent research has placed more focus on the recognition of nonverbal information, and has especially focused on emotion reaction. There exist several frameworks from various fields of academic study, such as cognitive science, linguistics, and psychology that can inform and augment analyses of sentiment, opinion, and emotion [45].

The main themes of sentiment analysis are to i) identify subjective information from text, i.e., the exclusion of 'neutral' or 'factual' comments that do not carry sentiment information, ii) identify sentiment polarity and iii) domain dependency. Spam and fake-news detection, abbreviation, sarcasm, word-negation handling, and much word ambiguity are the other wings of this in recent trends. Moreover, it is difficult to extract sentiment from different multimodal contexts (audio, video, and text), semantic (concept).

Subjectivity Analysis aims to identify whether a sentence expresses an opinion or not and if so, whether the opinion is *positive* or *negative*. In contrast, the emotions are the subjective feelings and thoughts and the strengths of opinions are closely related to the intensities of certain emotions, e.g., *joy* and *anger* [46]. Though the concepts of emotions and opinions are not equivalent, they have a large intersection of ideas. In addition, Affect Computing, a key area of research in computer science is a Natural Language Processing (NLP) technique for recognizing the emotive aspect of text.

Based on different aspects of design, application, sources of data, etc., sentiment analysis forebears a variety of challenges:

1. **Granularity**: Sentiment can be predicted at various levels: starting from sentiment associations of words and phrases; to sentiment of sentences, SMS, chats, and tweets; to sentiment in product reviews, blog posts, and whole documents. Often, the sentiment at higher granularity does not necessarily align with the composition of lower granularity.

2. **Sentiment of the speaker vs. of the listener**: Although sentiment may appear to be clear-cut at first glance, closer examination reveals that sentiment can be connected to any of the following: 1. One or more of the entities named in the utterance. 2. The speaker or writer. 3. The listener or reader. The vast bulk of sentiment-analysis research has concentrated on identifying the speaker's emotions, which is frequently accomplished by merely looking at the utterance. There are, however, a number of situations in which it is not evident if the speaker's sentiment and the sentiment expressed in the speech are the same. On the other hand, individuals can have various responses to the same statement, such as opposing viewpoints or competing sports fans.

Thus it is necessary to model listener profiles in order to model listener sentiment. The community has not done much study in this area.

3. **Aspect**: A product or service review can convey feelings on a variety of elements. For instance, a restaurant review may be complimentary of the service but unfavorable toward the food. Currently, there is a growing body of research on both the detection of product attributes in text and the assessment of sentiment toward these attributes.

It can be concluded that the perspectives of sociology, psychology, and commerce along with the close association among people, topic, and sentiment motivate us to investigate the inside of emotional changes of people over topic and time. Thus sentiment tracking not only aims to track a single user's comments on the same topic but also on different topics to analyze the changes in emotion with respect to topic and time. Tracking of mass emotions on a certain subject/topic/event over time is also considered as an important dimension of research.

1.3 Goals

Sentiment analysis from natural language texts is a multi-faceted and multi-disciplinary problem. Research efforts are being carried out for the identification of positive or negative polarity of the evaluative text and also for the development of devices that recognize human affect, display, and model emotions from textual contents. Identifying the strength of sentiment in figurative texts, fine-grained sentiment analysis on financial micro-blogs or news, identifying aspects and categories in reviews and their sentiment expressed, detecting the stance from the tweet data, detecting rumor and humor, identifying the psychological condition of persons from chats, even detecting sentiment in clinical texts and the moods from music, etc., are the recent trends in the field of sentiment analysis.

The developments in the area of sentiment analysis are also gaining ground along with the advents of social media as it becomes the voice of millions of people over the decades. Social-media text has special relations with the real-time events. Multilingual users, often have the tendency to mix two or more languages while expressing their opinion on social media, this phenomenon leads to the generation of a new code-mixed language. The code-mixed problem is well studied in the field of NLP and several basic tools like POS tagging and Parsing have been developed for the code-mixed data. The study of sentiment analysis in code-mixed data is in its early stages [47].

Social-networking site (SNS) usage has become the most popular activity on the recent Web [48]. On the other hand, its dark side is associated with numerous negative outcomes. According to the studies [49], there exists a significant relationship between the usage of online social networks (OSN) and mental diseases like *depression, aggression, anxiety, stress, compulsion, isolation,* etc. One study [50] shows that adolescents who are suffering from social-network addictions have a much higher risk of suicidal inclination than non-addictive users of OSN.

On the other hand, it has also been observed that during the last decade, online social-networking sites such as Facebook, Twitter, MySpace, and so on have made many changes in the way people communicate and interact. People share their day-to-day thoughts, experiences, relationships, likes, dislikes, opinions, and even emotions, etc., on social-networking sites. Online social networks have created a platform for humans to share information at an unprecedented scale. However, most of the data in such social networks are unstructured in nature. The distillation of knowledge from such a large amount of unstructured information, however, is an extremely difficult task, as the contents of today's Web are perfectly suitable for human consumption, but remain barely accessible to machines [51] [52].

1.4 Recent advances in sentiment-data analysis

Sentiment-analysis models can generally be classified into three major categories: knowledge-based approaches, machine-learning models, and hybrid models.

1. **Knowledge-based methods**, commonly referred to as symbolic AI, are methods that rely on a knowledge foundation. Knowledge bases are knowledge warehouses with underlying sets of rules, relations, and assumptions from which a computer system can draw. As knowledge-based methods frequently use a knowledge base to derive features, they are intimately linked to the input representation. Interpretability is one of the benefits of knowledge-based techniques. Specifically, the information utilized to generate the model output is usually clear to identify. Knowledge-based solutions often have simple underlying mechanisms, allowing for extremely transparent approaches to sentiment classification. Although knowledge-based solutions do not require any training, the creation of knowledge bases can take a long time. Knowledge-based methods can be further classified into three subcategories:

a. **Dictionary-driven**: The majority of early classification approaches relied on dictionaries. Dictionary-based approaches create a feature vector x from a record R containing an aspect a, where each element x_i indicates an emotion score, or orientation, of a word in the context about the aspect. WordNet [4] and SentiWordNet [5] are two dictionaries that can be utilized with sentiment classification. These dictionaries identify groups of words as well as the linguistic relationships that exist between them. WordNet, for example, divides nouns, verbs, adjectives, and adverbs into synsets, which are collections of synonyms or groupings of words with the same meaning. As words and their synonyms usually convey the same emotion, these relationships can be used for sentiment classification [3]. As a result, we begin with a collection of seed words for which the sentiment has already been determined. For example, positive seed words include *"good," "great,"* and *"perfect,"* whereas negative seed words include *"awful," "boring,"* and *"ugly"*. These seed words can then be used to assess the sentiment of words surrounding an aspect by looking up synsets in a dictionary such as WordNet. Positive sentiment is assigned to words that are synonyms of a positive seed word or antonyms of a negative seed word. SentiWordNet is based on this concept in part. Using a mix of a seed-set expansion strategy and a number of classification models, this dictionary provides a sentiment label (*"positive," "neutral"* or *"negative"*) for each of the synsets.

b. **Ontology-based**: In general, ontology is defined as an "explicit, machine-readable specification of a shared conceptualization" that specifies a set of items and relations that correspond to their qualities [6,7]. Ontology differs from a dictionary in that it captures linguistic relationships between words, whereas ontology represents relationships between real items. These relationships can be utilized to determine which words in the record are crucial in deciding how people feel about a particular element. One can use an existing ontology or construct one based on the domain at hand for sentiment classification [8]. The semantically interconnected web communities (SIOC) ontology [9], which gathers data from online web communities, and the ontology of emotions proposed in [10] are two examples of existing ontologies. However, rather than relying on pre-existing ontologies, most academics prefer to construct their own. This is due to the difficulty of finding an ontology that is relevant to a certain topic, as many existing ontologies encapsulate very generic notions. The structure of objects in a domain is captured by ontologies. These relationships can be utilized to determine what context the aspect belongs in [8]. The sentiment label can then be determined by using a method based on the context acquired from the ontology. Using a dictionary-based sentiment classifier, for example, while standard ontologies are valuable for defining relationships between items, sentiment information can be added into the ontology to help with sentiment analysis [11,12]. These sentiment ontologies focus on sentiment relationships between words or entities.

c. **Discourse-based**: A discourse tree based on rhetorical structure theory (RST) [13] is another sort of knowledge base that can be utilized for sentiment categorization. In order to divide phrases into simple discourse units, RST can be used to create a hierarchical discourse structure inside a record (EDU). Discourse trees provide sets of relations that can be utilized, like ontologies, to pick out the key words when putting a sentiment classification on an aspect. The hierarchical discourse relations in a record are denoted by a discourse tree that is built for the record. The authors of [14] employ an RST-based method to create a sub-tree of the discourse tree that comprises the discourse relations specifically related to the aspect in order to ascertain the context surrounding an aspect in the record. The context tree is a sub-tree that can be utilized to ascertain the sentiment classification of a feature. The authors of [14] employ a dictionary-based method to label the leaf nodes of the context tree with sentiment-orientation scores for sentence-level classification because the context tree is devoid of sentiment information. Simply, evaluating the sum of the sentiment scores calculated for the context tree will yield the aspect's sentiment classification. A similar strategy is applied in [15] along with a more complex method of scoring aggregation. In addition to RST, there are different varieties of discourse-structure theories [16]. Cross-document structure theory (CST) [17], which may be used to analyze the structure and discourse relationships between groups of documents, serves as an illustration of this. Social-media posts are brief documents that are frequently heavily connected; therefore cross-document structure analysis might be helpful in social-media analysis. The SMACk system [18], which analyses a cross-document structure based on abstract argumentation theory [19], is an intriguing example of this. Products, for instance, frequently receive numerous reviews from different consumers, some of whom may comment to one another. To enhance the aggregate of the sentiment stated toward the various aspects, the SMACk system analyzes the relationships between the various arguments offered in the evaluations [20].

2. **Machine-learning methods**, sometimes referred to as sub-symbolic AI, use a training dataset of feature vectors and match correct labels as opposed to knowledge-based approaches, which draw on knowledge bases to accomplish a sentiment classification. One can generally identify three broad trends here: traditional ML models, neural models, and, pre-trained language models.

a. **Traditional ML**: Models like Support Vector Machines, Decision Tree, Random Forest, etc., work on a set of manually engineered features extracted from the text to produce a mapping from the feature space to the label space. For sentiment analysis, support vector machine (SVM) models [21] have long been a preferred option [22–26]. By creating a hyperplane that divides data vectors corresponding to the various classes, SVM models are classifiers that distinguish between categories. In the case of sentiment classification, this essentially involves categorizing sentences/documents into sentiment classes (*positive, neutral,* and *negative*) based on the feature vector. Despite the fact that decision-tree models have not been widely used for classification, there are few works that have effectively used these models. The authors in [27] proposed an incremental decision-tree model that performs better than the SVM model that was previously mentioned. On several datasets, a decision tree is demonstrated to perform better than a number of alternative models, including an SVM, in [28]. SVM models, however, can perform better than decision-tree models for other issues [29]. The essential issue with decision trees is over-fitting, which can be particularly difficult for classification because of the large number of features that are frequently employed. Using a random forest model, which is a collection of decision trees, can help resolve this issue [30].

b. **Neural Networks**: Neural models like Convolutional Neural Networks (CNN), Recurrent Neural Networks (RNN), etc., provide further automation. Unlike traditional ML systems, these models do not require manual selection of features. Rather, they treat the text as a sequence of symbols and translate this into a sequence-learning task. RNNs, particularly LSTMs, have been used extensively for sentiment classification [29,31]. Motivated by the computer-vision community, CNNs have also been used in this arena [32], particularly due to the extra speedup and fewer trainable parameters they offer. Attention mechanisms have been proposed to circumvent the difficulty RNNs face to model long-distance intra-token dependencies [33,34].

c. **Pre-trained Language Models**: With the advent of Transformers [35], pre-training large neural models on a large corpus to build a generic language model and using them in downstream NLP tasks have become the most popular approach recently [36–38]. There are two distinct types of such PLMs, namely Masked Language Models and Causal Language Models. MLMs are pre-trained by predicting randomly masked input words in a sentence; examples include BERT [36], RoBERTa [37], etc. In contrast, CLMs are much like traditional language models that are trained on sentence-completion tasks auto-regressively, for example, GPT-3 [38]. The applications of these two types of models for sentiment classification differ as well due to their different pre-training strategies. MLMs are typically utilized as earlier neural models: given a sentence, an MLM produces a hidden representation that is fed to a feed-forward classification layer to predict the classes [39–41]. CLMs are being used in classification tasks very recently, using a method called *prompt-based learning*. Given the input sentence, the CLM is fine tuned to complete prompts like "The sentiment expressed is ___" using words like "*positive*", "*negative*" or "*neutral*", accordingly [42,43].

1.4.1 Industrial and academic developments

Advancements in the area of sentiment analysis can be depicted by their recognition under the umbrella of industry and academia as well. In the case of industrial needs, Sentiment Analysis is crucial since it reveals the things that consumers like and dislike about a company (as shown in Fig. 1.1). In situations like this, where businesses may make use of audience behaviors, responses, and responses to generated content, it becomes incredibly helpful. Additionally, it can examine how a client views a company's board of

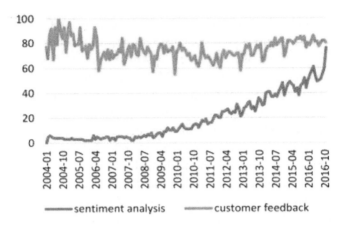

Figure 1.1 Sentiment Analysis based on Customer Feedback.

directors as well as other issues, services, and products. Through Sentiment Analysis, a company can/may:

- *Provide proactive solutions*: Business executives can utilize sentiment analysis to uncover the driving forces behind perceptions about a product or service that are either good, negative, or neutral. Blogs, reviews, forums, news articles, and social-media posts can all be used to find this information. Users can also track purchasing intent and benchmark competitors and marketplaces.
- *Provide audience insight*: Building a strong plan for future content and campaigns requires understanding how the audience responds to the pieces that are published. It is also possible to target particular client categories for future markets by using sentiment research to see which market segments respond well to advertisements.
- *Augment existing customer-service platforms*: The introduction of chatbots can undoubtedly enhance customer service by enabling a more individualized user experience. By using text mining to discover frequently asked queries, potential issues with the items could be found.

Recent advances include:

- The introduction of chatbots can undoubtedly enhance customer service by enabling a more individualized user experience. By using text mining to discover frequently asked queries, potential issues with the items could be found.[2]

[2] https://en.wikipedia.org/wiki/ChatGPT.

- With more than 90 million cars and other vehicles, the automotive industry is one of the major economic sectors in the world. Social-media data analysis can help marketers improve their marketing targets and objectives because the market is quite competitive. Unstructured tweets were analyzed using text mining and sentiment analysis in a recent study to uncover consumer perceptions of various automakers. According to the study, Audi received the most tweets with a favorable attitude, whereas Mercedes received the most tweets with a negative sentiment.[3]

- The insurance sector is another possible application area for NLP, sentiment analysis, and artificial intelligence. Insurance companies are notorious for their antiquated procedures, therefore using the afore-mentioned technologies to automate the procedures and lighten the strain on insurance agents would streamline the process and free up customers from having to deal with bureaucracy when filing claims. Some businesses that have used the technologies have noticed a consid-erable improvement in quality and processing speed.

- Chatbots are a popular example of how NLP and sentiment analysis are used. They function as a means of customer connection and operate through messaging apps. NLP and sentiment analysis are used by chat-bots to comprehend consumer requests and offer a more specialized level of service.

- Mood analysis from music is an emerging area in Music Information Retrieval (MIR). The popularity of downloading and purchasing of music from online music shops has been increasing. Similarly, with the rapid evolvement of technology, music is just a few clicks away, on almost any personal gadget, be it computers, portable music players, or smart phones. This fact underlines the importance of developing an automated process for its organization, management, search as well as generation of playlists and various other music-related applications. Recently, MIR based on emotions or moods has attracted researchers from all over the world because of its highly motivated implications in human–computer interactions.

- In the case of pandemics such as the COVID era, the utilization of sentiment and computational intelligence draws the most impor-tant system, i.e., the Healthcare Recommendation System (as shown

---

[3] https://www.linkedin.com/pulse/sentiment-analysis-applications-industry-vaikunta-raman.

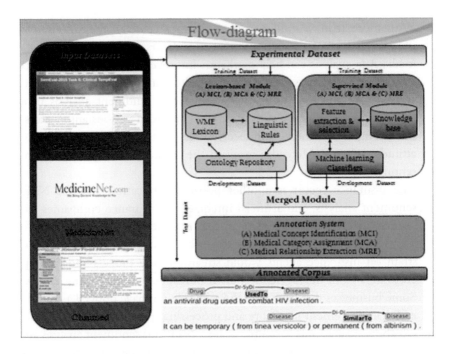

Figure 1.2 Overview of a Healthcare Recommendation System.

in Fig. 1.2) where you will receive enough guidance and support to cope with the primal emergencies.

1.5 Conclusions

Overall, the intents of the chapters in this book are designed in such a manner as to understand the fundamentals of the research topic of sentiment analysis and relate its impacts by employing and engaging strategies of computational intelligence. The challenges and applications are the two dimensions that attract each other to expedite the progress in this field with the new advents of intelligent methodologies. AI and its machine learning as well as deep-learning gadgets are being employed in a multi-modal fashion starting from texts, audio, and video to social-network graphs and virtual reality and for this very reason, the exploration of this area is becoming popular and purposeful, despite the challenging obstacles.

Every nook and corner of the world demands the tools and toys integrated with computational-intelligence techniques. Such techniques are not being developed under the umbrella of natural language processing solely but compiled with other accessories such as machine and deep learning. Hopefully, the various chapters in this book and their multifarious objectives will serve the purposes of the readers of all ages and professions and help their understanding in assessing the developments of the recent trends.

Sentiment Analysis is being practiced to date as a compensating study to overcome several multi-modal research problems. However, the emphasis became prominent and compulsory while dealing with social information shared across the globe. In order to guess the intuition of the web users on a large scale and to explore the unstructured corpus with a semantic axe for finding the emotions and psychology of people in general, the intelligent hands of machine learning and deep learning expedite the process of technological innovations on a large scale.

Hopefully, the next-generation machines will gain more intelligence in a lucid manner to predict emotions, feelings, and all types of affects. The ongoing technologies in terms of deep learning will pave the way for development of more nature-inspired approaches to the design of computationally intelligent sentiment-data analysis systems that will be capable of handling semantic knowledge and act as a platform to investigate concepts not only from linguistic patterns but also from audio, video, and social signals, etc.

References

[1] Bing Liu, Sentiment analysis and opinion mining, Synthesis Lectures on Human Language Technologies 5 (1) (2012) 1–167.
[2] Minqing Hu, Bing Liu, Mining and summarizing customer reviews, in: 10th ACM SIGKDD International Conference on Knowledge Discovery and Data Mining (KDD 2004), ACM, 2004, pp. 168–177.
[3] Minqing Hu, Bing Liu, Mining opinion features in customer reviews, in: 19th AAAI Conference on Artificial Intelligence (AAAI 2004), AAAI Press, 2004, pp. 755–760.
[4] George A. Miller, WordNet: a lexical database for English, Communications of the ACM 38 (11) (1995) 39–41.
[5] Stefano Baccianella, Andrea Esuli, Fabrizio Sebastiani, SentiWordNet 3.0: an enhanced lexical resource for sentiment analysis and opinion mining, in: 7th International Conference on Language Resources and Evaluation (LREC 2010), vol. 10, ELRA, 2010, pp. 2200–2204.
[6] Thomas R. Gruber, Toward principles for the design of ontologies used for knowledge sharing?, International Journal of Human-Computer Studies 43 (5–6) (1995) 907–928.
[7] Rudi Studer, V. Richard Benjamins, Dieter Fensel, Knowledge engineering: principles and methods, Data & Knowledge Engineering 25 (1–2) (1998) 161–197.
[8] Efstratios Kontopoulos, Christos Berberidis, Theologos Dergiades, Nick Bassiliades, Ontology-based sentiment analysis of Twitter posts, Expert Systems with Applications 40 (10) (2013) 4065–4074.

[9] SIOC, Semantically Interlinked Online Communities, http://sioc-project.org/, 2021.

[10] Kirk Roberts, Michael A. Roach, Joseph Johnson, Josh Guthrie, Sanda M. Harabagiu, EmpaTweet: annotating and detecting emotions on Twitter, in: 8th International Conference on Language Resources and Evaluation (LREC 2012), vol. 12, 2012, pp. 3806–3813.

[11] Xinhui Nie, Lizhen Liu, Hanshi Wang, Wei Song, Jingli Lu, The opinion mining based on fuzzy domain sentiment ontology tree for product reviews, Journal of Software 8 (11) (2013) 2682–2687.

[12] Katarzyna Wójcik, Janusz Tuchowski, Ontology based approach to sentiment analysis, in: 6th International Scientific Conference Faculty of Management Cracow University of Economics (CFM 2014), 2014.

[13] William C. Mann, Sandra A. Thompson, Rhetorical structure theory: toward a functional theory of text organization, Text-Interdisciplinary Journal for the Study of Discourse 8 (3) (1988) 243–281.

[14] Rowan Hoogervorst, Erik Essink, Wouter Jansen, Max Van Den Helder, Kim Schouten, Flavius Frasincar, Maite Taboada, Aspect-based sentiment analysis on the web using rhetorical structure theory, in: 16th International Conference on Web Engineering (ICWE 2016), in: LNCS, vol. 9671, Springer, 2016, pp. 317–334.

[15] Nuttapong Sanglerdsinlapachai, Anon Plangprasopchok, Ekawit Nantajeewarawat, Exploring linguistic structure for aspect-based sentiment analysis, Maejo International Journal of Science and Technology 10 (2) (2016) 142.

[16] Shengluan Hou, Shuhan Zhang, Chaoqun Fei, Rhetorical structure theory: a comprehensive review of theory, parsing methods and applications, Expert Systems with Applications 157 (2020) 113421.

[17] Dragomir Radev, Jahna Otterbacher, Zhu Zhang, CST Bank: a corpus for the study of cross-document structural relationships, in: Proceedings of the Fourth International Conference on Language Resources and Evaluation (LREC'04), Lisbon, Portugal, European Language Resources Association (ELRA), 2004.

[18] Mauro Dragoni, Célia da Costa Pereira, Andrea G.B. Tettamanzi, Serena Villata, SMACk: an argumentation framework for opinion mining, in: 25th International Joint Conference on Artificial Intelligence (IJCAI 2016), IJCAI, 2016, pp. 4242–4243.

[19] Phan Minh Dung, On the acceptability of arguments and its fundamental role in nonmonotonic reasoning, logic programming and n-person games, Artificial Intelligence 77 (2) (1995) 321–357.

[20] Mauro Dragoni, Celia da Costa Pereira, Andrea G.B. Tettamanzi, Serena Villata, Combining argumentation and aspect-based opinion mining: the SMACk system, AI Communications 31 (1) (2018) 75–95.

[21] Corinna Cortes, Vladimir Vapnik, Support-vector networks, Machine Learning 20 (3) (1995) 273–297.

[22] Mohammad Al-Smadi, Omar Qawasmeh, Mahmoud Al-Ayyoub, Yaser Jararweh, Brij Gupta, Deep recurrent neural network vs. support vector machine for aspect-based sentiment analysis of Arabic hotels reviews, Journal of Computational Science 27 (2018) 386–393.

[23] Tony Mullen, Nigel Collier, Sentiment analysis using support vector machines with diverse information sources, in: 2004 Conference on Empirical Methods in Natural Language Processing (EMNLP 2004), ACL, 2004, pp. 412–418.

[24] Bo Pang, Lillian Lee, Shivakumar Vaithyanathan, Thumbs up? Sentiment classification using machine learning techniques, in: 2002 Conference on Empirical Methods in Natural Language Processing (EMNLP 2002), ACL, 2002, pp. 79–86.

[25] Nipuna Upeka Pannala, Chamira Priyamanthi Nawarathna, J.T.K. Jayakody, Lakmal Rupasinghe, Kesavan Krishnadeva, Supervised learning based approach to aspect based sentiment analysis, in: 16th IEEE International Conference on Computer and Information Technology (CIT 2016), IEEE, 2016, pp. 662–666.

[26] R. Varghese, M. Jayasree, Aspect based sentiment analysis using support vector machine classifier, in: 2013 International Conference on Advances in Computing, Communications and Informatics (ICACCI 2013), 2013, pp. 1581–1586.

[27] Rajalaxmi Hegde, Seema S., Aspect based feature extraction and sentiment classification of review data sets using incremental machine learning algorithm, in: 3rd International Conference on Advances in Electrical, Electronics, Information, Communication and Bio-Informatics (AEEICB 2017), 2017, pp. 122–125.

[28] Md Shad Akhtar, Asif Ekbal, Pushpak Bhattacharyya, Aspect based sentiment analysis: category detection and sentiment classification for Hindi, in: 17th International Conference on Computational Linguistics and Intelligent Text Processing (CICLing 2016), in: LNCS, vol. 9624, Springer, 2016, pp. 246–257.

[29] Mohammad Al-Smadi, Mahmoud Al-Ayyoub, Yaser Jararweh, Omar Qawasmeh, Enhancing aspect-based sentiment analysis of Arabic hotels' reviews using morphological, syntactic and semantic features, Information Processing & Management 56 (2) (2019) 308–319.

[30] Leo Breiman, Random forests, Machine Learning 45 (1) (2001) 5–32.

[31] Sebastian Ruder, Parsa Ghafari, John G. Breslin, A hierarchical model of reviews for aspect-based sentiment analysis, in: 2016 Conference on Empirical Methods in Natural Language Processing (EMNLP 2016), ACL, 2016, pp. 999–1005.

[32] Budi M. Mulyo, Dwi H. Widyantoro, Aspect-based sentiment analysis approach with CNN, in: 5th International Conference on Electrical Engineering, Computer Science and Informatics (EECSI 2018), IEEE, 2018, pp. 142–147.

[33] Tao Shen, Tianyi Zhou, Guodong Long, Jing Jiang, Shirui Pan, Chengqi Zhang, DiSAN: directional self-attention network for RNN/CNN-free language understanding, in: 32nd AAAI Conference on Artificial Intelligence (AAAI 2018), AAAI Press, 2018, pp. 5446–5455.

[34] Yequan Wang, Minlie Huang, Xiaoyan Zhu, Li Zhao, Attention-based LSTM for aspect-level sentiment classification, in: 2016 Conference on Empirical Methods in Natural Language Processing (EMNLP 2016), ACL, 2016, pp. 606–615.

[35] Ashish Vaswani, Noam Shazeer, Niki Parmar, Jakob Uszkoreit, Llion Jones, Aidan N. Gomez, Łukasz Kaiser, Illia Polosukhin, Attention is all you need, in: Advances in Neural Information Processing Systems, vol. 30, 2017.

[36] Jacob Devlin, Ming-Wei Chang, Kenton Lee, Kristina Toutanova, BERT: pre-training of deep bidirectional transformers for language understanding, arXiv preprint, arXiv: 1810.04805, 2018.

[37] Yinhan Liu, Myle Ott, Naman Goyal, Jingfei Du, Mandar Joshi, Danqi Chen, Omer Levy, Mike Lewis, Luke Zettlemoyer, Veselin Stoyanov, RoBERTa: a robustly optimized BERT pretraining approach, arXiv preprint, arXiv:1907.11692, 2019.

[38] Tom B. Brown, Benjamin Mann, Nick Ryder, Melanie Subbiah, Jared Kaplan, Prafulla Dhariwal, Arvind Neelakantan, Pranav Shyam, Girish Sastry, Amanda Askell, Sandhini Agarwal, Ariel Herbert-Voss, Gretchen Krueger, Tom Henighan, Rewon Child, Aditya Ramesh, Daniel M. Ziegler, Jeffrey Wu, Clemens Winter, Christopher Hesse, Mark Chen, Eric Sigler, Mateusz Litwin, Scott Gray, Benjamin Chess, Jack Clark, Christopher Berner, Sam McCandlish, Alec Radford, Ilya Sutskever, Dario Amodei, Language models are few-shot learners, arXiv:2005.14165, July 2020.

[39] Manish Munikar, Sushil Shakya, Aakash Shrestha, Fine-grained sentiment classification using BERT, in: 2019 Artificial Intelligence for Transforming Business and Society (AITB), vol. 1, IEEE, 2019, pp. 1–5.

[40] Zhengjie Gao, Ao Feng, Xinyu Song, Xi Wu, Target-dependent sentiment classification with BERT, IEEE Access 7 (2019) 154290–154299.

[41] Alexander Rietzler, Sebastian Stabinger, Paul Opitz, Stefan Engl, Adapt or get left behind: domain adaptation through BERT language model finetuning for aspect-target sentiment classification, arXiv preprint, arXiv:1908.11860, 2019.

[42] Chengxi Li, Feiyu Gao, Jiajun Bu, Lu Xu, Xiang Chen, Yu Gu, Zirui Shao, SentiPrompt: Sentiment knowledge enhanced prompt-tuning for aspect-based sentiment analysis, arXiv preprint, arXiv:2109.08306, 2021.

[43] Ronald Seoh, Ian Birle, Mrinal Tak, Haw-Shiuan Chang, Brian Pinette, Alfred Hough, Open aspect target sentiment classification with natural language prompts, arXiv preprint, arXiv:2109.03685, 2021.

[44] E. Cambria, D. Das, S. Bandyopadhyay, F. Antonio, A Practical Guide to Sentiment Analysis, LNCS, ISBN 978-3-319-55392-4, 2017, with Springer publishing house in the series http://www.springer.com/series/13199.

[45] Jonathon Read, John Carroll, Annotating expressions of appraisal in English, in: Language Resources& Evaluation, 2010, https://doi.org/10.1007/s10579-010-9135-7.

[46] Bing Liu, Sentiment analysis and subjectivity, in: N. Indurkhya, F.J. Damerau (Eds.), Handbook of Natural Language Processing, 2nd ed., 2010, pp. 1–38.

[47] B.G. Patra, D. Das, A. Das, Sentiment analysis of code-mixed Indian languages: an overview of SAIL code-mixed shared task@ICON-2017, arXiv preprint, arXiv:1803.06745, Mar. 2017.

[48] R. Agarwal, E. Karahanna, Time flies when you're having fun: cognitive absorption and beliefs about information technology usage, MIS Quarterly 24 (2000) 665–694, https://doi.org/10.2307/3250951.

[49] C.S. Andreassen, Online social network site addiction: a comprehensive review, Current Addiction Reports 2 (2015) 175–184, https://doi.org/10.1007/s40429-015-0056-9.

[50] I.-H. Lin, et al., The association between suicidality and Internet addiction and activities in Taiwanese adolescents, Comprehensive Psychiatry 55 (2014) 504–510.

[51] E. Cambria, A. Hussain, Sentic computing, Cognitive Computation 7 (2015) 183–185, https://doi.org/10.1007/s12559-015-9325-0.

[52] Mika V. Mäntylä, Daniel Graziotin, Miikka Kuutila, The evolution of sentiment analysis—a review of research topics, venues, and top cited papers, Computer Science Review (ISSN 1574-0137) 27 (2018) 16–32, https://doi.org/10.1016/j.cosrev.2017.10.002.

CHAPTER 2

Natural language processing and sentiment analysis: perspectives from computational intelligence

Soumitra Ghosh[a], Asif Ekbal[a], and Pushpak Bhattacharyya[b]
[a]Department of Computer Science & Engineering, Indian Institute of Technology Patna, Patna, India
[b]Department of Computer Science & Engineering, Indian Institute of Technology Bombay, Powai, India

2.1 Introduction

People's ideas, feelings, and emotions are mined in this field based on perceptions of their behavior, which writings can collect, facial expressions, voices, music, and movements, among other things. In this chapter, we will just look at text-sentiment analysis. In recent years, text-sentiment analysis has become a hot subject. Text-sentiment analysis has been a common research subject since the mid-1990s; however, there is no organized hierarchy of tasks in this domain, and different tasks are referred to by various words. To discuss the precise meaning, for instance, sentiment analysis, opinion mining, and polarity classification are all used, even though they are not lexically or semantically sound. As a result, examining the sentiment of a text unit will entail looking at both the opinion and the emotion behind it.

Natural language processing (NLP) and machine-learning strategies for detecting emotions predictive of suicidal behavior are becoming increasingly common. Suicidal thoughts and acts refer to discussing or taking the step to cause self-harm with the intent of ending one's own life. For quite some time now, suicide has been the 10th leading cause of death in the United States.[1] While the last decade saw a fall in suicide rate across many countries, the United States has been an exception[2] in this case. In 2015, suicide and self-harm have cost the United States a whopping $69 bil-

---

[1] https://www.apa.org/monitor/2019/03/trends-suicide.
[2] https://www.cdc.gov/nchs/products/databriefs/db309.htm.

Computational Intelligence Applications for Text and Sentiment Data Analysis
https://doi.org/10.1016/B978-0-32-390535-0.00007-0
17

lion.[3] Approximately, 1400000 suicide attempts were estimated for the year 2017 and over 48k Americans committed suicide in the year 2018.[4] The numbers are not encouraging in the other countries, with developing and under-developed countries suffering the most. The fact that 90% of suicide victims had a diagnosable mental-health issue at the time of their deaths is more terrible than the statistics. Suicide-prevention efforts with improved access to mental-health treatment and awareness are the need of the hour.

Suicide notes serve as a rich source of emotionally charged content that accurately provides knowledge of the psychological processes of persons who died by suicide. Proper review and comprehension of such notes can aid in detecting at-risk subjects and providing appropriate care, thus preventing the act from occurring.

The precise explanations for the increase or decline of suicide rates are impossible to pinpoint. This is a complicated problem that involves a myriad of conflicting feelings [1] that a person with suicidal thoughts goes through. More often than not, at the individual level, multiple risk factors are involved as causes of suicide. Health factors (depression, substance use, mental illness, etc.) may be linked to situational factors (relationship difficulties, career stress, financial crisis, etc.) or past factors (depression, drug use, mental illness, etc.) (previous suicide attempts, history of suicide in the family, childhood abuse or trauma, etc.). Recent advances in internet technologies and the gaining popularity of several social-media platforms has brought a manifold increase in user activities leading to increased cases of cyberbullying [2] causing trauma to victims prompting some to take the ultimate step of ending their own lives.

Although closely related, sentiment and emotion do not always express the same effect. Since opinion and emotion are so closely connected, mixing them up is easy. For example, emotion sometimes motivates people to judge others and form views about them. A person's point of view can also evoke feelings in others. Conversely, a text device may express contrasting perspectives and emotions. "My family thinks it's a smart idea to continue my education abroad, but they miss me," for example, demonstrates both a positive and negative attitude toward the same subject. Sentiment can be considered a superset of emotion where the former is concerned with defining one's opinion or view. The latter is thrust upon identifying specific feelings experienced by a person [3]. The sentiment is often measured using polarities, which are positive and negative scores. A third classification

[3] https://afsp.org/suicide-statistics/.
[4] https://afsp.org/about-suicide/suicide-statistics/.

is neutral, which denotes something that is neither positive nor negative. Emotion, on the other hand, delves further into a person's complex spectrum of emotions. As a result, a positive sentiment label may be combined with a variety of emotion labels such as joy, thankfulness, pride, hopefulness, and so on. Similarly, negative sentiment can be associated with several emotion labels like anger, disgust, fear, sadness, etc. The emotional analysis provides the much-needed in-depth understanding of people's actions that cannot be mapped in terms of mere polarities (positive or negative). Both sentiment and emotion analysis are interesting applications in NLP that receive much attention.

In this chapter, we exploit the coexistence of emotion and sentiment in a classification scenario and investigate whether sentiment analysis plays a role in improving the performance of emotion recognition in suicide notes. Such an approach becomes essential when the available annotated data is scarce, and the performance of the existing systems needs to improve markedly. In this study, we consider the fine-grained emotion-annotated CEASE[5] [4] suicide-notes dataset. The dataset consists of emotion-annotated sentences from English suicide notes (2393 sentences from 205 suicide notes). CEASE is the only freely accessible emotion-annotated corpus of suicide notes, and it was recently launched [4] to promote study and advancement in emotion detection and suicide prevention. A fine-grained 15 emotion tagset[6] has been considered while annotating the corpus. We adopt a weak labeling scheme to generate the sentiment annotations corresponding to each instance in this corpus. For sentence-level emotion (primary task) and sentiment-detection tasks (secondary task), we construct multiple end-to-end deep neural-based multitask models (Convolutional Neural Network: CNN, Bidirectional Gated Recurrent Unit: Bi-GRU, and Bidirectional Long-Term/Short-Term Memory: Bi-LSTM), where both goals are trained jointly.

We build these multitask systems as the upgraded variants over the single-task (only emotion detection) systems and an extensive performance comparison among the single-task and the multitask systems show the latter to have superior classification performance with best-attained cross-validation accuracy of 60.76% using Bi-LSTM multitask system. We also equate the efficiency of our proposed method to the performance of many

---

[5] Resource available at: https://www.iitp.ac.in/~ai-nlp-ml/resources.html#CEASE.

[6] Emotion labels: forgiveness, happiness_peacefulness, love, pride, hopefulness, thankfulness, blame, anger, fear, abuse, sorrow, hopelessness, guilt, information, instructions.

feature-based machine-learning models and the system that reported results on this dataset to demonstrate the effectiveness of the proposed approach.

The following are the key contributions of our proposed work:

- To the best of our knowledge, we are the first to use multitask learning of suicide and emotion modeling on suicide notes.
- We effectively leverage weak supervision to annotate the CEASE dataset with near-appropriate sentiment labels.
- We propose a multitask learning system that improves overall success on the suicide-note emotion-classification task.

The remainder of the chapter is arranged in the following manner. A survey of current studies in the relevant domain is discussed in Section 2.2. Section 2.3 looks at some of the most commonly used emotion models in computational analysis and their limitations when applied to suicide data. Next, we discuss various aspects of the dataset considered in this work in Section 2.4. Here, we also discuss the annotation of the dataset with weakly labeled sentiment labels. In Section 2.5, we discuss the methodologies that we implement for our task. In Section 2.6, we discuss our considered baselines in brief. In Section 2.7, we go through the tests, effects, and interpretation. Finally, in Section 2.8, we conclude our research with a short discussion of the work's key shortcomings before identifying the direction of future research.

2.2 Related work

The first study on real-life suicide notes was conducted in the 1950s [5], and it found that those who die by suicide were not in their right minds. This project aimed to distinguish authentic notes from fakes by distinguishing those characteristics using discourse-analysis techniques. A pioneer in the field of suicidology, Shneidman's work prompted a large number of other studies, like distinguishing the genuineness of notes using text characteristics like modal and auxiliaries [6], language characteristics like Part-of-Speech variation, etc. [7,8]. A comparative study [9] of genuine suicide notes with letters written to friends and relatives showed that the content written under heightened drive levels is more stereotyped and disorganized with frequent conflicting responses. The majority of this study was focused on [5]'s limited corpus of 66 suicide notes.

Studies focusing on the emotional content of suicide notes started in the early 1960s [10,11] explored the various implied reasons for suicide and, on similar lines [12], studied the socioeconomic and psychological variables of suicide. On a set of 286 suicide notes (received from the Birmingham Coroner's Office) and another 33 actual and 33 fake notes, [13] conducted a comparative study of the topics used in real and simulated suicide notes (from Los Angeles). The research discovered overlapping and distinct features correlated with a group of notes. The authors in [14] analyzed the actual suicide notes to understand the mental state of a suicidal person at the moment of committing the act and found several behavioral differences based on gender among the deceased.

The authors in [15] observed trends that women attempt suicide more than men though the completion rate of suicide is higher for men than women. The authors in [16] studied 224 notes from 154 different topics and found some fascinating facts about the notes and their publishers. Most of the notes analyzed belonged to young married women who had never attempted suicide before and had no history of mental illness. Notes from young people were lengthier and emotionally richer (content-wise) than notes from their elders. While notes of older adults contained more objective information (like information and instruction), young people wrote emotionally richer content (mainly that of guilt and forgiveness). The authors in [17] noted that completers would exhibit a burden toward loved ones more so than attempters.

Mental-health workers [18–20] found that human annotators were outperformed by computer-learning methods in terms of classification precision to see whether machine-learning algorithms would distinguish actual and simulated suicide notes. The lack of suicide notes in the public domain (internet) has been a major reason for the limited application of computational methods in analyzing suicide notes. Track 2 of the 2011 i2b2 NLP Challenge [21] was created in this sense to kick-start innovation in emotion detection and suicide prevention. This competition presented a 900 suicide notes fine-grained emotion-annotated corpus in English. Notes were annotated at the sentence level with multi-label emotions from a rich set of 15 emotion classes: abuse, anger, blame, fear, forgiveness, guilt, happiness_peacefulness, hopefulness, hopelessness, love, pride, sorrow, thankfulness, information, and instructions. This dataset aided development in a variety of ways [22–26] from the standpoint of classification using various NLP techniques [27]. Multitask learning has applications in many recent studies [28,29] in sentiment and emotion analysis. The authors in [28] introduced a multitask system to address several problems in emotion and sentiment analysis (such as emotion classification and intensity, valence arousal, and emotion and sentiment dominance) across a wide spectrum of realms (tweets, Facebook posts, news headlines, blogs, etc.). In [29], the authors proposed a two-layered multitask attention-based deep-learning system for sentiment and emotion prediction. It leverages external knowledge information by using the Distributional Thesaurus to improve the system's performance.

Many researchers used artificial-intelligence and machine-learning methods to predict suicidal thoughts and provide early intervention to at-risk people in psychiatric and clinical trials [30], and confidential questionnaire answers [31]. They analyzed social-media evidence [32] to detect suicide ideation and provide early intervention to at-risk individuals. Online platforms for communication have enabled users to share their feelings, opinions, suffering, and sometimes suicidal thoughts anonymously. Data generated in these forums have enabled several agencies to build suicide-prevention tools (iBobbly [33], Woebot4 by Facebook) using NLP techniques to fight people's depression and anxiety and detect suicide ideation. Feature engineering [34,35], emotion analysis [36,37], and deep learning [38–40] are used to detect social material. Suicide, or at least an elevated risk of suicide, is linked to depression [41]. Young single females with a lack of basic education and a history of mental-health problems have become especially vulnerable to suicide [42]. As much as mental illness, there is more to the risk of suicide [43].

Understanding the importance of emotions in human behavior will contribute to creating more capable, adaptable Artificial-Intelligence (AI) systems. We use the 15 fine-grained emotion tags added in the i2b2 2011 shared-task challenge because of the high emotive material in suicide notes and the variety of emotions that cannot be limited to Ekman's [44] or Plutchik's [46] simple emotions. We construct three single-task deep learning-based (CNN, Bi-GRU, and Bi-LSTM) classifiers for emotion detection, as well as three multitask systems with a secondary task (sentiment detection) to complement the primary task (i.e., emotion recognition). We compare our proposed approach's performance with the existing work [4] and some popular machine-learning algorithms on the CEASE [4] dataset.

2.3 Popular emotion models in computational analysis

A mutually beneficial relationship has developed between computational science and emotion research in psychology, driven mainly by the massive scope of research on emotion and cognition. Over the years, many hypotheses of emotion have been proposed by eminent scholars and psychologists, and they can be divided into two categories: dimensional emotion models (which include an emotion spectrum with several dimensions) and discrete emotion models (which involves distinct emotion categories). This section will go through some of the most commonly used emotion models in numerical research.

2.3.1 Russell's circumplex model of emotions

Developed by James Russell, the Circumplex Model [45] is one of the most prominent dimensional models of emotion. As inferred from the name, the model arranges various emotional states across the circumference of a 2-dimensional (valence and arousal dimensions) circular space. Arousal refers to the degree of calmness or excitement, whereas valence refers to how good or negative one feels. Valence and arousal are often synonymously used with concepts of polarity and intensity, respectively. (See Fig. 2.1.)

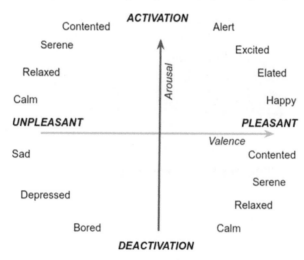

Figure 2.1 Pictorial representation of Russell's Circumplex Model of Affect.

Russell's circumplex model has been prevalent in psychologic and psycholinguistic studies and computational linguistics. Where continuous measures of valence and arousal are needed rather than separate emotional categories, the latter considers this model extremely useful.

2.3.2 Plutchik's wheel of emotions

Robert Plutchik created a model of emotions known as Plutchik's wheel of emotions [46] in the 1980s, representing eight primary bi-polar emotions (joy versus sadness; anger versus fear; trust versus disgust; and surprise versus anticipation) as well as eight derived emotions (from the basic ones). He arranged these emotions in a wheel-like structure, with similar emotions located adjacent to each other and opposite emotions in distant spaces. (See Fig. 2.2.)

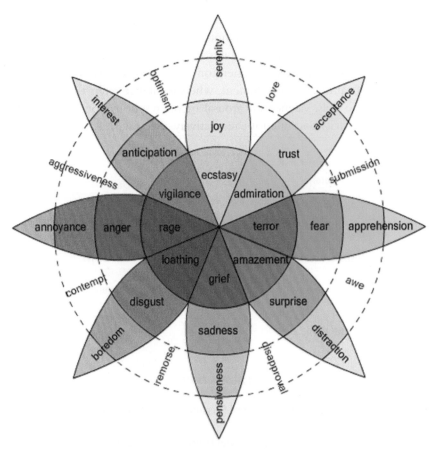

Figure 2.2 Pictorial representation of Plutchik's Wheel of Emotions. Image Courtesy: [46] https://www.jstor.org/stable/pdf/27857503.pdf.

The distance of a section of a petal from the center of the wheel determines how intense an emotion is; hence, emotions become less discernible the farther they are from the center of the wheel.

2.3.3 Ekman's basic emotions

The theory of basic emotions was first formulated by Silvan Tomkins [47] (in the early 1960s). It was later concretized by Paul Ekman (one of Tomkins' mentees), who defined six fundamental emotions (anger, disgust, fear, happiness, sadness, and surprise) [48] as distinct classes, as opposed to Russell's circumplex model's continuous existence. Anger–disgust and fear–surprise are closely related emotions within these basic emotions. The basic emotions of Ekman are well known in computational research and are widely used in emotion analysis, especially in emotion-recognition tasks.

While these models are commonly used in many emotion-processing activities, they are inadequate to capture the full spectrum of distinct emotions in most suicide notes. Abuse, blame, guilt, hopefulness, hopelessness, and thankfulness are common and essential in many suicide notes, but they are not captured by the popular emotion models mentioned above. This leads us to consider a fine-grained emotion tagset to suit our requirement, which we discuss in the following section.

2.3.4 Hourglass of emotions

The Hourglass of Emotions [49] is a brain-inspired and scientifically grounded theory that argues that the mind is made up of several different devices, and that emotional states are the product of turning one set on and off. Six degrees of activation (measuring the strength of an emotion) distinguish an affective variable, referred to as "sentic levels," which represent the expressed/perceived emotion's intensity thresholds.

The 'sentic vector,' a four-dimensional float vector, can potentially synthesize the whole continuum of emotional experiences regarding Pleasantness, Attention, Sensitivity, and Aptitude. The vertical axis in the model reflects the strength of the various affective axes, while the radial dimension represents the stimulation of various emotional configurations (as illustrated in Fig. 2.3). The model is built on a pattern used in color theory and science to draw decisions about blends, or the emotions that appear when two or more basic emotions are combined, similar to how red and blue make purple. The Hourglass paradigm is also used for polarity-detection tasks and emotion detection.

2.4 Dataset description

In this work, we consider our recently introduced dataset CEASE [4] corpus that contains 2393 fine-grained emotion annotated sentences from

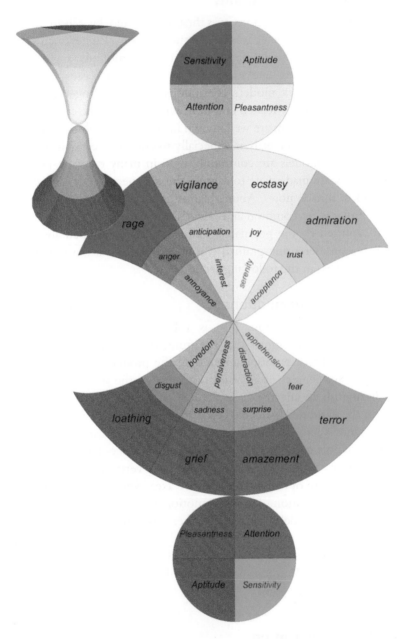

Figure 2.3 Hourglass of Emotions. Image Courtesy: [49].

205 suicide notes. There are 15 distinct emotion labels, namely (forgiveness, happiness_peacefulness, love, pride, hopefulness, thankfulness, blame, anger, fear, abuse, sorrow, hopelessness, guilt, information, instructions), and each sentence is labeled with at most one emotion. Fig. 2.4 depicts the data distribution over the various sentiment and emotion classes in the CEASE dataset. In 2011 i2b2 Shared Task [21] introduced a fine-grained emotion-annotated corpus of 900 suicide notes to develop an automated sentiment-classification system. Our consideration of the 15-emotion tagset is motivated by this work.

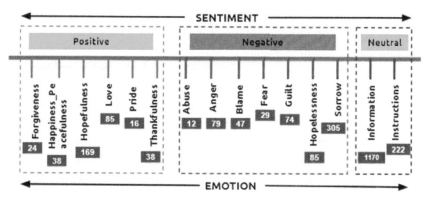

Figure 2.4 A Mapping between Emotion classes to the closest Sentiment equivalent categories. The numeric values in boxes reflect the number of instances in the dataset that belong to a given class.

Existing works related to content analysis of suicide notes depend heavily on the notes introduced in [14] and the i2b2 Shared Task [21]. The former is a minimal resource containing 66 notes and the latter, though relevant and resourceful, is currently unavailable for future research. The CEASE Corpus was introduced to fill this void and facilitate research and development with forensic records such as suicide notes.

2.4.1 Corpus preparation

We prepared the corpus in [4] by collecting data in two distinct phases. In the first phase, transcripts of suicide notes were searched in the internet (news-websites, blogs, articles, etc.) and saved in text format. Around half of the total notes collected to build the corpus were collected in this manner. To reduce the chances of crawling any fake or doctored suicide notes, excerpts published in the popular websites[7] were considered only. In the second phase, 138 suicide notes were collected from a book titled '...Or Not to Be: A Collection of Suicide Notes' by Marc Etkind [50]. It contained a compilation of several suicide notes from various sources, a brief description of the deceased, and the circumstances during the act.

The entire book was scanned and images generated were converted to plain text using a free third-party online OCR software. The author's comments were removed from the transcripts, and only suicide texts were retained. OCR-related errors were corrected, and the notes were sentence tokenized. Basic cleaning and pre-processing (removal of punctuation marks, redundant blank spaces removal, lowercase conversion, contractions handling ("I'm" for "I am", "shan't" for "shall not", etc.), etc.) were performed, and the resultant sentences were supplied for annotation.

Three distinct annotators, each with a postgraduate degree and experience in performing similar annotation tasks labeled each text in the dataset. They were instructed to assign no more than one emotion label from the list of 15 emotions for each sentence. A majority-vote method was employed to decide on the final emotion classification for each text. Sentences that had no common emotion category were not considered for inclusion in the final annotated dataset. On the annotated dataset, an average Kappa value of 0.71 was observed, indicating fair inter-rater agreement. Table 2.1 displays a few annotated sentences from the CEASE corpus.

2.4.2 Descriptive statistics of the corpus

We shared some exciting insights in [4] about the notes collected for building the corpus. Among the notes collected, the most vulnerable age interval seemed to be between 20 and 50. The number of male notes was more significant than the number of female notes. Compared to older people, young people (aged 11 to 30) typically wrote longer notes than older people (aged above 60). Often, notes for individuals under the age of 20 and above 80 are hard to come by.

---

[7] List of a few sources:
  https://www.huffpost.com/entry/cora-delille-suicide_n_5366546,
  https://edition.cnn.com/2018/08/20/us/aaron-hernandez-suicide-note-baez-book/index.html,
  https://www.jconline.com/story/news/local/2013/03/18/a-letter-found-in-angel-greens-room/28936361/,
  https://www.phrases.org.uk/quotes/last-words/suicide-notes.html.

Table 2.1 Annotation samples of some emotion classes.

Emotion	Sentence
Abuse	My first memories as a child are of being raped repeatedly.
Anger	All you want in life is partying, your women, and your selfish motives.
Blame	You are much too ignorant and self-concerned to even attempt to listen or understand, everyone knows that.
Fear	I just do not care anymore. I need to go; I am so scared now.
Hopelessness	After three and a half years I find I can no longer go on with this pain and agony.
Sorrow	I may look human from the outside but my inside is empty, stupid, dull-witted, and self-isolating.
Thankfulness	Thank you for caring and feeding and loving me for 14 years.

2.4.3 Generation of sentiment labels using weak supervision

For the sentiment task, we leverage a weak labeling scheme on the CEASE dataset to produce sentiment labels corresponding to each instance in the dataset. We categorize the emotion classes into three groups [24], signifying the 3 sentiment classes (positive, negative, and neutral). The 2 objective emotion classes (information and instruction) are added together to form the Neutral class in the sentiment task. The remaining 13 subjective emotion classes are categorized into positive and negative classes. Classes like Anger, Fear, Blame, Guilt, Hopelessness, Sorrow, and Abuse constitute the Negative class, and classes like Hopefulness, Happiness_Peacefulness, Pride, Forgiveness, Love, and Thankfulness comprise the Positive class for the sentiment-classification task.

The distribution of instances around the sentiment groups is heavily skewed, with about 16%, 26%, and 58% of the instances belonging to positive, negative, and neutral classes, respectively. While this form of weak annotation results in some noises, it saves time and effort by eliminating the need to redo annotations from scratch. Additionally, it preserves the conventional association between various emotions and the polarity categories that go along with them.

2.5 Proposed methodology

We built 3 deep-learning-based architectures (CNN, BiGRU and Bi-LSTM), each for the single-task and multitask variant for the emotion-classification problem. We rely on pre-trained word embeddings for word representations followed by sentence-encoding layers. The resultant sentence representation is passed through an attention layer to focus on the important information in the sentence. The attended vector is passed through a couple of fully connected (FC) layers and finally through the output layer(s) with Softmax activation. ·

2.5.1 Word-embedding representation

Pre-trained word embeddings assist in capturing the words' syntactic and semantic nuances. The models are fed the embedded representation of the words in a sentence. The word embeddings were learnt using the Common Crawl corpus (42 billion tokens) and came from GloVe[8] [51]. To ensure that input sequences are all the same length, padding arrays of zeros are utilized. An embedding matrix is used to hold the embedding vectors for the words in our training set. We put this embedding matrix into a Keras[9] Embedding layer and set the trainable attribute to *False* in order to prevent the weights and embedding vectors from being updated during training. In order to extract the semantic information from the given message, the sentence encoders pass the embedded representations along.

2.5.2 Base models
2.5.2.1 Convolutional Neural Network (CNN_STL)

Due to its potential to deliver good classification outcomes, frequently comparable to state-of-the-art architectures, Convolutional Neural Networks [54] have been used extensively in many studies on sentiment classification [52,53], making it a logical choice to act as a strong benchmark for modern text-classification architectures.

We use a convolutional layer with 150 filters (rather than the 100 filters used in [4]) to create a single-task CNN (CNN_STL)-based system that slides over 2, 3, and 4 words in parallel. The layers' outputs are combined (added) to create a new output of the same form as each layer's output. The convoluted features are max-pooled (pool size = 2) to create a function vector of lower dimensionality. This is then transferred through an attention layer focusing on the sentence's insightful material. The attention layer's output is routed through two connected layers (each with 100 neurons and ReLU activation) and a softmax-activated output layer (with 15 neurons).

---

[8] GloVe: http://nlp.stanford.edu/data/wordvecs/glove.42B.300d.zip.
[9] A high-level neural-network API: https://keras.io/.

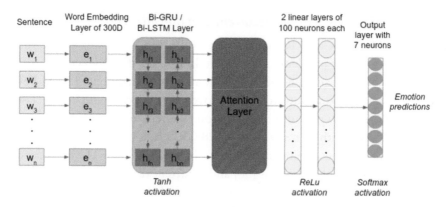

Figure 2.5 Single-task architecture.

2.5.2.2 Bidirectional Long Short-Term Memory (BiLSTM_STL)

Long Short-Term Memory (LSTM) networks [55] are a form of recurrent neural network that overcomes some of the drawbacks of typical recurrent neural networks. Any LSTM unit's cell state and three gates (forget, input, and output) allow the network to monitor the information flow through it (from previous and current timesteps) and effectively manage the vanishing-gradient problem, as well as remember long-term dependencies in text sequences. We develop a Bidirectional LSTM-based single-task (BiLSTM_STL) system for emotion detection that steps through the input sequence in both directions (forward and backward) at the same time, as depicted in Fig. 2.5. We use the summation operation to combine the outputs of the two networks and generate a single representation for each word. We use the summation operation to combine the outputs of the two networks and generate a single representation for each word. The word embeddings are passed through a single 128-unit Bi-LSTM layer (as opposed to a Bi-LSTM layer followed by an LSTM layer in [4]) that outputs the sentence's semantic representation, which is then passed through an attention layer that pays attention to informative content in the sentence. The rest of the architecture follows similarly as described for the CNN_STL system from the attention layer onwards. We use recurrent activation as Tanh and dropout [56] and recurrent dropout of 25% each in the LSTM units to prevent overfitting. The outputs from the forward and the backward LSTM units are merged using the sum operation.

2.5.2.3 Bidirectional Gated Recurrent Unit (Bi-GRU_STL)

Like LSTMs, the Gated Recurrent Unit (GRU) [57] can also handle the vanishing-gradient problem and preserve long-term dependencies in text sequences. GRU is considered a better variation of traditional LSTM because of its simple architecture (only two gates: update and reset), fast execution, and low memory consumption. We replace the LSTM layer in Bi-LSTM_STL with a similar layer of 128 GRU cells (refer to Fig. 2.5) and keep the rest of the architecture intact to build Bi-GRU_STL. To reduce overfitting, we employ dropout [56] and recurrent dropout of 25% each in the GRU units. Unlike the use of two successive layers of GRU (a Bi-GRU layer followed by a GRU layer) in [4], we drop the single GRU layer, thus making the model more straightforward as we have limited instances (the dataset size is small) to learn upon.

2.5.3 Attention

We use an attention function [58] after the word-encoding layer in our models that produces an attended sentence vector to concentrate on the terms that add the most to the sentence context.

$$u_{it} = tanh\left(W_w h_{it} + b_w\right) \tag{2.1}$$

$$\alpha_{it} = \frac{exp\left(u_{it}^T u_w\right)}{\sum_t exp\left(u_{it}^T u_w\right)} \tag{2.2}$$

$$s_i = \sum_t \left(\alpha_{it} * h_{it}\right) \tag{2.3}$$

where u_{it} is the hidden representation of h_{it} (word representation from the word-encoding layer), u_w is the context vector, α_{it} is the attention weight for a word, and s_i is the output-sentence vector from the attention layer.

2.5.4 Loss function

We consider Categorical Cross-entropy as the loss function since both the sentiment and emotion task deal with a single-label classification problem. That is, one instance can belong to one class only. The loss function can be realized by the formula:

$$F\left(a, p\right) = \sum_{j=0}^{X} \sum_{i=0}^{Y} \left(a_{ij} * log\left(p_{ij}\right)\right) \tag{2.4}$$

The real value is a, and the expected value is p. The double summations from $j = 0$ to X and $I = 0$ to Y, respectively, are over the number of instances (I) and groups (Y). The neural network returns a vector of Y probabilities representing probability of an instance belonging to any of the classes.

2.5.5 Multitask framework

Multitask learning enables a single neural-network model to learn several tasks simultaneously and, more often than not, improve upon both individual tasks' performance compared to when learned separately.

Problem Definition: Our problem is formulated as follows:

Let $(i_p, e_p, s_p)_{p=1}^{I}$ be a set of I instances or sentences with the corresponding emotion labels of E classes and sentiment labels of S classes, where $e_p \in E$ and $s_p \in S$. Our multitask learning framework aims to find a feature that maps each instance $i_p \in I$ to its related emotion label e_p and sentiment label s_p.

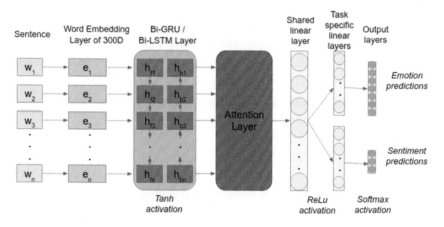

Figure 2.6 Multitask Architecture.

The final two layers of our STL architecture are tweaked by replacing the last entirely connected layer with two separate task-specific linear layers, followed by their respective output layers. The architecture of our multitask platform for Bi-GRU_MTL and Bi-LSTM_MTL systems is seen in Fig. 2.6. Instead of the Bi-GRU/BiLSTM layer, the CNN_MTL can be realized using the same architecture by combining a convolutional and pooling layer. The task-specific layers have 100 neurons each, and their corresponding output layers have 15 and 3 neurons representing the emotion and sentiment task, respectively. Similar to the base-model architectures, we use ReLU [59] activation in the Convolutional layer of CNN_MTL and Tanh activation in the GRU and LSTM units of Bi-GRU_MTL and Bi-LSTM_MTL, respectively. To reduce the effect of overfitting, we add a 25% dropout [55] after the attention layer and even before the output layer in any model.

Calculation of Loss: The formula below calculates the sum of the optimization losses for the network. This layer produces a probability distribution over the emotion labels. Our loss function is composed of two cross-entropy losses (one for each task) with different weights as follows:

$$L = a * E_{cel}(i, e) + b * S_{cel}(i, s) \qquad (2.5)$$

where E_{cel} represents the cross-entropy loss for emotion classification, and S_{cel} represents the cross-entropy loss for sentiment classification. a and b are the weights to control the importance of the two parts of losses. We use the Adam [60] algorithm to minimize the numerical loss function L.

If appropriate annotated data on similar data is available, our suggested multitask learning (MTL) setup can easily be expanded to help other associated auxiliary tasks (anxiety, depression, post-traumatic stress disorder (PTSD), etc.) that often occur together.

2.6 Baselines

To analyze the performance of our proposed approaches, we consider similar baselines as were used in our earlier work reported in [4] with the CEASE dataset. We also draw relevant performance comparisons with our current system and our previous work [4]. We train the machine-learning models on the features, such as NLTK Part-of-Speech (PoS) tags,[10] MPQA Subjectivity Lexicons,[11] Opinion Lexicons,[12] NRC Emotion Lex-

---

[10] https://www.nltk.org/book/ch05.html.
[11] http://mpqa.cs.pitt.edu/lexicons/subj lexicon/.
[12] https://www.cs.uic.edu/~liub/FBS/sentiment-analysis.html.

icons and NRC Hashtag Emotion Lexicons,[13] Vader[14] [60], Afinn[15] [61], Word ngrams ($n = 1$ to 4), and Character n-grams ($n = 1$ to 4).

The following is the list of baselines considered in this work:

- *Bernoulli Naive Bayes classifier (BNB):* Naive Bayes techniques are supervised learning algorithms built on the Bayes theorem with the "naive" assumption that a pair of features are conditionally independent given the value of the class variable. We use the Bernoulli variant of Naive Bayes. A Bayesian probabilistic classifier driven by the assumption that the attributes are binary-valued variables and the characteristics are conditionally autonomous, rather than the Multinomial Naive Bayes classifier used in [4]. Despite their oversimplified expectations, naive Bayes classifiers have performed admirably in various real-world applications, most notably document classification and spam filtering. They just need a small amount of training data to approximate the necessary parameters.

- *The Support Vector Machine classifier (SVM)* algorithm decides the best hyperplane for classifying the groups. Support Vector Machines [62] are a numerical learning theory-based technique for reducing systemic damage. The basic theory of SVM is to locate the judgment boundary that maximizes the distance between two groups. Support vectors are the vectors that characterize this decision boundary. Test samples are categorized according to predetermined class categories using a classification model created by the SVM algorithm, which is a non-probabilistic linear classifier. SVM's fundamental concepts are broken down into three steps:
  1. determining the best decision boundary that maximizes the difference between two groups;
  2. optimizing the same (a) for non-linear separable problems;
  3. data is converted to a high-dimensional space so linear and non-linear separable instances can be conveniently classified.

- *Random Forest classifier (RF)* builds multiple decision trees on several randomly selected subsets of the training dataset. It outputs the prediction on the test data by applying a voting technique on all the outputs of the decision trees. Random forest is a supervised learning tool that can be used for both grouping and regression. Using data samples selected

---

[13] http://sentiment.nrc.ca/lexicons-for-research/.
[14] https://github.com/cjhutto/vaderSentiment.
[15] https://github.com/fnielsen/afinn.

at random, random forests build decision trees, obtain predictions from each tree, and then vote on the best outcome. It also acts as a potent signal of the function's worth. Random forests have various uses, including recommendation engines, image recognition, and feature selection. It can be used to detect illegal online activities, distinguish trustworthy loan borrowers, and forecast diseases. The Boruta algorithm, which selects essential features in a dataset, is built around it.

- *Logistic Regression classifier (LR):* Logistic regression is used to predict the chances of classification problems for two possible outcomes. It is a linear regression model extension for classification problems. While the linear regression model is efficient for regression, it fails miserably when it comes to classification. A logistic regression is a method for classifying data. The logistic regression model applies the logistic function to squeeze the output of a linear equation between 0 and 1, as opposed to fitting a straight line or hyperplane to the output of a linear equation. As in the multinomial variation of LR, we employ softmax activation with a cross-entropy loss function in the output layer.
- *CNN:* The architecture is similar to that of CNN_STL, as discussed earlier, with only a difference in the number of filters considered. Unlike our consideration of 150 filters in CNN_STL and CNN_MTL, [4] used 100 filters.
- *GRU:* The architecture is similar to that of BiGRU_STL, as discussed earlier, with an extra single GRU layer (128 GRU cells) after the Bi-GRU layer.
- *LSTM:* The architecture is similar to that of BiLSTM_STL, as discussed earlier, with an extra single LSTM layer (128 LSTM cells) after the Bi-LSTM layer. Also, in this case, regularization parameters such as recurrent activation, dropout, and dropout in LSTM cells are not considered.

2.7 Experiments, results, and analysis

2.7.1 Experimental setting

Our systems are implemented using Keras with a Tensorflow backend and GPU support. At different phases of our implementations, we additionally make use of the well-known Python package Scikit-learn[16] [63].

---

[16] https://scikit-learn.org/stable/.

For the CNN-based models, we tried multiple convolutional (conv) and pooling (pool) layers combination in succession (conv–pool–conv–pool) [28]. We observed better performance with a single conv–pool layer. Also, we observe superior performance when we use a single Bi-LSTM/BiGRU layer instead of stacked Bi-LSTM/Bi-GRU layers as in [28]. We empirically found that passing the output of the attention layer through a shared fully connected layer followed by the task-specific layers resulted in better performance than using only task-specific layers without any shared fully connected layer as in [28]. Unlike having task-specific attention blocks and limited information sharing up to encoding layers [29], our proposed approach allows for learning the similarities/overlap between the two correlated tasks until the last fully connected shared layer. Since data size is considerably smaller with a range of fine-grained classes for emotion, this architecture takes support from the sentiment task, which is comparatively of low complexity comprising 3 classes and a quantifiable number of instances.

We compute the accuracy for the classification (emotion class) task for evaluation. To build the training and test sets for our tests, we split the CEASE dataset in an 80:20 ratio. We also conduct 10-fold cross-validation to prevent overfitting on the whole dataset. Since the emotion prediction is the primary output and the sentiment prediction is the auxiliary output, we set the loss-weights parameter in the Keras compile function to [1, 0.3][17] to weight the model output losses accordingly. The specifics of several hyperparameters for our developed deep-learning system training are shown in Table 2.2. We report the macro-averaged Precision, Recall, and F1 scores on the test dataset due to the highly skewed distribution of the different classes in our dataset.

2.7.2 Evaluation metrics

The results that are accurately predicted are true positives and true negatives. We try to keep false positives and negatives to a minimum.

True Positives (TP) – These are the predicted positive values, which suggest that both the actual and projected class values are positive. The predicted class value confirms the actual class value, which shows that the passenger survived.

---

[17] [1, 0.3] produced the best results among the following considered ratio pairs: [1, 0.1], [1, 0.3], [1, 0.5], [1, 0.7], [1, 1].

Table 2.2 Details of various hyper-parameters related to our experiments.

Parameters	Details
Convolutional Filters	150 filters of size 2, 3, and 4 in parallel
Shared Layers	1 CNN (conv–pool) layer
	1 LSTM layer (128 neurons)
	1 GRU layer (128 neurons)
	Base models - 2 FC layers (100 neurons each)
	Multitask models - 1 FC layer (100 neurons)
Task-Specific layers	Multitask models – 1 FC layer (100 neurons)
Output layer(s)	Base models – 1 output layer (15 neurons)
	Multitask models – 2 output layers (one with 15 and another with 3 neurons)
Hidden Activations	ReLU [58]
Output Activations	Softmax for both Emotion and Sentiment task
Batch Size	16
Epochs	30
Dropout [55]	25%
Loss	Categorical Cross-Entropy for both Emotion and Sentiment task
Loss Weights	[1, 0.3]
Optimizer	Adam [59]

True Negatives (TN) – The values of the actual class and the anticipated class are both zero. Suppose, for instance, that both the actual and the anticipated classes report that this passenger did not survive.

False Positives (FP) – These are when the present and predicted classes are not the same. For example, if the actual class indicates that this passenger died, but the predicted class indicates that this passenger will survive.

False Negatives (FN) – This is when a class is predicted to be negative, but the actual class is positive. For instance, if the passenger's actual class value indicates that they survived, the predicted class value would suggest that they have died.

Accuracy, Precision, Recall, and F1 score can all be calculated once we have a firm grasp of these four criteria.

Accuracy – Accuracy, which is effectively the proportion of accurately predicted observations to all observations, is the efficiency statistic that makes the most sense to people. Accuracy is a useful statistic, but only when datasets are symmetric and false positives and false negatives are roughly equal in number. It counts how many positive and negative observations were accurately categorized. On unbalanced problems, you should not use the accuracy measure. Then, by merely classifying all observations as the majority class, obtaining a high accuracy ranking is simple,

$$Accuracy = \frac{TP + TN}{TP + FP + FN + TN} \tag{2.6}$$

Precision – Precision is defined as the proportion of accurately predicted positive observations to all positively predicted observations. How many of the passengers who were reported as have survived actually did so is the subject of this calculation. A low false-positive rate is related to precision,

$$Precision = \frac{TP}{TP + FP} \tag{2.7}$$

Recall (Sensitivity) – Recall is the ratio of correctly predicted positive observations to all other observations in the class. It answers the following question: How many of the passengers truly survived were labeled?

$$Recall = \frac{TP}{TP + FN} \tag{2.8}$$

F1 score – The weighted average of accuracy and recall is known as the F1 Score. As a result, both false positives and false negatives are included in this metric. Despite being less intuitive than precision, F1 is typically more useful. This is particularly true if there is an uneven distribution of classes. As the costs of false positives and false negatives are equal, accuracy performs better,

$$F1\ Score = \frac{2 * \left(Recall * Precision\right)}{\left(Recall + Precision\right)} \tag{2.9}$$

2.7.3 Experimental results and discussion

The assessment of our proposed models based on per-class accuracy, recall, and F1 scores is shown in Table 2.3. Table 2.4 displays the outcomes of the sentiment challenge from the multitasking models, with the Bi-LSTM_MTL solution obtaining the highest test accuracy of 68.12%. The metrics' per-class values show that the number of instances available for a particular class significantly impacts its efficiency.

In Table 2.5, we report the test accuracies and the 10-fold cross-validation accuracies attained by our proposed single-task and multitask

Table 2.3 Emotion Task Results: Per-class Precision, Recall, and F1 scores of the single-task (STL) and the multitask (MTL) deep-learning models. Values in bold show the maximum attained P-R-F scores (macro- and weighted) among all the approaches.

Sentiment	CNN_STL			CNN_STL			Bi-GRU_MTL			Bi-GRU_MTL			Bi-GRU_MTL			Bi-LSTM_MTL		
	P	R	F	P	R	F	P	R	F	P	R	F	P	R	F	P	R	F
Forgiveness	60	60	60	80	80	80	80	80	80	100	100	100	83	100	91	56	100	71
Happiness	22	25	24	20	12	15	100	12	22	67	25	36	33	25	29	29	100	27
Hopefulness	43	44	43	43	38	41	62	29	40	62	29	40	50	44	47	45	44	45
Love	64	82	72	80	71	75	77	59	67	63	71	67	69	53	60	56	82	67
Pride	00	00	00	00	00	00	00	00	00	00	00	00	00	00	00	00	00	00
Thankfulness	67	75	71	100	75	86	67	75	71	83	62	71	100	62	77	100	75	86
Abuse	33	33	33	00	00	00	00	00	00	00	00	00	00	00	00	00	00	00
Anger	53	56	55	64	56	60	67	50	57	53	62	57	69	56	62	53	62	57
Blame	11	10	11	33	20	25	50	10	17	00	00	00	33	10	15	12	20	15
Fear	50	33	40	100	17	29	00	00	00	00	00	00	50	33	40	50	33	40
Guilt	71	67	69	71	67	69	60	60	60	77	67	71	59	67	62	79	73	76
Hopelessness	38	18	24	50	18	26	00	00	00	00	00	00	45	29	36	44	47	46
Sorrow	53	28	37	37	25	29	33	23	27	43	10	16	38	54	45	57	39	47
Information	66	81	73	64	85	73	61	89	72	59	93	72	69	78	73	70	74	72
Instructions	65	44	53	73	42	54	40	51	60	75	33	46	68	42	52	61	56	58
macro-avg	**46**	**44**	**44**	**54**	**40**	**44**	**45**	**35**	**36**	**45**	**37**	**38**	**48**	**41**	**43**	**49**	**49**	**47**
weighted-avg	**59**	**60**	**58**	**59**	**61**	**58**	**55**	**60**	**55**	**55**	**60**	**53**	**60**	**61**	**60**	**62**	**62**	**61**

Table 2.4 Sentiment Task Results from multitask models: Per-class Precision, Recall and F1 scores. Values in bold show the maximum value for a particular metric in that row.

| | CNN_MTL | | | Bi-GRU_MTL | | | Bi-LSTM_MTL | | |
Sentiment	*P*	*R*	*F*	*P*	*R*	*F*	*P*	*R*	*F*
Positive	67	59	63	76	50	60	59	62	60
Negative	57	37	45	58	41	48	58	56	57
Neutral	71	85	75	69	85	76	75	75	75
macro-avg	65	60	62	**68**	59	61	64	64	64
weighted-avg	67	**68**	66	67	**68**	66	**68**	**68**	**68**
Accuracy	67.90			67.70			**68.12**		

approaches. We also report the results from the baseline models (BNB, SVM, RF, and LR and results from [4]). All our deep-learning methods perform considerably better than the classical machine-learning-based baselines. Also, our single-task deep-learning models (CNN_STL, Bi-GRU_STL, and Bi-LSTM_STL) score marginally better than similar approaches (CNN, GRU and LSTM) reported in [4] on the same CEASE dataset. This may be attributed to our consideration of shallower BiGRU and Bi-LSTM layers and richer feature representation for CNN-based models than [4]. All 3 proposed multitasking models outperform their single-task variants and the considered baselines with a best-attained cross-validation accuracy of 60.76%. Our best model, a simple BiLSTM-based multitasking model, can also beat the top-performing model reported in [4], which is an ensemble-based model. The explicit nature of instances in suicidal texts enables our models to achieve commendable per-class performances for even some under-represented classes. Table 2.6 shows several cases in which the single-task model misclassifies, but the multitask version correctly classifies.

2.7.4 Error analysis

Due to the under-representation of the majority of emotionally intense classes, it appears that the class imbalance issue is the main obstacle to reaching good class-wise accuracies or F1 scores. Pride and abuse are two classes that no model can correctly classify. The lack of sufficient instances in these classes may be attributed as the reason for such an outcome. Table 2.7 displays sample misclassified instances from the test set for

Table 2.5 Accuracy scores on the test set (Test set Acc.) and Average Accuracy values of 10-fold cross-validation (10F-CV Avg Acc.) are shown. The italicized values reflect the multitask models' better scores over the single-task versions. The values in bold reflect the highest possible ratings.

Models	Test set Acc. (%)	10F-CV Avg Acc. (%)
BNB	46.17	46.34
SVM	45.13	50.53
RF	52.59	54.20
LR	53.00	56.98
CNN	59.54	59.43
GRU	58.70	58.54
LSTM	58.08	57.96
CNN_STL	*60.10*	*60.23*
Bi-GRU_STL	*59.83*	*59.92*
Bi-LSTM_STL	*59.63*	*59.38*
CNN_MTL	*60.87*	*60.72*
Bi-GRU_MTL	*60.46*	*60.66*
Bi-LSTM_MTL	***61.49***	***60.76***

Table 2.6 Annotation samples of some emotion classes.

Sentence	Wrong predictions from BiLSTM_STL	Correct predictions from BiLSTM_MTL
Seriously there is nothing to be done. Hello.	Information	Hopelessness
< name > today you have suspected me without any reason as no act of mine is wrong.	Sorrow	Blame
I just became increasingly scared that you would hurt me mentally or physically.	Guilt	Fear
Shoot the 1st basket!	Information	Instruction
Though I am about to kick the bucket, I am as happy as ever.	Information	Happiness_Peacefulness

each of our three multitask models (CNN_MTL, Bi-GRU_MTL, and Bi-LSTM_MTL).

Also, it is observed that sentiment prediction is correct for some instances, whereas the corresponding emotion prediction is incorrect.

Table 2.7 Annotation samples of some emotion classes.

Sentence	Actual Emotion	Predicted Emotion	Predicted Sentiment
I believe that it is advisable if one's inclinations lead to the antisocial side.	Hopefulness	Pride	Negative
Their generosity, devotion, love, and tact made it possible for me to accept their financial help over a long period of time.	Thankfulness	Blame	Positive
I cannot begin to fathom the countless agonies down the road.	Sorrow	Guilt	Neutral
I am not sure why I am writing this.	Information	Pride	Neutral
And about bud, I want to dismiss every idea about him.	Information	Happiness_Peacefulness	Negative

For example, consider the sentence:

I am not sure why I am writing this.

The predicted sentiment is *Neutral,* whereas the predicted emotion label is *Pride.* This is because the sentiment task has fewer classes than the emotion task, enabling it to train better with less confusion among the available classes. This can be realized in Tables 2.3 and 2.4. We equate our multitask model predictions to single-task model predictions and conduct qualitative error analysis on them. We find that multitask learning outperforms single-task learning in certain situations (correct or similar to gold labels).

2.8 Conclusion

The consideration of deep-learning approaches in research on suicide offers new opportunities for improvement in existing emotion-detection tools related to forensic texts. Also, it detects suicidal ideation among at-risk individuals providing scope for timely suicide prevention. In this work, we leverage the effectiveness of multitask learning by jointly training two correlated tasks, emotion (primary task) and sentiment (auxiliary task) prediction, to enhance the performance of existing deep neural-based single-task architectures. We have proposed 3 multitask systems for sentiment and emotion detection from real-life suicide notes (at the sentence level) based on 3 independent deep-learning approaches. These multitask models are built upon their single-task variants, which also serve as the baselines along with 4 other popular machine learning classifiers. We consider the CEASE [4] dataset, a publicly available standard dataset of 2393 fine-grained emotion annotated sentences from 205 real-life suicide notes. When comparing the efficiency of our proposed methods to the baselines, we found that all multitasking systems outperformed their single-task equivalents and outperformed deep-learning models by a significant margin. The Bi-LSTM_MTL model has the best cross-validation accuracy of 60.76%.

In future work, we want to use social-media evidence to investigate the impact of depression as a source of suicidal ideation. We will also look for trends in writings on social media and suicide messages. Further, we intend to expand the CEASE dataset with more annotated suicide notes and extend the annotation scheme to a multilabeling one with added Valence, Arousal, and Dominance dimensions.

Acknowledgments

The authors gratefully acknowledge the help of MeitY, the Government of India, and the Government of Bihar for the project titled 'Development of CDAC Digital Forensic Centre with AI related Information Support Tools.' The authors would like to express their gratitude to the linguists Akash Bhagat, Suman Shekhar (IIT Patna), and Danish Armaan (IIEST Shibpur) for their contributions in labeling the tweets.

References

[1] R.C. O'Connor, M.K. Nock, The psychology of suicidal behaviour, Lancet Psychiatry 1 (1) (2014) 73–85.

[2] S. Hinduja, J.W. Patchin, Bullying, cyberbullying, and suicide, Archives of Suicide Research 14 (3) (2010) 206–221.

[3] K. Roberts, M.A. Roach, J. Johnson, J. Guthrie, S.M. Harabagiu, EmpaTweet: annotating and detecting emotions on Twitter, in: LREC'12, Citeseer, 2012, pp. 3806–3813.

[4] S. Ghosh, A. Ekbal, P. Bhattacharyya, CEASE, a corpus of emotion annotated suicide notes in English, in: Proceedings of the 12th Language Resources and Evaluation Conference, European Language Resources Association, Marseille, France, May 2020, pp. 1618–1626, https://www.aclweb.org/anthology/2020.lrec-1.201.

[5] E.S. Shneidman, N.L. Farberow, Clues to suicide, Public Health Reports 71 (2) (1956) 109.

[6] A.M. Edelman, S.L. Renshaw, Genuine versus simulated suicide notes: an issue revisited through discourse analysis, Suicide & Life-Threatening Behavior 12 (2) (1982) 103–113.

[7] L.A. Gottschalk, G.C. Gleser, An analysis of the verbal content of suicide notes, British Journal of Medical Psychology 33 (1960) 195–204.

[8] J. Tuckman, R.J. Kleiner, M. Lavell, Emotional content of suicide notes, The American Journal of Psychiatry 116 (1) (1959) 59–63.

[9] C.E. Osgood, E.G. Walker, Motivation and language behavior: a content analysis of suicide notes, Journal of Abnormal and Social Psychology 59 (1) (1959) 58.

[10] A. Capstick, Recognition of emotional disturbance and the prevention of suicide, British Medical Journal 1 (5180) (1960) 1179.

[11] F. Wagner, Suicide notes, Danish Medical Journal 7 (1960) 62–64.

[12] E.S. Shneidman, N.L. Farberow, A socio-psychological investigation of suicide, in: Perspectives in Personality Research, Springer, 1960, pp. 270–293.

[13] J.J. Shapero, The language of suicide notes, Ph.D. dissertation, University of Birmingham, 2011.

[14] E.S. Shneidman, Suicide notes reconsidered, Psychiatry 36 (4) (1973) 379–394.

[15] S.S. Canetto, D. Lester, The Epidemiology of Women's Suicidal Behavior, Springer Publishing Co, 1995.

[16] T. Ho, P.S. Yip, C. Chiu, P. Halliday, Suicide notes: what do they tell us?, Acta Psychiatrica Scandinavica 98 (6) (1998) 467–473.

[17] T.E. Joiner, J.W. Pettit, R.L. Walker, Z.R. Voelz, J. Cruz, M.D. Rudd, D. Lester, Perceived burdensomeness and suicidality: two studies on the suicide notes of those attempting and those completing suicide, Journal of Social and Clinical Psychology 21 (5) (2002) 531–545.

[18] J.P. Pestian, P. Matykiewicz, J. Grupp-Phelan, Using natural language processing to classify suicide notes, in: Proceedings of the Workshop on Current Trends in Biomedical Natural Language Processing, Association for Computational Linguistics, 2008, pp. 96–97.

[19] J. Pestian, P. Matykiewicz, Classification of suicide notes using natural language processing, in: Proceedings of ACL Bio NLP, vol. 967, 2008.

[20] J. Pestian, H. Nasrallah, P. Matykiewicz, A. Bennett, A. Leenaars, Suicide note classification using natural language processing: a content analysis, Biomedical Informatics Insights 3 (2010) BII–S4706.

[21] J.P. Pestian, P. Matykiewicz, M. Linn-Gust, B. South, O. Uzuner, J. Wiebe, K.B. Cohen, J. Hurdle, C. Brew, Sentiment analysis of suicide notes: a shared task, Biomedical Informatics Insights 5 (2012) BII–S9042.

[22] R. Wicentowski, M.R. Sydes, Emotion detection in suicide notes using maximum entropy classification, Biomedical Informatics Insights 5 (2012) BII–S8972.

[23] A. Kovačević, A. Dehghan, J.A. Keane, G. Nenadic, Topic categorisation of statements in suicide notes with integrated rules and machine learning, Biomedical Informatics Insights 5 (2012) BII–S8978.

[24] H. Yang, A. Willis, A. De Roeck, B. Nuseibeh, A hybrid model for automatic emotion recognition in suicide notes, Biomedical Informatics Insights 5 (2012) BII–S8948.

[25] K. Roberts, S.M. Harabagiu, Statistical and similarity methods for classifying emotion in suicide notes, Biomedical Informatics Insights 5 (2012) BII–S8958.

[26] B. Desmet, V. Hoste, Emotion detection in suicide notes, Expert Systems with Applications 40 (16) (2013) 6351–6358.

[27] J. Lopez-Castroman, B. Moulahi, J. Azé, S. Bringay, S. Deninotti, S. Guillaume, E. Baca-Garcia, Mining social networks to improve suicide prevention: a scoping review, Journal of Neuroscience Research 98 (2020) 616–625.

[28] S. Akhtar, D. Ghosal, A. Ekbal, P. Bhattacharyya, S. Kurohashi, All-in-one: emotion, sentiment and intensity prediction using a multi-task ensemble framework, IEEE Transactions on Affective Computing 13 (2022) 285–297.

[29] A. Kumar, A. Ekbal, D. Kawahra, S. Kurohashi, Emotion helps sentiment: a multi-task model for sentiment and emotion analysis, in: 2019 International Joint Conference on Neural Networks (IJCNN), IEEE, 2019, pp. 1–8.

[30] V. Venek, S. Scherer, L.-P. Morency, J. Pestian, et al., Adolescent suicidal risk assessment in clinician-patient interaction, IEEE Transactions on Affective Computing 8 (2) (2017) 204–215.

[31] D. Delgado-Gomez, H. Blasco-Fontecilla, A.A. Alegria, T. Legido-Gil, A. Artes-Rodriguez, E. Baca-Garcia, Improving the accuracy of suicide attempter classification, Artificial Intelligence in Medicine 52 (3) (2011) 165–168.

[32] G. Liu, C. Wang, K. Peng, H. Huang, Y. Li, W. Cheng, SocInf: membership inference attacks on social media health data with machine learning, IEEE Transactions on Computational Social Systems 6 (5) (2019) 907–921.

[33] J. Tighe, F. Shand, R. Ridani, A. Mackinnon, N. De La Mata, H. Christensen, Ibobbly mobile health intervention for suicide prevention in Australian Indigenous youth: a pilot randomised controlled trial, BMJ Open 7 (1) (2017) e013518.

[34] B. O'dea, S. Wan, P.J. Batterham, A.L. Calear, C. Paris, H. Christensen, Detecting suicidality on Twitter, Internet Interventions 2 (2) (2015) 183–188.

[35] H.-C. Shing, S. Nair, A. Zirikly, M. Friedenberg, H. Daume III, P. Resnik, Expert, crowdsourced, and machine assessment of suicide risk via online postings, in: Proceedings of the Fifth Workshop on Computational Linguistics and Clinical Psychology: From Keyboard to Clinic, 2018, pp. 25–36.

[36] F. Ren, X. Kang, C. Quan, Examining accumulated emotional traits in suicide blogs with an emotion topic model, IEEE Journal of Biomedical and Health Informatics 20 (5) (2015) 1384–1396.

[37] L. Yue, W. Chen, X. Li, W. Zuo, M. Yin, A survey of sentiment analysis in social media, Knowledge and Information Systems (2018) 1–47.

[38] A. Benton, M. Mitchell, D. Hovy, Multi-task learning for mental health using social media text, arXiv preprint, arXiv:1712.03538, 2017.

[39] S. Ji, C.P. Yu, S.-f. Fung, S. Pan, G. Long, Supervised learning for suicidal ideation detection in online user content, Complexity 2018 (2018) 6157249.

[40] S. Ji, G. Long, S. Pan, T. Zhu, J. Jiang, S. Wang, Detecting suicidal ideation with data protection in online communities, in: International Conference on Database Systems for Advanced Applications, Springer, 2019, pp. 225–229.

[41] J. Joo, S. Hwang, J.J. Gallo, Death ideation and suicidal ideation in a community sample who do not meet criteria for major depression, Crisis 37 (2) (2016) 161–165.

[42] M.K. Nock, G. Borges, E.J. Bromet, J. Alonso, M. Angermeyer, A. Beautrais, R. Bruffaerts, W.T. Chiu, G. De Girolamo, S. Gluzman, et al., Cross-national prevalence and risk factors for suicidal ideation, plans and attempts, British Journal of Psychiatry 192 (2) (2008) 98–105.

[43] A.J. Ferrari, R.E. Norman, G. Freedman, A.J. Baxter, J.E. Pirkis, M.G. Harris, A. Page, E. Carnahan, L. Degenhardt, T. Vos, et al., The burden attributable to mental and substance use disorders as risk factors for suicide: findings from the global burden of disease study 2010, PLoS ONE 9 (4) (2014) e91936.

[44] P. Ekman, An argument for basic emotions, Cognition and Emotion 6 (3–4) (1992) 169–200.

[45] J.A. Russell, A circumplex model of affect, Journal of Personality and Social Psychology 39 (6) (1980) 1161.

[46] Robert Plutchik, The nature of emotions: human emotions have deep evolutionary roots, a fact that may explain their complexity and provide tools for clinical practice, American Scientist 89 (4) (2001) 344–350.

[47] S.S. Tomkins, Affect Imagery Consciousness: Volume I: The Positive Affects, Springer Publishing Company, 1962.

[48] P. Ekman, E.R. Sorenson, W.V. Friesen, Pan-cultural elements in facial displays of emotion, Science 164 (3875) (1969) 86–88.

[49] Zhaoxia Wang, Seng-beng Ho, Erik Cambria, A review of emotion sensing: categorization models and algorithms, Multimedia Tools and Applications 79 (2020) 35553–35582.

[50] M. Etkind, ...Or Not to Be: A Collection of Suicide Notes, Riverhead Books, New York, NY, Feb 1997.

[51] J. Pennington, R. Socher, C. Manning, GloVe: global vectors for word representation, in: Proceedings of the 2014 Conference on Empirical Methods in Natural Language Processing (EMNLP), 2014, pp. 1532–1543.

[52] M.S. Akhtar, A. Kumar, A. Ekbal, P. Bhattacharyya, A hybrid deep learning architecture for sentiment analysis, in: Proceedings of COLING 2016, the 26th International Conference on Computational Linguistics: Technical Papers, 2016, pp. 482–493.

[53] P. Singhal, P. Bhattacharyya, Borrow a little from your rich cousin: using embeddings and polarities of English words for multilingual sentiment classification, in: Proceedings of COLING 2016, the 26th International Conference on Computational Linguistics: Technical Papers, 2016, pp. 3053–3062.

[54] Y. Kim, Convolutional neural networks for sentence classification, arXiv preprint, arXiv:1408.5882, 2014.

[55] S. Hochreiter, J. Schmidhuber, Long short-term memory, Neural Computation 9 (8) (1997) 1735–1780.

[56] N. Srivastava, G. Hinton, A. Krizhevsky, I. Sutskever, R. Salakhutdinov, Dropout: a simple way to prevent neural networks from overfitting, Journal of Machine Learning Research 15 (1) (2014) 1929–1958.

[57] K. Cho, B. Van Merrienboer, D. Bahdanau, Y. Bengio, On the properties of neural machine translation: encoder-decoder approaches, arXiv preprint, arXiv:1409.1259, 2014.

[58] Z. Yang, D. Yang, C. Dyer, X. He, A. Smola, E. Hovy, Hierarchical attention networks for document classification, in: Proceedings of the 2016 Conference of the North American Chapter of the Association for Computational Linguistics: Human Language Technologies, 2016, pp. 1480–1489.

[59] X. Glorot, A. Bordes, Y. Bengio, Deep sparse rectifier neural networks, in: Proceedings of the Fourteenth International Conference on Artificial Intelligence and Statistics, 2011, pp. 315–323.

[60] D.P. Kingma, J. Ba, Adam: a method for stochastic optimization, arXiv preprint, arXiv: 1412.6980, 2014.

[61] C.J. Hutto, E. Gilbert, VADER: a parsimonious rule-based model for sentiment analysis of social media text, in: Eighth International AAAI Conference on Weblogs and Social Media, 2014.

[62] Corinna Cortes, Vladimir Vapnik, Support-vector networks, Machine Learning 20 (3) (1995) 273–297.

[63] F. Pedregosa, G. Varoquaux, A. Gramfort, V. Michel, B. Thirion, O. Grisel, M. Blondel, P. Prettenhofer, R. Weiss, V. Dubourg, et al., Scikit-learn: machine learning in Python, Journal of Machine Learning Research 12 (85) (Oct 2011) 2825–2830.

CHAPTER 3

Applications and challenges of SA in real-life scenarios

Diptesh Kanojia[a] and Aditya Joshi[b]
[a]Surrey Institute for People-centred AI, Guildford, United Kingdom
[b]SEEK, Melbourne, VIC, Australia

The previous chapter describes sentiment analysis (SA) and its allied sub-problems via the perspective of computational intelligence. At its heart, SA is a prediction problem over text. Given a piece of text, the task is to predict sentiment (positive/negative/neutral) or emotion (happy/sad/angry and so on), etc. Aspect-based SA, domain-specific SA can be viewed as sub-tasks in SA – each bringing additional challenges providing opportunities for innovative architectures.

However, any area of technology is centered around two pillars: innovation and usefulness. The two are interleaved in that one drives the other. The case is no different for SA. The innovation and advancements in SA can be attributed to the availability of benchmark datasets, most notably for English as a part of the GLUE benchmark [109] or Sentiment Treebank. SA has witnessed a development of large-scale datasets and lexicons. For example, Amazon made their review dataset public [75] providing an impetus to research in aspect-based SA. The sentiment tree bank provided a tree-based dataset of sentences and phrases labeled for sentiment. As a result, SA attracted the attention of [101]. There were datasets to train large-scale neural models, and the public availability of the datasets meant reproducibility and comparison of proposed approaches were achieved.

While the availability of benchmark datasets spawned innovation in SA, this chapter is about the second pillar: usefulness. We visualize the usefulness of SA in the form of its last-mile applications. The phrase 'last mile' is often used in the context of e-commerce websites: websites that sell products to consumers. The Cambridge dictionary describes 'last mile' as the last stage in a process, especially of a customer buying goods. In the context of SA, the last mile are the applications of SA to the real world. The usefulness of SA is manifested in the real-world applications of SA: from helping stock traders make purchase decisions to mining continuous streams of social-media data for intelligence on public-health outbreaks. In this chapter, we

Computational Intelligence Applications for Text and Sentiment Data Analysis
https://doi.org/10.1016/B978-0-32-390535-0.00008-2

49

cover these applications of SA in real-life scenarios: health, culture, social policy, human safety, and other areas of NLP research.

Fig. 3.1 is a perspective of what constitutes an application of SA. SA is at the center of the figure. It is conflated to mean SA, emotion analysis, aspect-based SA and other sub-areas of SA. The focus of this chapter is, however, the connections of SA with these other areas that are positioned around it: society, health, safety, culture, business, and other areas of NLP.[1] Each of these form forthcoming sections of the chapter. In each section, we address questions pertinent to the specific domain. For example, how can SA be applied to improve the health of individuals and a community? How can SA be applied to aid businesses achieve their objectives? The areas discussed in the chapter are real-life scenarios: scenarios impacting individuals, communities or organizations.

At the outset, it is important to note that an application does not only mean the domain of the dataset used. A new application domain may provide unique opportunities to improve SA. For example, ontologies created by medical experts are unique to the health domain and have been shown to be immensely useful as structured knowledge bases for SA applications in health. Therefore, in addition to applications of SA, we also highlight particular challenges and opportunities for these applications to demonstrate that an effective application often needs application-based understanding and adaptation of SA.

In each of the following sections, we describe applications and challenges of SA in real-world scenarios, as illustrated in Fig. 3.1.

3.1 Health

Advances in science and technology that have been applied and deployed to improve the health and well-being of individuals and the society have always received attention. SA is no exception. Health-related textual datasets may be generated by medical professionals in the form of clinical notes or by individuals in the form of social-media posts. SA applied to each of these can be useful in many ways. In this section, we now discuss some of these applications.

---

[1] This is not the complete list of applications of SA. A few applications such as education technology or disaster management are not included in the chapter. However, we believe that the applications covered in the chapter are representative of the majority of the applications, and provide a sense of the utility of SA.

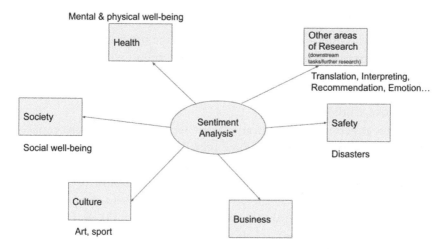

*Conflated term: Intended to cover emotion/opinion/aspect detection

Figure 3.1 Applications of SA.

3.1.1 Challenges

The immediately apparent difficulty in applying SA to health-related problems is the availability of datasets. Medical datasets may not always be available in digitized form in some regions of the world. Similarly, privacy and confidentiality of medical data prevents making it accessible for research or deployment. However, some benchmark datasets such as MIMIC are available for research purposes. An alternative to the medical datasets are user-generated datasets such as tweets. Since official medical datasets are confidential, tweets posted by people can be a useful alternative. The epidemiology community, therefore, refers to tweets as 'open-source data'.

However, using tweets for healthcare applications of SA has its own challenges. Social-media usage is popular in certain demographics, potentially based on their age or acquaintance with technology. As a result, as a volume, social-media-based datasets may not be representative of a community, reflecting a selection bias.

3.1.2 Applications

In situations where medical transcripts and data by medical practitioners is available, Denecke and Deng [21] identify the following avenues for application of SA using medical transcripts:

1. **Change in health status:** The medical practitioner may note whether a patient felt better or worse. This may be done using sentiment words. This sentiment may be expressed towards entities such as the pharmacological interventions used for treatment.
2. **Critical events:** Medical emergencies can be reported through strong negative sentiment.
3. **Patient experience:** A medical practitioner may report patient experience as the patient describes how they are feeling during an appointment.

The points above hold true for user-generated medical data as well. Discussion forums on the internet for people suffering from certain medical conditions allow people to share experiences with each other. SA applied on these discussion forums can help to identify what measures are working for people – and what are not.

In addition, since social media is widely used, people often report their health conditions in the form of social-media posts such as tweets. Social-media-based epidemic intelligence is the use of social-media posts to monitor initiation, prevalence and spread of epidemics in the real world [46]. By its very definition, the word 'disease' signifies a situation where a person is not ('dis') at 'ease' with themselves. As a result, people experiencing illnesses typically express negative sentiment, at least implicitly negative. Social-media-based epidemic intelligence (SMEI) is a quintessential application of SA applied to the world of health/healthcare.

At the heart of SMEI is the task of predicting whether a tweet mentioning an illness-related word is a report of the illness. Such a tweet has been called a personal-health mention. For example, a tweet 'This fever is killing me' is a report of an illness, while 'Fever, cough, and loss of taste are common symptoms of COVID-19' is not a report of an illness, although both contain the symptom word 'fever'. The task of computationally detecting personal-health mentions is called personal-health mention classification. Personal-health mention classification uses features based on sentiment, as given in Joshi et al. [46]: the number of negative words, the implied sentiment, and so on. Alternatively, sentiment information can be incorporated into a neural architecture. Biddle et al. [7] concatenate word representations with sentiment distributions obtained from three sentiment lexicons. This is then passed to sequential layers such as LSTM before the prediction is made.

The second step in SMEI is health-event detection. It uses time-series monitoring in order to predict an outbreak in the number of personal-

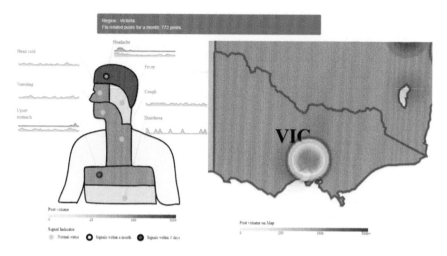

Figure 3.2 Social-Media-based Epidemic Intelligence.

health mentions (say, within a time period). SMEI can potentially detect short-term outbreaks as well as the beginning of long-term epidemics. SMEI can eventually be deployed in a dashboard that monitors social-media posts in the geography of interest. One such dashboard is 'Watch The Flu' [43] that automatically monitors tweets posted from within Australia, identifies the ones that are personal-health mentions (via classification) for influenza symptoms and then detects potential spikes in symptoms reports (via time series monitoring). A screenshot from their paper is given in Fig. 3.2.

SA also assumes importance in terms of the aspects towards which the sentiment is expressed. For example, vaccination-sentiment detection involves detection of sentiment towards vaccines [57]. Similarly, Social Media Monitoring 4 Health (SMM4H) workshop conducts shared tasks for health-related tweets [65]. The reported systems regularly report the use of SA-based enhancements for tasks such as adverse drug-reaction detection, vaccination-behavior detection, and so on.

The COVID-19 pandemic is an unprecedented pandemic that resulted in worldwide infections, deaths, lockdowns, and economic slowdowns. In Kruspe et al. [56], SA (using a neural network) is applied to multi-lingual tweets from around the world. The paper shows how sentiment towards the pandemic changed in different parts over the world over time. An application of SA such as this provides a zeitgeist of the impact of the COVID-19 pandemic. A figure from this paper is included as Fig. 3.3.

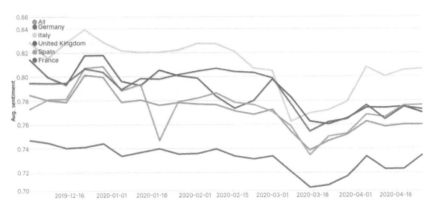

Figure 3.3 Sentiment changes in different countries during the COVID-19 pandemic.

SA of tweets during the time of a pandemic can help to understand issues being experienced by people. An example in the context of COVID-19 is Kleinberg et al. [54]. The paper reports a COVID-19 Real-world Worry Dataset. The datasets contains tweets posted from within UK during the time of the COVID-19 pandemic. In the introductory paper, the authors use topic modeling and lexical analysis using Linguistic Inquiry and Word Count (LIWC) in order to understand issues and concerns as expressed in the tweets.

3.2 Social policy

SA holds an important place in the social-conversation space as combined with text mining from the social-media domain. It can be a really powerful tool to gather public opinion. Early research in this area [50] argues that this is an interdisciplinary field that crosses the boundaries of artificial intelligence and natural language processing – the domains to which it is known to belong to. As the digitization of public opinion via forums like Reddit and Twitter are becoming more popular, with more and more people gaining access to the internet, we see a shift in the strategies employed by governments of the world that take these digital media into account. The analysis of sentiment towards political discourse is also important as sentiment/emotion expressed towards a political scenario are polar in nature. People express opinions in favor or against a political decision or even the rulings of courts in many countries. Therefore, it is widely believed and also already acceptable to use SA-based tools and research for measuring the sentiment of people towards social policy. A social issue is an issue that relates to people's personal lives and interactions. The impact of public opinion on social issues and on policy makers operates in a similar manner to those of product reviews for manufacturers. Current governments and organizations engaging with social issues can analyze public criticisms or supports for a particular policy and consider public opinions in making decisions. Politicians can receive electorates' opinions concerning important issues and their expectations. However, social issues are very different from products and services. The divide on social issues can be much larger in people compared to the divide in opinion on a product. Such opinions can also be very nuanced and may be expressed neither in complete favor nor completely against a social policy, which is also a challenge faced by SA research when applied to the social-policy domain. People who voice their opinions on social-media platforms also tend to use *hashtags, slangs, mixed language*, i.e., code-mixing/switching, and inconsistent *variants of words* in a language that are technical challenges to further mining the social opinion of a populace. There are conversations in comments and on Twitter threads that imbibe a context for humans, whereas this context combined with the background knowledge of the subject matter is impossible for machines to comprehend and take into account, which is mining social opinions. Despite these challenges, the applications of SA research to the social-policy domain continues to thrive and has allowed so many research questions to stem from this field, which we will discuss further in the next subsection.

3.2.1 Applications in social policy

Social media provides opportunities for policy makers to gauge public opinion. However, the large volume and a variety of expressions on social media have changed traditional policy analysis and public-sentiment assessment. The applications of SA research in this area have an immense contribution in gauging the social and political sentiment of a populace. For example, Adams-Cohen [1] show how public opinion shifted post-legalization of same-sex marriage in the United States. They used Twitter to analyze public opinion after the Supreme Court ruling and observed how states affected by the ruling carried a more negative sentiment towards the subject. Court rulings on social policy can polarize the public as the mandate might not be culturally acceptable by the layman. Crossley et al. [19] proposed a tool they call SEANCE for sentiment, social cognition, and social-order analysis. This tool offers various features for the analysis of data collected from various social-media forums. Existing research has also presented arguments that political scientists have done little in the way of rigorous analysis towards the sentiment/mood of the general public [24]. However, SA research, due to automated computational approaches, is able to do this without the manually conducted political surveys and opinion polls. With the rapid growth of social-media content and usage, policy makers and even ordinary citizens are able to efficiently obtain voluminous data about public sentiment. Opinion leaders, authorities, and activists who share their ideas on Twitter are often followed closely by thousands of users. These leaders provide valuable content as well as linkage information that can offer insights for policy decision making [17]. It is well documented that online forums like Twitter affect the political discourse and raises questions that need answers from the governments [80]. These questions can be related to incidents that happen rarely or can be related to the long-term political decisions or a potential problem for the country in the long term (aging population [81]). SA research has focused on public opinion about rural issues as well – issues pertaining to a section of the population that has limited access to the internet where these issues are discussed, which is ironic to think about [11,61,99,100,107]. Social or political campaigns run by the governments/politicians are also topics of discussion amongst the online population that can help predict the public opinion towards a campaign [12,15,35,94,103]. The analysis of online text or opinion can help create a positive impact on the policy as governments can be better informed about public opinion. Such content can be useful for government agencies, as it can help them understand the needs and problems of society to formulate effective public policies. The constantly increasing complexity of social problems and needs makes this political content even more valuable, as it contains extensive knowledge concerning such problems, which can be quite useful for understanding and managing their complexity [14]. Online media can affect and help form social policies, as evident by these significant number of studies in this domain. However, the mining of sentiment/opinion from public forums does not come without its own set of challenges, which we discuss in brief in the next subsection.

3.2.2 Challenges in social policy

Social media is full of opinions, emotions, and sentiments expressed largely in the forms of text. This voluminous amount of text, however, can be expressed in different ways, which is largely considered a challenge by the researchers in the SA domain [106]. A whole subspace of SA researchers have dedicated themselves to identifying genuine users and account holders as compared to what are known as fake or 'troll' accounts online. Fake accounts on social media are run via politically motivated organizations with the help of a large number of employees and also by 'bots' which can help further any agenda. Here are some of the research challenges faced by SA researchers when collecting the data from social-media forums:

Identification of Users: While traditional data-collection methods like surveying and interviewing largely relied upon manual collection of data, it could collect authentic data. However, with the advent and easy access to social media, it is an important challenge to determine which accounts carry the opinions of genuine social-media users. Flores-Saviaga et al. [27] note that political trolls initiate online discord not only for the laughs but also for ideological reasons. They uncover that the most active users employed distinct discursive strategies to mobilize participation and also deployed technical tools like bots to create a shared identity and sustain engagement. In fact, they themselves face a challenge as they build their own 'troll' community while simultaneously disrupting others.

User Privacy: Privacy concerns and related risks are a cause of concern for researchers and for the public. The danger of spatial information disclosure becomes more serious when people use mobile devices and "check-in" through social media to reveal their physical locations. Although a large-scale opinion-mining research practice may ignore such data, released datasets may contain sensitive information, and hence, researchers face an additional challenge in terms of anonymization of data streams used for research. This information can at times also reveal medical records and public-health data, which should not be shared without ensuring either the consent of the patient or proper anonymization techniques.

Noisy Data: The rapid growth of social media has also led to a rapid increase in spam and online marketing of content that is prevalent in social conversations. This noise may create a hurdle for SA research that tries to capture a genuine opinion of social-media users. Non-relevant posts and comments, marketing messages, bots, 'clickbaits' and advertisements lead to a lot of noisy data, which needs to be removed before the analysis of user data generated via social-media forums.

Mental Health: Mental illness is a serious and widespread health challenge today. Many people suffer from depression, and only a fraction opt to receive adequate treatment. The role of this need for validation via social-media posts has been investigated by many researchers [5,20]. Advocates of mental health and policy makers have expressed concerns regarding the potential negative impact of social media on an overall young population.

Although much of the public narrative on such negative effects implies that its mere exposure is related to common mental-health problems, the evidence suggests that quality rather than quantity of use is more crucial. For example, existing research argues that the use of social media for negative social comparison, which, alongside rumination, leads to depression.

Language: SA research is a part of the NLP domain and suffers from similar technical challenges in terms of the language used to express opinions on the internet. Automatically detecting the sentiment or opinion from online forums is challenging in terms of the language used on social media. For example, emotions are not stated explicitly with the content. Social-media text can express frustration, depression, anger, joy, sarcasm and so on in varying degrees that are implicitly captured in the text. Certain words that carry negation towards the sentence can be very impactful towards the sentiment but are not used to capture the sentence polarity. The use of creative and non-standard language, which includes hashtags and abbreviations, popular among a young generation, can also convey sentiment and emotion that need to be captured. Para-linguistic information like facial expressions is often ignored as SA research primarily deals with text, but this information also carries sentiment that should be captured. Cross-cultural differences in emotions expressed towards a particular situation can also lead to ambiguity that sometimes, even humans cannot comprehend. Of course, the lack of labeled sentiment data is also a huge challenge that leads to the use of semi-supervised and unsupervised approaches that can not be relied upon fully.

The mining of opinion or sentiment from the social-media text, especially when social policy is concerned, faces hurdles due to such challenges. As research in SA progresses, new sub-problems like aggression/hate-speech detection, offensive-language identification, and emotion analysis have emerged, which attempt to tackle these in a very "one-problem-at-a-time" way. Hopefully, in the near future, the solutions to these challenges will also emerge slowly and help us garner actual public opinion about social policies from the internet.

3.3 E-commerce / industry

Customer reviews over online e-commerce platforms have become a common source of product feedback for consumers and manufacturers alike. Similarly, services like Yelp (www.yelp.com), Zomato (www.zomato.com), and TripAdvisor (www.tripadvisor.com) are commonly available for customer feedback on restaurants and travel destinations. Social-media platforms like Facebook and Instagram are also known hosts to pages and channels that provide feedback on restaurants and travel destinations. These review sources also act as an important part of the *'feedback loop'* for e-commerce platforms and manufacturers to improve the overall product quality based on certain aspect-level reviews. Recent research shows that fine-grained aspect-based SA has penetrated SA research in NLP [3,25,34,42,95]. In this section, we discuss how SA has gained importance in the e-commerce domain and also provide an outline of the challenges posed for this research.

3.3.1 Applications in e-commerce

Customers who buy products online often rely on other customers' reviews found over e-commerce platforms, more than reviews found in specialist magazines. These reviews often prove to be important recommendations for books, mobiles, laptops, clothing etc., and seem reliable as they are written by product users, in most cases. In fact, short reviews form a separate category of their own and are known as 'tips'. For example, *"I love this phone! The battery life and camera quality have won me over."* can be considered a review, whereas *"Great battery. Nice camera. Photos are good"* is considered a 'tip' or short recommendation [75]. The significantly increased exposure to digital technology and the penetration of the Internet in rural areas in recent years has led to a vast number of expressed opinions over products. In particular, customers express opinions on several aspects of products, services, blogs, and comments that are deemed to be influential, especially when making purchase decisions based on product reviews [96]. This is in contrast to the traditional surveys and questionnaires that participants had to fill without any personal motivation, thus resulting in the sub-optimal collected information.

Many potential consumers read these opinionated reviews, resulting in an influenced buying behavior [6]. From the point of view of a consumer, the information provided by past consumers of a product is regarded as more trustworthy than the information provided by its manufacturer. Also, from a manufacturer point of view, 1) understanding the product performance in a real-world setting, 2) improving some aspects of existing products, and furthermore, 3) understanding how the information in product reviews interacts with each aspect of the product or the service, enables the manufacturer to take advantages of these reviews and improve sales.

Recent NLP research on aspect-based SA (ABSA) has been driving the efforts of the e-commerce industry to analyze product reviews and gain the insights discussed above. While performing aspect-based SA, three distinguishable processing steps can be 1) identification of aspects and sentiment expressed, 2) classification of sentiment for each aspect, and 3) aggregation of the overall sentiment in the review. However, some studies only focus on one of them and do not perform all three of these steps. **The first step** involves the detection of aspects from the review text, which can be performed with the help of different approaches namely frequency-based, syntax-based, supervised machine-learning-based, unsupervised machine-learning-based, and hybrid approaches. **The second step** that entails the classification of sentiment, can also be performed with the help of various approaches, namely dictionary-based, supervised machine-learning-based, and unsupervised machine-learning-based approaches. Additionally, there are methods that perform the detection of aspects and the analysis of sentiment using a joint method via different approaches such as syntax-based, supervised machine-learning-based, unsupervised machine-learning-based, and hybrid approaches. We will discuss each of these approaches in brief here.

Hu and Liu [37,38] observe that reviews contain a limited set of vocabulary, which is used more often, as likely aspects, in the reviews. Such frequent words inspired a straightforward approach for aspect detection based on nouns and compound nouns in the review. However, such an approach has clear shortcomings in terms of the existence of other nouns in the review, which are frequently used but are not aspects. Similarly, there are implicit aspects in the reviews that can not be detected via such an approach. Hai et al. [30] propose an approach to detect such implicit aspects with the help of association-rule mining. They restrict sentiment words in the text to appear as rule antecedents only, and aspect words to appear as rule consequents, and generate association rules to find aspects based on pre-identified sentiment words.

Syntax-based methods, on the other hand, focus on syntactical relations to find aspects present in a review text. One of the simplest approaches is to tag the text with part-of-speech categories for each token in the review and then identify the adjectives that modify a potential 'aspect'. For example, the phrase 'lovely ambience' where the 'ambience' of a location is the aspect. Zhao et al. [116] discuss how syntactic patterns in the text could be utilized to extract aspects using a tree-kernel function. Similarly, Qiu et al. [84], propose a method for aspect extraction that uses a double-propagation algorithm for sentiment word expansion and aspect detection (later extended by Zhang et al. [115] and Qiu et al. [85]). This method treats aspect detection and sentiment-lexicon expansion as inter-related problems and features the use of a sentiment lexicon to find more aspects, and with additional aspects, this method is able to further find more sentiment lexicon.

Among the machine-learning-based methods to detect aspects in a text, a limited number of supervised methods have been explored. Aspect detection can be modeled as a sequence-labeling problem but supervised learning heavily relies on features extracted from the text; features that can provide more information than simple bag-of-words or part-of-speech tagged tokens in the text. However, a Conditional Random Field (CRF)-based method has been utilized to perform this task [41]. This method utilizes multiple features from the text, including the tokens, their part-of-speech tags, dependency relations between aspect token and sentiment lexicon, and the context of the aspect token. However, as compared to supervised learning-based methods, unsupervised learning-based methods have been more popular for the task of aspect detection. Most of the unsupervised methods utilize some variation of Latent Dirichlet Association (LDA) to explore the review text [10].

The use of LDA to detect fine-grained aspects in a review text is not straightforward, as it is more suited to work with large documents that have multiple topics. LDA utilizes a bag-of-words approach at the document level and hence succeeds in detecting global topics, which is not very useful for detecting aspects. Therefore, for finding local aspects to a particular review, researchers combine LDA with a Hidden Markov Model (HMM) to distinguish between aspect tokens and other background lexicons [58]. An extension to LDA, known as Multi-grain LDA (MG-LDA), also attempts to solve the global vs. local topics by having a fixed set of global topics and a dynamic set of local topics. For the local topics, the document is modeled as a set of sliding windows. This allows for a window overlap to sample one topic from multiple windows and the inherent bag-of-words modeling in LDA to have a larger set of words [9,67]. Then, there are the other variants that try to apply LDA at the sentence level [63], estimating the emphasis of aspects [110], adding syntactic dependencies [114], aspect taxonomy construction based on syntactic rules [64] and incorporating product categories to alleviate the 'cold-start' problem caused due to a limited number of reviews [70]. These efforts towards mining fine-grained aspects from reviews on e-commerce platforms show how research in SA is directly applicable in a real-world setting. At this point in the chapter, we encourage the reader to learn more about hybrid methods for aspect mining from reviews. These methods combine multiple approaches like serial hybridization [82,86,113], and parallel hybridization [8] to mine aspects. We shall now move on to discussing the second part of ABSA, which is SA/classification.

SA, in the context of this discussion, becomes the task of assigning a sentiment label or a score to each aspect in the review text. On E-Commerce platforms, each review text may contain multiple aspects or, in some cases, none of them. Therefore, SA research applied to such reviews should be robust to be able to handle any corner cases. The earlier methods for this task attempted to utilize dictionaries like Wordnets to find adjectives and label them as sentiment class (i.e., positive or negative). There are various heuristics among the early dictionary-based methods where the distance from a sentiment word would determine the appropriate sentiment class for the sentence [38,69,117]. However, as compared to aspect detection, sentiment classification can be easily modeled as a supervised learning task due to the reduction in the number of labels. Hence, we discuss the supervised machine- and deep-learning-based methods briefly below.

Supervised methods for machine and deep learning have been significantly more successful for SA in the e-commerce domain. These methods can easily incorporate information from the tokens in the review text as features, and raw scores based on the sentiment lexicon can be used to compute additional feature values. Blair-Goldensohn et al. [8] employ such a method and a MaxEnt classifier to obtain sentiment scores. Similarly, SVM is used by Yu et al. [113] to classify text into positive or negative labels by using a parse tree and reasonably assuming that each sentiment word found in the text should be within a distance of five 'parse-steps' of an aspect. Choi and Cardie [16] perform SA on very short expressions and associate these short expressions to aspects in the text. Many researchers use bag-of-words as features for supervised sentiment classification, but many argue that such models are too simple to be applied to a domain as vast as e-commerce. We highlight the challenges of using such approaches in the e-commerce domain in the next subsection and also discuss some proposed solutions. However, as opposed to the consistently tested classification-based methods, various researchers have attempted using a regression-based method to obtain sentiment scores. This does allow the sentiment-score generation to be a little more fine grained, but eventually the authors try to group the sentiment scores in five classes akin to the five-star rating system. Lu et al. [63] use a support vector regression model to obtain a sentiment score for each aspect. This model allows the sentiment score to be modeled as a real number in the zero to five rating interval. Similarly, with the help of PRanking [18], a perceptron-based online learning method, Titov and Mc-Donald [105] perform SA given the topic clusters using an LDA-like model. The input to this method is different n-grams along with binary features that describe LDA clusters. This method is interesting as it involves the construction of a feature vector for each sentence based on the absence or presence of a certain word–topic–probability combination and then groups these probabilities into 'buckets'. The PRanking algorithm takes the feature vector and learned weights as inputs to arrive at a number, which is checked against the boundary value to be divided into one of the five classes for a sentiment score.

Unsupervised methods, however, are not widely used for sentiment classification. With the help of parsed syntactic dependencies, one can find a potential sentiment phrase in the vicinity of a pre-detected aspect. Such a sentiment word carrying a polarity can be used to arrive at a decision regarding the overall sentiment of the aspect, namely positive or negative [82]. The research in SA has also attempted to borrow from the area of computer vision, specifically, an unsupervised method known as relaxation labeling [39]. The relaxation-labeling technique helps assign a polarity label to each sentiment phrase while adhering to a set of specified constraints, which can be obtained based on the semantic orientation of adjectives [32]. The final output for any unsupervised method is also the same, either a positive or a negative label for each review text.

The methods discussed above provide an insight into the research area of aspect-based SA and how they can be used in the e-commerce domain. Depending on the availability of data samples and available methods, SA research has been prevalent in shaping the online platforms that are now a part of our daily lives. Improving customer experience and building product brands are two very simple use-cases of this research in a real-world scenario. E-commerce giants also use SA to gain a competitive edge and engage with customers based on their SA research. However, no area of research or research methodologies exist without challenges of their own. In the upcoming section, we discuss these challenges in detail and show how SA research has tried to tackle some of them.

3.3.2 Challenges in e-commerce

The premise for the SA research carried out by NLP researchers and e-commerce industries is the trustworthiness and reliability of these reviews posted by customers. However, the trust in these reviews is often misplaced due to 'fake reviews'. For example, some authors glorify their own books in reviews on an e-commerce platform. This phenomenon is also known as **'sock-puppetry'**. Unfortunately, fake reviews can be produced in different ways such as,

- product manufacturers may hire a group of individuals to post positive reviews of their products on online platforms;
- service providers like hoteliers and restaurant owners may glorify their services from multiple accounts/handles;
- authors who can post glorifying reviews about their work on online platforms via different handles/channels/social-media influencers, and lastly;
- any of these parties can also hire people to post negatively about their competition's products and rate them lower on purpose.

Such fake reviews need to be identified and filtered before processing product reviews for the sentiment. One of the major challenges for SA research is the identification of these deceptive reviews. The essence of generating a sentiment towards a product/service is trusting the 'crowd-sourcing' phenomenon, and this trust can easily be broken with deceptive content on e-commerce platforms. Such phenomena have been exposed by campaigners such as crime writer Jeremy Duns, who found a number of fellow authors involved in such practices.[2] Consider a scenario where you are trying to launch a product as a startup, and you have established competitors in the market. If a competitor decides to hire a chain of people who post negatively about your product/service, your product may not be able to penetrate the market at all. To make matters worse, this can lead actual users to believe your product is not worth investing their money in at all.

Identification of fake reviews has been addressed as a problem by the research community in various papers [26,78]. However, the research in this area had been limited to the identification of deceptive language [68, 74] whether they were computational methods or linguistic approaches to style detection. However, Fornaciari and Poesio [28] discuss a large dataset

---

[2] Amy Harmon, "Amazon Glitch Unmasks War Of Reviewers", New York Times, February 14, 2004.

containing 'real-life' examples of deceptive uses of language in a corpus they call "DeRev" (abbreviated from "Deceptive Reviews"). They created this dataset in collaboration with Jeremy Duns and other 'sock-puppet hunters' and showed how computational approaches to identify fake reviews can be helped with such a dataset. Similarly, Liu et al. [62] identify some indicators of fake reviews in the text based on spammer behavior. More recently, research has attempted to identify fake reviews in the e-commerce domain using a dataset containing text from multiple sub-domains and using an integrated neural network to help resolve the problem [2].

Apart from a social challenge like 'sock-puppetry', there are always computational and linguistic challenges to any problem. For example, the domain specificity in product reviews has always existed as a 'hard-to-swallow pill' for the researchers in the ABSA domain. Reviews in different domains adhere to different vocabulary and terminology, which makes it a challenge. Researchers have also attempted to find suitable cross-domain training that can help save time by training SA models in a particular do-main and utilizing it for another domain [97,98]. The ABSA task is a very complex endeavor in itself, and the addition of cross-domain challenges to it just makes it more challenging. Narayanan et al. [73] proposed that in-stead of focusing on a one-size-fits-all solution, researchers should focus on the many sub-problems.

There are many critical issues when implementing an LDA-based method for ABSA [105]. The simple bag-of-words approach discussed in the section above also presents different challenges, and researchers have tried to use compositional semantics to help resolve some of them. Compositional semantics states that the meaning of an expression is a function of the meaning of its parts and the syntactic rules by which these are combined. Wilson et al. [112] propose a learning algorithm that combines multiple lexicons (positive, negative, neutral) and use a compositional inference model with rules incorporated to update the deployed SVM algorithm for this task. Moreover, the language used by a genuine user of a product can be sarcastic towards the product while writing a review that seems positive at the outset. Computational approaches struggle at detecting sarcasm/irony in text, and sarcasm detection is a known challenge for researchers in the area of SA [45]. Irony in the written text is a pervasive characteristic of reviews found online, and the subjectivity (or ambiguity) in the language used with online reviews is also a major challenge [87,88]. Despite the challenge described above, there has been a constant push by research in the NLP and the SA domain to help develop generic models that can help solve the challenges in this domain. We hope that this push to solve multiple sub-problems eventually leads to solving these problems.

3.4 Digital humanities

Digital humanities is the confluence of computational methods (such as NLP) and areas of humanities. Digital humanities in the context of text-based datasets may analyze these datasets to understand the evolution of languages and the evolution of biases within the datasets. However, in the context of this chapter, we focus on approaches that use SA for digital humanities. Literary works such as books, plays, and movies may be sources of entertainment, but are also reflective of the prevalent society. Analysis of literary works using computational methods can be useful to understand these literary works, compare them and analyze patterns between literary works of the same period or by the same author. For example, an interesting question may be to understand underlying common patterns and similarities between characters and plays by William Shakespeare. Similarly, another interesting application would be to analyze the Indian epics, Ramayana and Mahabharata, and compare their storylines in the context of emotion trajectories of the characters. Closer to a deployment setting, Martinez et al. [66] show how violence rating can be predicted using the script of a movie. Each utterance is represented as a concatenation of lexical and sentiment/violence-related features. A recurrent neural network captures the linear nature of utterances in a conversation. The final prediction is an attention-based classifier based on the neural representations of the utterances.

However, in the rest of this section, we discuss the applications of SA to applications in digital humanities. Specifically, we focus on works that focus on literature, sport, and art.

Datasets used for the purpose of emotion analysis may be provided for other areas of NLP. For example, Gorinski and Lapata [29] present a corpus of movie scripts and use it for the purpose of summarization. Similarly, online portals such as the Internet Movie Script Database (https://www.imsdb.com/) (for movie scripts), Project Gutenberg (https://www.gutenberg.org/) (for books) may also be crawled in order to create relevant datasets.

3.4.1 Applications

Application of SA to art works can help to understand potential user experience. For example, what is the trajectory of emotions that a user will experience when reading a certain book or watching a certain movie? Understanding this may be useful to understand the impact of an art work on a person experiencing it. Kim and Klinger [53] present a detailed survey of sentiment and emotion-analysis approaches applied to literary works. They highlight broad categories of approaches in the area as:

1. **Classification-based formulations**: This includes tasks such as prediction of emotion of a literary work (for example, a poem), or whether or not a story has a happy ending.

2. **Temporal sentiment changes**: This involves tasks dealing with understanding how sentiment changes over time in a given literary work. The word 'time' here refers to the course of the literary work.

3. **Relationships between characters**: This involves tasks dealing with understanding relationships between characters in a literary work. This may be interlayed with temporality where the changes in relationships between characters are tracked over time.

4. **Understanding prevalent biases**: SA applied to literary works may uncover underlying biases. For example, an emotion analysis of characters followed by marginalization (in the probabilistic sense) over certain attributes may help to understand their portrayal. For example, it may help to understand if people of certain genders are portrayed as more angry or sad than others.

In order to analyze emotion-related dynamics in literary works, Hipson and Mohammad [33] present a set of metrics known as utterance emotion dynamics (UED). They show how UED metrics can be calculated and can be useful in order to understand emotion dynamics in a narrative such as a book, play or a movie. Some UED metrics that can be used to analyze emotion in a literary work are:

1. Emotion-word density: This is the proportion of emotion words uttered by a character within a certain time interval.

2. Emotional arc: The emotional arc of a character is the path taken by the character over the course of the literary work. For example, the character may start off in a happy state. Then, during the course of the narrative, an unpleasant incident occurs with them, following which they become sad and angry. As the events unfold, the character becomes happy at the end of the story.

3. Home base, variability, and displacement count: The three metrics indicate (respectively): what is the most common emotional state of a character, how much does their emotional state vary, and how often does it vary. Home base can be viewed as the most common emotional state of a character, while variability indicates how much their emotional state differs in the story. Displacement count is the number of times the character experiences an emotion displacement in the story.

4. Peak distance and rise/recovery rates: Peak distance indicates how far a character in a play deviates from their most common emotional state. Rise rate indicates how soon they achieve the peak distance, while recovery rate indicates how quickly they come back to their home base. This metric potentially refers to the ups and downs in a story.

The metrics above provide a structured framework to analyze literary works using emotion analysis. Nalisnick and Baird [72] apply SA to analyze Shakespeare's plays. The SA approach in itself is rather simple. The sentiment values of words in an utterance are looked up in a sentiment lexicon, and the sentiment is attributed as a directed relationship between the character who spoke a certain utterance and the character who spoke the next utterance in the conversation. However, the key analysis proceeds in two dimensions: relationships between characters and time in the play. As a result, the paper describes how sentiment and affinity relationships between characters change over the course of a play. Joshi et al. [48] perform a similar temporal analysis for the commentary of a cricket match. A cricket match is played over a sequence of delivery of balls. The commentary captures what happens in each of the balls. Based on what the commentator said to report each of the deliveries, the EmoGram analyzes how exciting different cricket matches were.

Literary works may also provide a proxy for real life. If a dataset of real-world data is not available, creative works can serve as a useful dataset. For example, Joshi et al. [47] present an approach for sarcasm detection in conversations. Since a dataset from conversational data is not available and since they hope for a certain class distribution in the dataset, they use transcripts of the TV Show 'Friends'. Every utterance in this dataset is manually annotated with a sarcasm label. Then, sequence-labeling algorithms are used to predict sarcasm in every utterance, using features from the utterance and utterances in its neighborhood.

Finally, digital humanities can also use SA to create a multimedia anthology of the society. An example of this is the 'We Feel' dashboard [59]. We Feel is an interactive dashboard maintained by the State Library of New

South Wales, Australia. In order to maintain a historical anthology as seen on social media, We Feel monitors tweets, detects topics from the tweets, and also records the emotion experienced by people. The We Feel dashboard contains an emotion flower – which visualizes emotion changes in tweets posted from Australia and around the world.

3.5 Other research areas

There are multiple other areas of research where the analysis of sentiment can help improve the output. In this section, we delineate such areas and try to cover the known applications of SA to other research areas and the challenges it brings forth in the said research domain. Many of the research areas we cover here belong to the NLP domain, but not all. As we discussed earlier, the recent SA research-based models attempt to determine the text's polarity and intensiveness. Various algorithms divide the text into different polarities and try to learn a sentiment towards a product, a topic, a policy, and so on. However, we have not yet discussed how this research applies to other areas and how these areas use automatic SA of text to perform the tasks pertaining to these areas. Let us briefly discuss such areas and see how SA applies to them.

3.5.1 Applications to other research areas

SA can benefit many research areas, including research in the non-computational domain. As deployable sentiment-based models become easier to use, researchers in various domains like psychology, interpreting studies, translation, explainability, and so on, have used these models to build up their research. One of the more recently investigated areas by many NLP and Deep-Learning researchers is Explainable AI (XAI). XAI research has used SA as a classification task that can help explain the decision of a neural-network-based model in past research [4,31]. Explaining and justifying recommendations to users has the potential to increase the transparency and reliability of such models [76]. Existing research has tried to learn user preferences and writing styles from crowd-sourced reviews to generate explanations in the form of natural language, i.e., synthesized review generation [22,77]. However, a large portion of the review text used for the SA task does not contain many features that can help identify the cause of decision making towards either the positive or the negative class. Therefore, Ni et al. [76] extract fine-grained aspects from justifications provided in the sentiment text to come up with user personas and item profiles consisting of a set of representative aspects. They discuss two different neural-network-based models that can provide justifications based on different aspects as a reference and provide justifications based on existing justification templates in the data for the sentiment text/instances that do not provide justifications. Similarly, Han et al. [31] contrast between the use of gradient-based saliency maps [60] and the use of Influence Functions to provide explanations for decisions made by SA models. Gradient-based saliency maps can also be visualized with the help of existing tools like LIME [89]. This method computes squared partial derivatives obtained by standard gradient back-propagation. On the other hand, Layer-wise Relevance Propagation (LRP) has also been commonly used to explain the decisions of a SA model [40,51,93,118]. With this method, each layer neuron in the neural network is provided with a relevance score back-propagating from the final layer to the input layer neurons. However, XAI is not the only research area that SA has been utilized for further research. Let us delve into some of the other past research where SA has proven to be a useful area in terms of existing research and model deployability:

Psychology: Jo et al. [44] argue how the sentiment expressed in a text can be used to predict the emotional state of a person and not the sentiment of a text. They build neural-network-based models to perform SA and attempt to model the emotional state of a person. Based on a similar context, Provoost et al. [83] present an exploratory study on how SA can allow more empathetic automatic feedback in online cognitive behavioral therapy (iCBT) interventions for people with psychological disorders, including depression.

Translation: The translation of sentiment is a known problem within the deep-learning-based translation models. Much research has shown that perturbing the input to such translation models, i.e., reversing the polarity or the sentiment carried by the original input sentence results in incorrect output translation where the correct sentiment or polarity (especially negation) is not carried forward [36,49,71,90–92,102] including research from the statistical machine-translation era [111].

Interpreting: Carstensen and Dahlberg [13] argue how interpreting during a court session, i.e., legal interpreting required the use of emotions by human interpreters to make it better. As automated methods for interpreting become more used in this area, such models will need to take the 'sentiment' expressed by various parties into account. Similarly, interpreting in the healthcare domain can lead to situations of distress among both the interpreter [55] and the person describing their illness [104]. The person describing their illness can modify their emotions if they feel distressed describing their ailment to the medical professional, which is being interpreted due to a language barrier [79,108].

Sociology: Karamibekr and Ghorbani [50] discuss the use of SA for social issues. They discuss how SA of social issues can affect social policy and the political scenario of a country. They present their views on how SA is not only important to the product-review domain, and the applications of SA research should not be limited to the e-commerce domain. A more descriptive discussion on how SA is essential for social policy can be found in Section 3.2 in this chapter.

With the aforementioned applications of SA research in various domains, we further discuss some challenges towards applying sentiment research in these areas.

3.5.2 Challenges for SA research in other areas

Applying SA research in other domains comes ubiquitously for NLP research domains like Translation, Question Answering, Conversational Agents, and so on. However, it is incredibly challenging if SA research is used for the XAI domain. Visualization of neural models in NLP is a challenge because of the following factors [60]:

Compositionality: It is not clear how vector-based models achieve 'compositionality' i.e., building sentence vector/meaning from the vector/meaning of words and phrases.

Interpretability: The 'interpretability' and 'causality' of the decision making is questioned on many occasions making them less 'reliable' for real-world applications like decisions on parole applications[3] and many more.

Complexity: Deep-learning models have become increasingly complex, and unfortunately, their inscrutability has grown in tandem with their predictive power [23]. As multi-layered neural models (e.g., BiLSTM, Multimodal models) are deployed for solving problems in the AI domain; they become more and more complex to explain.

Hidden Layers: The very black-box nature of neural models is due to the existence of hidden layers in the neural architectures constantly used for solving NLP problems/tasks.

Researchers have argued about the very definition of *interpretability* or *causality* for neural models. *Interpretability* is used to confirm other impor-

---

[3] MIT Technology Review: Criminal Justice.

tant desiderata of ML/DL-based models or NLP systems. There exist many auxiliary criteria like the notion of *fairness* or *unbiasedness* towards protected groups that needs further investigation to ensure they are not discriminated against by other groups. *Causality* is sometimes defined as the predicted change in output due to a perturbation that may occur in the input for a real-world NLP system, and SA research has always played a prominent role in the development of important XAI concepts that are now fundamental to the NLP research in the XAI domain. Some areas such as *fairness* and *privacy* have formalized the criteria for causality in their research. These formalizations have allowed for more rigorous research in these fields. In many areas such as psychology, however, such formalization remains elusive, and arguments are presented on the lines of "explanations may highlight an incompleteness" [52]. However, research from the SA domain combined with XAI can assist in qualitatively ascertaining whether other desiderata such as fairness, reliability, transparency, and so on, are met. Given that much SA research is performed on limited datasets, there are many challenges towards actually using these models in a real-world scenario but nonetheless, this research can be used as a proof-of-concept to build more "mature" DL-based models that can help solve real-world problems. In the next section, we summarize this chapter and briefly discuss the research presented above.

3.6 Summary

Applications of sentiment analysis (SA) to real-life scenarios are the last mile for SA: they make the research in SA useful for specific real-world tasks. In this chapter, we describe five applications of SA. The first one is health. In terms of health, we describe applications such as social-media-based epidemic intelligence, while highlighting challenges around selection bias. The next application is social policy, wherein we describe how SA can be used that understands public sentiment about social issues while highlighting issues such as noisy data and privacy. The next application is e-commerce that focuses on the use of SA for business objectives. This area in particular witnesses a breadth of SA techniques for specific business problems such as aspect-based SA. It is also important, however, to note that fake reviews are an issue that such an application must deal with. The next application of SA is digital humanities where we describe approaches that use SA on literary works and other cultural artifacts for an improved understanding of the artwork. Finally, we also describe how SA has impacted other areas of

NLP such as translation and interpretation, requiring a focus on compositionality and interpretability that are crucial for both SA and the related NLP task.

As SA continues to be deployed in several applications impacting businesses, individuals, and the society, the applications described in this chapter provide an introductory perspective to the breadth of SA and the impact SA has had on several real-life scenarios.

References

[1] N.J. Adams-Cohen, Policy change and public opinion: measuring shifting political sentiment with social media data, American Politics Research 48 (2020) 612–621, https://doi.org/10.1177/1532673X20920263.

[2] S.N. Alsubari, S.N. Deshmukh, M.H. Al-Adhaileh, F.W. Alsaade, T.H. Aldhyani, Development of integrated neural network model for identification of fake reviews in e-commerce using multidomain datasets, Applied Bionics and Biomechanics 2021 (2021).

[3] S. Angelidis, M. Lapata, Summarizing opinions: aspect extraction meets sentiment prediction and they are both weakly supervised, in: Proceedings of the 2018 Conference on Empirical Methods in Natural Language Processing, Association for Computational Linguistics, Brussels, Belgium, 2018, pp. 3675–3686, https://aclanthology.org/D18-1403, https://doi.org/10.18653/v1/D18-1403.

[4] L. Arras, G. Montavon, K.R. Müller, W. Samek, Explaining recurrent neural network predictions in sentiment analysis, arXiv preprint, arXiv:1706.07206, 2017.

[5] C. Berryman, C.J. Ferguson, C. Negy, Social media use and mental health among young adults, Psychiatric Quarterly 89 (2018) 307–314.

[6] B. Bickart, R.M. Schindler, Internet forums as influential sources of consumer information, Journal of Interactive Marketing 15 (2001) 31–40.

[7] R. Biddle, A. Joshi, S. Liu, C. Paris, G. Xu, Leveraging sentiment distributions to distinguish figurative from literal health reports on Twitter, in: Proceedings of the Web Conference 2020, 2020, pp. 1217–1227.

[8] S. Blair-Goldensohn, K. Hannan, R. McDonald, T. Neylon, G. Reis, J. Reynar, Building a sentiment summarizer for local service reviews, in: Proceedings of WWW 2008 Workshop on NLP Challenges in the Information Explosion Era (NLPIX), 2008.

[9] D.M. Blei, P.J. Moreno, Topic segmentation with an aspect hidden Markov model, in: Proceedings of the 24th Annual International ACM SIGIR Conference on Research and Development in Information Retrieval, 2001, pp. 343–348.

[10] D.M. Blei, A.Y. Ng, M.I. Jordan, Latent Dirichlet allocation, Journal of Machine Learning Research 3 (2003) 993–1022.

[11] L. Botterill, The role of agrarian sentiment in Australian rural policy, in: Tracking Rural Change: Community, Policy and Technology in Australia, New Zealand and Europe, ANU E Press, Canberra, 2009, pp. 59–78.

[12] W. Budiharto, M. Meiliana, Prediction and analysis of Indonesia presidential election from Twitter using sentiment analysis, Journal of Big Data 5 (2018) 1–10.

[13] G. Carstensen, L. Dahlberg, Court interpreting as emotional work: a pilot study in Swedish law courts, No Foundations: An Interdisciplinary Journal of Law and Justice 14 (2017) 45–64.

[14] Y. Charalabidis, M. Maragoudakis, E. Loukis, Opinion mining and sentiment analysis in policy formulation initiatives: the EU-community approach, in: International Conference on Electronic Participation, Springer, 2015, pp. 147–160.

[15] Y. Chen, E.A. Silva, J.P. Reis, Measuring policy debate in a regrowing city by sentiment analysis using online media data: a case study of Leipzig 2030, Regional Science Policy & Practice 13 (2021) 675–692.

[16] Y. Choi, C. Cardie, Learning with compositional semantics as structural inference for subsentential sentiment analysis, in: Proceedings of the 2008 Conference on Empirical Methods in Natural Language Processing, 2008, pp. 793–801.

[17] W. Chung, D. Zeng, Social-media-based public policy informatics: sentiment and network analyses of us immigration and border security, The Journal of the Association for Information Science and Technology 67 (2016) 1588–1606.

[18] K. Crammer, Y. Singer, et al., Pranking with ranking, in: Nips, 2001, pp. 641–647.

[19] S.A. Crossley, K. Kyle, D.S. McNamara, Sentiment analysis and social cognition engine (seance): an automatic tool for sentiment, social cognition, and social-order analysis, Behavior Research Methods 49 (2017) 803–821.

[20] M. De Choudhury, Role of social media in tackling challenges in mental health, in: Proceedings of the 2nd International Workshop on Socially-Aware Multimedia, 2013, pp. 49–52.

[21] K. Denecke, Y. Deng, Sentiment analysis in medical settings: new opportunities and challenges, Artificial Intelligence in Medicine 64 (2015) 17–27.

[22] L. Dong, S. Huang, F. Wei, M. Lapata, M. Zhou, K. Xu, Learning to generate product reviews from attributes, in: Proceedings of the 15th Conference of the European Chapter of the Association for Computational Linguistics: Volume 1, Long Papers, 2017, pp. 623–632.

[23] F. Doshi-Velez, B. Kim, Towards a rigorous science of interpretable machine learning, arXiv:1702.08608, 2017.

[24] R.H. Durr, What moves policy sentiment?, American Political Science Review 87 (1993) 158–170.

[25] F. Fan, Y. Feng, D. Zhao, Multi-grained attention network for aspect-level sentiment classification, in: Proceedings of the 2018 Conference on Empirical Methods in Natural Language Processing, Association for Computational Linguistics, Brussels, Belgium, 2018, pp. 3433–3442, https://aclanthology.org/D18-1380, https://doi.org/10.18653/v1/D18-1380.

[26] S. Feng, R. Banerjee, Y. Choi, Syntactic stylometry for deception detection, in: Proceedings of the 50th Annual Meeting of the Association for Computational Linguistics (Volume 2: Short Papers), 2012, pp. 171–175.

[27] C. Flores-Saviaga, B. Keegan, S. Savage, Mobilizing the trump train: understanding collective action in a political trolling community, in: Proceedings of the International AAAI Conference on Web and Social Media, vol. 12, 2018, https://ojs.aaai.org/index.php/ICWSM/article/view/15024.

[28] T. Fornaciari, M. Poesio, Identifying fake Amazon reviews as learning from crowds, in: Proceedings of the 14th Conference of the European Chapter of the Association for Computational Linguistics, Association for Computational Linguistics, 2014, pp. 279–287.

[29] P. Gorinski, M. Lapata, Movie script summarization as graph-based scene extraction, in: Proceedings of the 2015 Conference of the North American Chapter of the Association for Computational Linguistics: Human Language Technologies, 2015, pp. 1066–1076.

[30] Z. Hai, K. Chang, J.j. Kim, Implicit feature identification via co-occurrence association rule mining, in: International Conference on Intelligent Text Processing and Computational Linguistics, Springer, 2011, pp. 393–404.

[31] X. Han, B.C. Wallace, Y. Tsvetkov, Explaining black box predictions and unveiling data artifacts through influence functions, arXiv preprint, arXiv:2005.06676, 2020.

[32] V. Hatzivassiloglou, K. McKeown, Predicting the semantic orientation of adjectives, in: 35th Annual Meeting of the Association for Computational Linguistics and 8th Conference of the European Chapter of the Association for Computational Linguistics, 1997, pp. 174–181.

[33] W.E. Hipson, S.M. Mohammad, Emotion dynamics in movie dialogues, arXiv preprint, arXiv:2103.01345, 2021.

[34] M. Hoang, O.A. Bihorac, J. Rouces, Aspect-based sentiment analysis using BERT, in: Proceedings of the 22nd Nordic Conference on Computational Linguistics, Linköping University Electronic Press, Turku, Finland, 2019, pp. 187–196, https://aclanthology.org/W19-6120.

[35] T. Hoffmann, "Too many Americans are trapped in fear, violence and poverty": a psychology-informed sentiment analysis of campaign speeches from the 2016 US Presidential Election, Linguistics Vanguard 4 (2018).

[36] M.M. Hossain, A. Anastasopoulos, E. Blanco, A. Palmer, It's not a non-issue: negation as a source of error in machine translation, arXiv preprint, arXiv:2010.05432, 2020.

[37] M. Hu, B. Liu, Mining and summarizing customer reviews, in: Proceedings of the Tenth ACM SIGKDD International Conference on Knowledge Discovery and Data Mining, 2004, pp. 168–177.

[38] M. Hu, B. Liu, Mining opinion features in customer reviews, in: AAAI, 2004, pp. 755–760.

[39] R.A. Hummel, S.W. Zucker, On the foundations of relaxation labeling processes, IEEE Transactions on Pattern Analysis and Machine Intelligence (1983) 267–287.

[40] T. Ito, K. Tsubouchi, H. Sakaji, T. Yamashita, K. Izumi, Concept cloud-based sentiment visualization for financial reviews, in: The International Conference on Decision Economics, Springer, 2019, pp. 183–191.

[41] N. Jakob, I. Gurevych, Extracting opinion targets in a single and cross-domain setting with conditional random fields, in: Proceedings of the 2010 Conference on Empirical Methods in Natural Language Processing, 2010, pp. 1035–1045.

[42] J. Jiang, A. Wang, A. Aizawa, Attention-based relational graph convolutional network for target-oriented opinion words extraction, in: Proceedings of the 16th Conference of the European Chapter of the Association for Computational Linguistics: Main Volume, Association for Computational Linguistics, 2021, pp. 1986–1997, https://aclanthology.org/2021.eacl-main.170, https://doi.org/10.18653/v1/2021.eacl-main.170.

[43] B. Jin, A. Joshi, R. Sparks, S. Wan, C. Paris, C.R. MacIntyre, 'Watch the flu': a tweet monitoring tool for epidemic intelligence of influenza in Australia, in: Proceedings of the AAAI Conference on Artificial Intelligence, 2020, pp. 13616–13617.

[44] H. Jo, S.M. Kim, J. Ryu, What we really want to find by sentiment analysis: the relationship between computational models and psychological state, arXiv preprint, arXiv:1704.03407, 2017.

[45] A. Joshi, P. Bhattacharyya, M.J. Carman, Automatic sarcasm detection: a survey, ACM Computing Surveys (CSUR) 50 (2017) 1–22.

[46] A. Joshi, S. Karimi, R. Sparks, C. Paris, C.R. Macintyre, Survey of text-based epidemic intelligence: a computational linguistics perspective, ACM Computing Surveys 52 (2019), https://doi.org/10.1145/3361141.

[47] A. Joshi, V. Tripathi, P. Bhattacharyya, M. Carman, Harnessing sequence labeling for sarcasm detection in dialogue from TV series 'Friends', in: Proceedings of the 20th SIGNLL Conference on Computational Natural Language Learning, 2016, pp. 146–155.

[48] A. Joshi, V. Tripathi, R. Soni, P. Bhattacharyya, M.J. Carman, EmoGram: an open-source time sequence-based emotion tracker and its innovative applications, in: Workshops at the Thirtieth AAAI Conference on Artificial Intelligence, 2016.

[49] D. Kanojia, M. Fomicheva, T. Ranasinghe, F. Blain, C. Orăsan, L. Specia, Pushing the right buttons: adversarial evaluation of quality estimation, in: Proceedings of the Sixth Conference on Machine Translation, Association for Computational Linguistics, 2021, pp. 625–638, https://aclanthology.org/2021.wmt-1.67.

[50] M. Karamibekr, A.A. Ghorbani, Sentiment analysis of social issues, in: 2012 International Conference on Social Informatics, IEEE, 2012, pp. 215–221.

[51] H. Kaur, S.U. Ahsaan, B. Alankar, V. Chang, A proposed sentiment analysis deep learning algorithm for analyzing COVID-19 tweets, Information Systems Frontiers (2021) 1–13.

[52] F. Keil, L. Rozenblit, C. Mills, What lies beneath? Understanding the limits of understanding, in: Thinking and Seeing: Visual Metacognition in Adults and Children, 2004.

[53] E. Kim, R. Klinger, A survey on sentiment and emotion analysis for computational literary studies, arXiv preprint, arXiv:1808.03137, 2018.

[54] B. Kleinberg, I. van der Vegt, M. Mozes, Measuring emotions in the COVID-19 real world worry dataset, in: Proceedings of the 1st Workshop on NLP for COVID-19 at ACL 2020, Association for Computational Linguistics, 2020, https://aclanthology.org/2020.nlpcovid19-acl.11.

[55] P. Korpal, A. Jasielska, Investigating interpreters' empathy: are emotions in simultaneous interpreting contagious?, Target. International Journal of Translation Studies 31 (2019) 2–24.

[56] A. Kruspe, M. Häberle, I. Kuhn, X.X. Zhu, Cross-language sentiment analysis of European Twitter messages during the COVID-19 pandemic, arXiv preprint, arXiv:2008.12172, 2020.

[57] P.E. Kummervold, S. Martin, S. Dada, E. Kilich, C. Denny, P. Paterson, H.J. Larson, Categorizing vaccine confidence with a transformer-based machine learning model: analysis of nuances of vaccine sentiment in Twitter discourse, JMIR Medical Informatics 9 (2021) e29584.

[58] H. Lakkaraju, C. Bhattacharyya, I. Bhattacharya, S. Merugu, Exploiting coherence for the simultaneous discovery of latent facets and associated sentiments, in: Proceedings of the 2011 SIAM International Conference on Data Mining, SIAM, 2011, pp. 498–509.

[59] M.E. Larsen, T.W. Boonstra, P.J. Batterham, B. O'Dea, C. Paris, H. Christensen, We feel: mapping emotion on Twitter, IEEE Journal of Biomedical and Health Informatics 19 (2015) 1246–1252.

[60] J. Li, X. Chen, E. Hovy, D. Jurafsky, Visualizing and understanding neural models in NLP, arXiv preprint, arXiv:1506.01066, 2015.

[61] Y.H. Li, J. Zheng, Z.P. Fan, L. Wang, Sentiment analysis-based method for matching creative agri-product scheme demanders and suppliers: a case study from China, Computers and Electronics in Agriculture 186 (2021) 106196.

[62] P. Liu, Z. Xu, J. Ai, F. Wang, Identifying indicators of fake reviews based on spammer's behavior features, in: 2017 IEEE International Conference on Software Quality, Reliability and Security Companion (QRS-C), 2017, pp. 396–403, https://doi.org/10.1109/QRS-C.2017.72.

[63] B. Lu, M. Ott, C. Cardie, B.K. Tsou, Multi-aspect sentiment analysis with topic models, in: 2011 IEEE 11th International Conference on Data Mining Workshops, IEEE, 2011, pp. 81–88.

[64] Z. Luo, S. Huang, F.F. Xu, B.Y. Lin, H. Shi, K. Zhu, Extra: extracting prominent review aspects from customer feedback, in: Proceedings of the 2018 Conference on Empirical Methods in Natural Language Processing, 2018, pp. 3477–3486.

[65] A. Magge, A. Klein, A. Miranda-Escalada, M. Ali Al-Garadi, I. Alimova, Z. Miftahutdinov, E. Farre, S. Lima López, I. Flores, K. O'Connor, D. Weissenbacher, E. Tutubalina, A. Sarker, J. Banda, M. Krallinger, G. Gonzalez-Hernandez, Overview of the sixth social media mining for health applications (#SMM4H) shared tasks at NAACL 2021, in: Proceedings of the Sixth Social Media Mining for Health (#SMM4H) Workshop and Shared Task, Association for Computational Linguistics, Mexico City, Mexico, 2021, pp. 21–32, https://aclanthology.org/2021.smm4h-1.4, https://doi.org/10.18653/v1/2021.smm4h-1.4.

[66] V.R. Martinez, K. Somandepalli, K. Singla, A. Ramakrishna, Y.T. Uhls, S. Narayanan, Violence rating prediction from movie scripts, in: Proceedings of the AAAI Conference on Artificial Intelligence, 2019, pp. 671–678.

[67] Q. Mei, X. Ling, M. Wondra, H. Su, C. Zhai, Topic sentiment mixture: modeling facets and opinions in weblogs, in: Proceedings of the 16th International Conference on World Wide Web, 2007, pp. 171–180.

[68] R. Mihalcea, C. Strapparava, The lie detector: explorations in the automatic recognition of deceptive language, in: Proceedings of the ACL-IJCNLP 2009 Conference Short Papers, 2009, pp. 309–312.

[69] S. Moghaddam, M. Ester, Opinion digger: an unsupervised opinion miner from unstructured product reviews, in: Proceedings of the 19th ACM International Conference on Information and Knowledge Management, 2010, pp. 1825–1828.

[70] S. Moghaddam, M. Ester, The FLDA model for aspect-based opinion mining: addressing the cold start problem, in: Proceedings of the 22nd International Conference on World Wide Web, 2013, pp. 909–918.

[71] S.M. Mohammad, M. Salameh, S. Kiritchenko, How translation alters sentiment, Journal of Artificial Intelligence Research 55 (2016) 95–130.

[72] E.T. Nalisnick, H.S. Baird, Character-to-character sentiment analysis in Shakespeare's plays, in: Proceedings of the 51st Annual Meeting of the Association for Computational Linguistics (Volume 2: Short Papers), 2013, pp. 479–483.

[73] R. Narayanan, B. Liu, A. Choudhary, Sentiment analysis of conditional sentences, in: Proceedings of the 2009 Conference on Empirical Methods in Natural Language Processing, 2009, pp. 180–189.

[74] M.L. Newman, J.W. Pennebaker, D.S. Berry, J.M. Richards, Lying words: predicting deception from linguistic styles, Personality & Social Psychology Bulletin 29 (2003) 665–675.

[75] J. Ni, J. Li, J. McAuley, Justifying recommendations using distantly-labeled reviews and fine-grained aspects, in: Proceedings of the 2019 Conference on Empirical Methods in Natural Language Processing and the 9th International Joint Conference on Natural Language Processing (EMNLP-IJCNLP), Association for Computational Linguistics, Hong Kong, China, 2019, pp. 188–197, https://aclanthology.org/D19-1018, https://doi.org/10.18653/v1/D19-1018.

[76] J. Ni, J. Li, J. McAuley, Justifying recommendations using distantly-labeled reviews and fine-grained aspects, in: Proceedings of the 2019 Conference on Empirical Methods in Natural Language Processing and the 9th International Joint Conference on Natural Language Processing (EMNLP-IJCNLP), 2019, pp. 188–197.

[77] J. Ni, J. McAuley, Personalized review generation by expanding phrases and attending on aspect-aware representations, in: Proceedings of the 56th Annual Meeting of the Association for Computational Linguistics (Volume 2: Short Papers), 2018, pp. 706–711.

[78] M. Ott, Y. Choi, C. Cardie, J.T. Hancock, Finding deceptive opinion spam by any stretch of the imagination, arXiv preprint, arXiv:1107.4557, 2011.

[79] C. Out, M. Goudbeek, E. Krahmer, Do speaker's emotions influence their language production? Studying the influence of disgust and amusement on alignment in interactive reference, Language Sciences 78 (2020) 101255, https://doi.org/

10.1016/j.langsci.2019.101255, https://www.sciencedirect.com/science/article/pii/S0388000119302815.

[80] J.H. Parmelee, S.L. Bichard, Politics and the Twitter Revolution: How Tweets Influence the Relationship Between Political Leaders and the Public, Lexington Books, 2011.

[81] G. Petonito, G.W. Muschert, Silver alert programs: an exploration of community sentiment regarding a policy solution to address the critical wandering problem in an aging population, in: Handbook of Community Sentiment, Springer, 2015, pp. 253–266.

[82] A.M. Popescu, O. Etzioni, Extracting product features and opinions from reviews, in: Natural Language Processing and Text Mining, Springer, 2007, pp. 9–28.

[83] S. Provoost, J. Ruwaard, W. van Breda, H. Riper, T. Bosse, Validating automated sentiment analysis of online cognitive behavioral therapy patient texts: an exploratory study, Frontiers in Psychology 10 (2019), https://doi.org/10.3389/fpsyg.2019.01065, https://www.frontiersin.org/article/10.3389/fpsyg.2019.01065.

[84] G. Qiu, B. Liu, J. Bu, C. Chen, Expanding domain sentiment lexicon through double propagation, in: Twenty-First International Joint Conference on Artificial Intelligence, 2009.

[85] G. Qiu, B. Liu, J. Bu, C. Chen, Opinion word expansion and target extraction through double propagation, Computational Linguistics 37 (2011) 9–27.

[86] S. Raju, P. Pingali, V. Varma, An unsupervised approach to product attribute extraction, in: European Conference on Information Retrieval, Springer, 2009, pp. 796–800.

[87] A. Reyes, P. Rosso, Making objective decisions from subjective data: detecting irony in customer reviews, Decision Support Systems 53 (2012) 754–760.

[88] A. Reyes, P. Rosso, D. Buscaldi, From humor recognition to irony detection: the figurative language of social media, Data & Knowledge Engineering 74 (2012) 1–12.

[89] M.T. Ribeiro, S. Singh, C. Guestrin, "Why should I trust you?" Explaining the predictions of any classifier, in: Proceedings of the 22nd ACM SIGKDD International Conference on Knowledge Discovery and Data Mining, 2016, pp. 1135–1144.

[90] H. Saadany, C. Orasan, Is it great or terrible? Preserving sentiment in neural machine translation of Arabic reviews, arXiv preprint, arXiv:2010.13814, 2020.

[91] H. Saadany, C. Orasan, E. Mohamed, A. Tantawy, Sentiment-aware measure (SAM) for evaluating sentiment transfer by machine translation systems, arXiv preprint, arXiv:2109.14895, 2021.

[92] M. Salameh, S. Mohammad, S. Kiritchenko, Sentiment after translation: a case-study on Arabic social media posts, in: Proceedings of the 2015 Conference of the North American Chapter of the Association for Computational Linguistics: Human Language Technologies, 2015, pp. 767–777.

[93] J.F. Sánchez-Rada, G. Vulcu, C.A. Iglesias, P. Buitelaar, EUROSENTIMENT: linked data sentiment analysis, in: International Semantic Web Conference (Posters & Demos), 2014, pp. 145–148.

[94] R. Sandoval-Almazan, D. Valle-Cruz, Sentiment analysis of Facebook users reacting to political campaign posts, Digital Government: Research and Practice 1 (2020) 1–13.

[95] M. Schmitt, S. Steinheber, K. Schreiber, B. Roth, Joint aspect and polarity classification for aspect-based sentiment analysis with end-to-end neural networks, in: Proceedings of the 2018 Conference on Empirical Methods in Natural Language Processing, Association for Computational Linguistics, Brussels, Belgium, 2018, pp. 1109–1114, https://aclanthology.org/D18-1139, https://doi.org/10.18653/v1/D18-1139.

[96] K. Schouten, F. Frasincar, Survey on aspect-level sentiment analysis, IEEE Transactions on Knowledge and Data Engineering 28 (2015) 813–830.

[97] L.R. Schultz, M. Loog, P.M. Esfahani, Distance based source domain selection for sentiment classification, arXiv preprint, arXiv:1808.09271, 2018.

[98] A. Sheoran, D. Kanojia, A. Joshi, P. Bhattacharyya, Recommendation chart of domains for cross-domain sentiment analysis: findings of a 20 domain study, in: Proceedings of the 12th Language Resources and Evaluation Conference, European Language Resources Association, Marseille, France, 2020, pp. 4982–4990, https://aclanthology.org/2020.lrec-1.613.

[99] M. Singh, V. Goyal, S. Raj, Sentiment analysis of English-Punjabi code mixed social media content for agriculture domain, in: 2019 4th International Conference on Information Systems and Computer Networks (ISCON), IEEE, 2019, pp. 352–357.

[100] P. Singh, R.S. Sawhney, K.S. Kahlon, Sentiment analysis of demonetization of 500 & 1000 rupee banknotes by Indian government, ICT Express 4 (2018) 124–129.

[101] R. Socher, A. Perelygin, J. Wu, J. Chuang, C.D. Manning, A.Y. Ng, C. Potts, Recursive deep models for semantic compositionality over a sentiment treebank, in: Proceedings of the 2013 Conference on Empirical Methods in Natural Language Processing, 2013, pp. 1631–1642.

[102] G. Tang, P. Rönchen, R. Sennrich, J. Nivre, Revisiting negation in neural machine translation, Transactions of the Association for Computational Linguistics 9 (2021) 740–755.

[103] D.K. Tayal, S.K. Yadav, Sentiment analysis on social campaign "Swachh Bharat Abhiyan" using unigram method, AI & Society 32 (2017) 633–645.

[104] E. Tiselius, E. Hägglund, P. Pergert, Distressful situations, non-supportive work climate, threats to professional and private integrity: healthcare interpreting in Sweden, in: Handbook of Research on Medical Interpreting, IGI Global, 2020, pp. 54–79.

[105] I. Titov, R. McDonald, Modeling online reviews with multi-grain topic models, in: Proceedings of the 17th International Conference on World Wide Web, 2008, pp. 111–120.

[106] M.H. Tsou, Research challenges and opportunities in mapping social media and big data, Cartography and Geographic Information Science 42 (2015) 70–74.

[107] A. Vagrani, S. Bijarnia, P.V. Ilavarasan, S. Masiero, Appraising WhatsApp in the Indian context: understanding the rural sentiment, in: International Conference on Social Implications of Computers in Developing Countries, Springer, 2020, pp. 142–156.

[108] C. Valero-Garcés, Emotional and psychological effects on interpreters in public services a critical factor to bear in mind, Translation Journal 9 (3) (2016) 1–13.

[109] A. Wang, A. Singh, J. Michael, F. Hill, O. Levy, S. Bowman, Glue: a multi-task benchmark and analysis platform for natural language understanding, in: Proceedings of the 2018 EMNLP Workshop BlackboxNLP: Analyzing and Interpreting Neural Networks for NLP, 2018, pp. 353–355.

[110] H. Wang, Y. Lu, C. Zhai, Latent aspect rating analysis without aspect keyword supervision, in: Proceedings of the 17th ACM SIGKDD International Conference on Knowledge Discovery and Data Mining, 2011, pp. 618–626.

[111] D. Wetzel, F. Bond, Enriching parallel corpora for statistical machine translation with semantic negation rephrasing, in: Proceedings of the Sixth Workshop on Syntax, Semantics and Structure in Statistical Translation, 2012, pp. 20–29.

[112] T. Wilson, J. Wiebe, P. Hoffmann, Recognizing contextual polarity in phrase-level sentiment analysis, in: Proceedings of Human Language Technology Conference and Conference on Empirical Methods in Natural Language Processing, 2005, pp. 347–354.

[113] J. Yu, Z.J. Zha, M. Wang, T.S. Chua, Aspect ranking: identifying important product aspects from online consumer reviews, in: Proceedings of the 49th Annual Meeting of the Association for Computational Linguistics: Human Language Technologies, 2011, pp. 1496–1505.

[114] T.J. Zhan, C.H. Li, Semantic dependent word pairs generative model for fine-grained product feature mining, in: Pacific-Asia Conference on Knowledge Discovery and Data Mining, Springer, 2011, pp. 460–475.

[115] L. Zhang, B. Liu, S.H. Lim, E. O'Brien-Strain, Extracting and ranking product features in opinion documents, in: Coling 2010: Posters, 2010, pp. 1462–1470.

[116] Y. Zhao, B. Qin, S. Hu, T. Liu, Generalizing syntactic structures for product attribute candidate extraction, in: Human Language Technologies: The 2010 Annual Conference of the North American Chapter of the Association for Computational Linguistics, 2010, pp. 377–380.

[117] J. Zhu, H. Wang, B.K. Tsou, M. Zhu, Multi-aspect opinion polling from textual reviews, in: Proceedings of the 18th ACM Conference on Information and Knowledge Management, 2009, pp. 1799–1802.

[118] C. Zucco, H. Liang, G. Di Fatta, M. Cannataro, Explainable sentiment analysis with applications in medicine, in: 2018 IEEE International Conference on Bioinformatics and Biomedicine (BIBM), IEEE, 2018, pp. 1740–1747.

CHAPTER 4

Emotions of students from online and offline texts

Rishi Dey[a], Rounak Dutta[b], and Chitrita Chaudhuri[c]
[a]Indian Statistical Institute, Kolkata, India
[b]Livpure Smart Homes Pvt. Ltd., Bengaluru, India
[c]Department of Computer Science and Engineering, Jadavpur University, Kolkata, India

4.1 Introduction

With the advent of electronic media, everyone who can afford to use it has become totally dependent on it for communicating their opinions and observations indiscriminately. Even under extraordinary situations, like the present one faced by the entire global community, where pandemics have rendered social distancing compulsory, this is one space that continues to touch the mental pulse of the throng.

In common parlance, mood indicates the frame of a human mind, and this often fluctuates with the change in its settings. Pleasant experiences invoke an uplift of spirit, while anything that threatens its peace has an entirely reverse effect. Rapid transition from the neutral to either of these two end states may be described by the term 'swing'. As we often see in the physical world around us, a swinging action may lead to overturning the cart itself – which, in the present context, indicates disturbing the mental balance of a person, causing immense damage to life and sanctity.

Not all people suffer from drastic mood swings. This only proves that the ballasts of certain persons are more strongly grounded than their unfortunate brethren. The guiding factor lies in another oft-used term: the 'temperament', which helps to guard the favored few from external stimulus. Such persons may be described as less sentimental. While variety always serves better to remove monotony, one must remember to monitor the more sensitive souls in order to prevent their catastrophic reactions to surrounding actions. Hence, the categories need to be sorted out in advance, and the mood swings of the weaker group monitored continuously to detect the troughs.

However, such constant vigilance is not easy to achieve, especially under circumstances the world has been going through in the last few years. One

Computational Intelligence Applications for Text and Sentiment Data Analysis
https://doi.org/10.1016/B978-0-32-390535-0.00009-4

tends to become more aloof and detached from the human society during disturbed situations such as these. However, the recent trend is to lay bare one's heart in the social media, if nowhere else. The mobile is one's nearest and dearest friend nowadays. Perhaps the electronic screen acts as a veil and enables one to lower the mask one wears in company – just an allegoric reference, of course!

This set a team of young researchers to think afresh – can the feature be utilized to achieve fruitful results? They decided to capture the social-media messages of their friends, in order to evaluate the frequencies and amplitudes of the mood swings lying therein. The pertinent candidates, handpicked for this study, further assisted the team by providing their handwritten signature images. These images helped in determining some relevant characteristic traits as indicated by the discipline of graphology.

The scheme originated with a work previously presented by some members of the research team in the IEEE 9th International Conference on Advanced Computing (IACC) [1]. The earlier endeavor aimed at establishing an efficient Lexical Analyzer to predict human emotion from text retained from Social-Media messages as well as those generated from Graphology-based rules. It compared the results with the efforts of Human Annotators as well.

Based on the evident efficacy of the tool, the current objective is to target it towards a section of the society who is at a higher risk of succumbing to environmental pressures, namely students. In a nutshell, the idea is to achieve this goal by studying their Social-Media conversations and signatures.

Here, the work is presented in two separate phases. The first phase deals with Natural Language Processing (NLP) and continuous extraction of sentiment polarities expressed by chats within a closed WhatsApp group using a suitable Lexical Analyzer such as the SentiWordNet [2–4]. The tendency to deviate towards the negative polarity is particularly studied, as it is believed to indicate a poorer mental health not capable of coping with the rigors of external stress.

The second phase discusses methods for discerning specific features from real-world handwritten signature images of the participants with the aid of technology. The field of Graphology suggests that humans divulge much of their personality quirks unconsciously through their adopted hands while writing or signing. Signature analysis is one of the most effective and reliable indicators for prediction of the same – as it is believed to be capable of revealing some home truths such as fear, honesty, and many other individual traits. The particular parameters considered here are Baseline and Writing Pressure [5,6]. The proposed tool then finds the correlation between the mood-swing frequencies determined in the first phase with the characteristic trends obtained from the second phase, to finally identify candidates who may be suffering from acute malaise.

In Section 4.2 are considered some relevant studies that have already been explored in the respective fields of Sentiment and Signature Analysis, the latter based on the fields of Image Processing and Graphology. Section 4.3 introduces some basic concepts in each of these specific disciplines that form the foundation of the present work. In Section 4.4 are detailed the methodologies used to determine the key features in both phases of the system tool. Section 4.5 describes the results obtained from the two phases through charts and tables. It also provides summaries on the basis of dataset and characteristic traits. The last section, Section 4.6, draws conclusions on the outcome of some of the experiments conducted to establish the connection between a person's writing hand, the words he/she may be using, and the mental state the person may be in. This section also hints at future scopes of improvements in this research domain.

One last detour before venturing into the details of the topic being discussed: usually people would like to know at the outset whether they would benefit at all by perusing through an article or not. So here is a short preface indicating who the authors feel may find their time well spent going ahead with the exercise.

First and foremost, are the young researchers working in relevant domains, and already initiated into the basics of text analytics, image processing, and machine learning. It is felt that this would serve as a first glimpse of the vast possibilities that exist in this particular research field. For them we recommend a thorough reading of the whole of this chapter. The second group who may be interested in the outcome of the study are the clinical psychologists and practicing psychiatrists – they can concentrate on the last two sections, where the results have been presented and discussed. To the vast majority of the remaining readers, our entreaty is that they should not quit without visiting at least the concluding section. They can re-check any of the other sections in retrospect, as most of the content has been discussed in an overtly simplified manner to suit the palate of the mass. With that we come to the end of our detour and wish all our readers a happy journey through the rest of this document.

4.2 State-of-the-art

Texts within the Web data have long been explored by NLP experts as a ready source in diverse fields ranging from opinion mining, aimed at achieving success in business, to resolving controversial ownership disputes in legal cases. The usage of such a rich repertoire for assisting the psychoanalysts in categorizing the population on the basis of their sentiment polarity has been a natural evolution under the circumstance. Following are described some of the articles associated with this interesting area of research – which furthermore lent themselves as the stepping stones for the first phase of the present work.

A system modeled by Marks et al. [7] picks out specific parts of speech within a sentence, the verbs, adverbs, nouns, and adjectives, and mines out information regarding the attitude of each actor inside the considered text. Here, the identity of the attitude holder and the positivity (or negativity) of the attitude itself play an important role in bringing out the overall semantic categorization. Utilizing negation words to reverse the sentiment polarity of a sentence has been studied by Hogenboom et al. [8] in their work involving movie reviews. They considered the impact of such a negation word, followed by bi-grams, in changing the meaning of a remark. Another study carried out by Dadvar et al. [9] experimented with variable-sized text windows within a sentence to assess the correctness metric in determining the right polarity. They concluded that standard techniques may fail, if subtle nuances exist within sentiment expressions. Forming an ensemble from three basic classifiers – Naïve Bayes, Maximum Entropy, and Support Vector Machines – Xia et al. [10] used part of speech and word relations to find sentiment. A comparison between the performance of Naïve Bayes and Maximum Entropy classifiers on bi-grams and tweets led Parikh et al. [11] to infer the supremacy of the first model. Another study by Gamallo et al. [12] classifies pure English language tweets on the three basic polarities using a Naïve Bayes model. They also built a separate bipolar model excluding the neutral type.

Since phase 2 of the present research deals with behavior prediction through Signature Analysis some reliable studies are described next to augment the process of assessing human temperament through their signatures. Plamondon et al. [13] excavate distinctive characteristics, from signature images available online, by applying diverse mechanisms. For the present purpose, the current strategies can be comprehensively separated into two categories – one involving attribute-specific and the other method-specific activities. Attribute-specific strategies utilize a vector portrayal comprising the global attributes obtained from the signatory's pen motions as presented by Ketabdar et al. [14]; on the other hand, the method-specific activities capture the local attributes of the autograph to identify a signatory through sequential time stamps and are adopted by several others like Fairhurst et al. in [15], Jain et al. in [16], and Nalwa in [17] to mention a few.

Another research group, Madabusi et al. [18] employ a relative incline-based calculation for both online and offline autograph authentication. Here, they fragment the autograph image and apply optimized functionality on each fragment using a Hidden Markov Model strategy. In this process, the slants between consecutive fragments are determined only after normalizing the original image. In yet another venture, Tong et al. [19] analyzed the autograph images dynamically to authenticate them based on some characteristic strokes within the images. Each such stroke yields fresh attributes that, along with space- and time-domain specifications of the autograph images, help to transform them into the template form. The framework is named Dynamic Signature Verification (DSV). The constituent subsystems in it, four in all, deal with the following tasks – the first one acquires the autograph images, the second one pre-processes them, the third extracts the features from the pre-processed images, and the last one executes the authentication process.

Mohamed et al. [20] describe an automated baseline-extraction scheme involving vector rules utilized to identify net-based autograph signatories. For this purpose, twenty signatories were randomly picked from various walks of life. Validation of the scheme was achieved by asking pointed questions from a pre-selected questionnaire regarding the baseline of each autograph image. Answers to these questions were obtained from individuals, who were all qualified experts to identify signatories from their marks. Ultimately, the responses from the schematic system were assessed against the human graphologists' decisions. Assuming these expert opinions to be correct, the system exhibited a high identification accuracy rate of 90%.

However, the above-mentioned studies, while probing deep into features extracted through image analysis, miss out on predicting the behaviors of the signatories using the rules of graphology, which is the main focus of the second phase of the present endeavor. Hence, the remaining part of this survey below indicates some recorded studies in the domain of graphology.

The first of the papers [21] studied in context utilizes graphology and graphometry-based features for authentic signature images to train a classifier built using a Hidden Markov Model (HMM) principle. It assesses the false-positive error rates when the system is fed with forged signatures of different types for a person. The dataset consists of 5600 signature images collected at 300 dpi, 256 gray levels. Truly speaking, it is the second paper [22] in this sequence that starts analyzing personality traits using the tools available in standard graphology. A training dataset of 100 handwriting samples is used here to create feature vector matrices from processed images analyzed by professional graphologists to map each one to a class value. The K-Nearest-Neighbor classification technique predicts the personality traits or class values of new samples using similarity matrix principles.

The third paper [23] discusses the art of deciphering personality traits thoroughly, with clear pictorial representation of the graphological significance of handwritten text images within tabular entries. The system block diagram at the end summarizes how the scanned JPEG images of the handwritten texts are pre-processed and segmented prior to the required feature-extraction step. Thereafter, ANN classification, built with specific features extracted using GSC algorithm [24], is used to arrive at suitable predictions of a personality-trait class. There is a language bias present in the fourth paper investigated [25] – as it deals with texts written using Farsi, and holds for the Arabic script too. Although Farsi text is written right to left and is inherently cursive, the paper remains interesting as most of the feature-extraction techniques from text images scanned at 300 dpi format remain the same as for English scripts and are described in some detail. Researchers use Support Vector Machines (SVM) with a Radial Basis Function (RBF) kernel for mapping features to a higher-dimension space. This helps to generate a hyperplane in this higher-dimension space that successfully segregates one personality class from another for the training-set data.

The next paper [26] uses Convolutional Neural Networks (CNN) at two stages: the first for the feature-extraction phase, which utilizes a convolution and pooling process with a deep-learning Rectified Linear Unit (ReLU) defined as $f(x) = \max(0, x)$; and the second for the actual classification phase implemented using a standard technique such as Multi-Layer Perception (MLP). The pooling at the first stage reduces the size of the feature space, and thus reduces computational load, and also prevents overfitting. At the second stage the Softmax layer assigns decimal probabilities to each class in the multi-class problem under consideration. The experimental results indicate variation of stochastic gradient schemes versus adaptive learning rates with different training to test ratios. Ultimately, the process claims perceptible improvements in accuracy of classification and processing speed, as compared to previous Artificial Neural Network (ANN)-based endeavors.

4.3 Some basic concepts

The basics of the domains related to the present work are introduced here briefly for the uninitiated: *Natural Language Processing, Image Processing*, and *Graphology-oriented Feature Extraction*.

4.3.1 Natural language processing (NLP)

NLP is the study of the computational treatment of natural (or human) language – which, in other words, teaches computers how to understand and generate human languages. NLP forms one strong area under the Machine-Learning regime, and utilizes most of its tools and techniques. In recent times, more sophistication and performance benefits have been achieved by applying deep-learning methodologies in NLP as well. The specific application with which the first phase of the present work deals is *Sentiment Analysis*. Sentiment analysis is a comprehensive term that loosely encompasses tasks associated with the mechanized observations gleaned from the general-public's response regarding a particular phenomenon or occurrence. In its basic elementary form it is a common text-categorization act that implements subjectivity analysis at the statement level, with the detection of three types of crude emotional scores – positive, negative, and neutral.

These scores can be applied at different grades of granularity, starting at the word or n-gram level, to the sentence level, ending at the document level. There are several tools available at the lowest level, out of which the SentiWordNet is chosen due to performance benefits attained through it in the preliminary motivating work [1]. SentiWordNet provides users with clusters of synonymous words ready to be used in sentiment-analysis exercises. Sample tuples in the SentiWordNet are shown in Table 4.1, and the column details are explained thereafter.

The first column of Table 4.1 contains the part-of-speech tag (POS) to which the relevant word belongs – 'V' here stands for verb and 'N' for noun. The second column holds the specific identifying number pertaining to the word according to SentiWordNet. The 3rd and 4th columns preserve real-value positive and negative scores for the term. Entries in the 5th column can consist of a single word (known as a *unigram* in NLP parlance), or a multiword-expression (likewise known as an *n-gram* in the computational linguistics community). SentiWordNet clusters words with similar sentiment orientation together into different sets. These may be a set of synonyms representing a concept, a grammatical class, and a definition Gloss, as exemplified in Table 4.1.

Table 4.1 Examples from SentiWordNet.

POS	ID	PosScore	NegScore	SysnSet Terms	Gloss
V	02526085	0.125	0.125	Accomplish	To gain with effort; "she achieved her goal despite setbacks"
N	14541044	0	0.75	Danger	a cause of pain or injury or loss; "he feared the dangers of traveling by air"

4.3.2 Image processing

The discipline of Image Processing demands some specific tasks to be performed on an image so that the image itself may become augmented or some intrinsic detail may be obtained from it. It involves signal-processing techniques to be applied on an incoming analog or digital image and produces either the enhanced image or its attributes. This fast-evolving basic area of research is demanding much attention from Computer Scientists and Engineers in recent years.

In the present context, the input consists of digital images specifically. Following are the constituent steps involved with the technology:

- First, sophisticated tools are employed to acquire the image.
- Next, the acquired image is either processed or analyzed, as required.
- Finally, either the processed image, or an output signifying the analysis, is generated.

It is too vast a topic to be covered in detail and only the relevant techniques employed in the present work are discussed in the Methodology section. Those interested to study the subject in more detail may refer to standard literature [27].

4.3.3 Graphology-oriented feature extraction

Following is a discussion that aims to explain how the art of graphology meets the science of rule-based taxonomy, and how human inhibitions and biases are overset by machine intelligence.

In the preparatory school, each child is taught to write neatly and in a particular manner. However, in most cases, the child outgrows the learnt patterns, and each individual forms a unique style of its own. This formation of style is a continuous affair, and is often acquired and influenced by the personal traits of the individual. At the end of the day, writing still remains a natural ability that transcends existing barriers of gender, ethnicity, skin color, or ideology.

In essence, Graphology provides an unprejudiced and non-invasive framework to assess the characteristics of an individual even in one's absence. One part of Graphology deals with the humanities disciplines of sociology and culture – as these aspects tend to influence the writing capability and style to a great extent. It is the aim of this part to consider the overall setting in which the handwritten words appear. The other part deals with the scientific aspects – such as the correct estimation of the written structures like slants, angles, and spacing of characters within words or between words and lines as a whole, as well as evaluating the writing pressure, with appropriate amplification and accuracy measures implemented as required.

The three components of writing involve pen motion, spacing, and structure. It is the job of the graphologist to consider how these components vary in a handwritten text, and interpret the psychological implications of the same. Specialists in the domain are able to attain great perfection in deciphering the mental attributes of writers from these factors. The present research is oriented towards making the machine adept at the same task.

4.3.4 Rule-based classifier

Knowledge regarding an entity is often acquired very conveniently from logical sets of Rules involving the characteristics of the entity. Such knowledge, expressed in the form of a set of IF-THEN rules, where each rule leads to a class value, composes the Rule-Based Classifier [28]. In the scenario under consideration, classification or class evaluation is synonymous with finding the behavioral traits of a person from some indicative patterns observed in his/her writing style or signature. The following demonstrative discussion explains the procedure.

An IF-THEN rule is an expression of the form:

IF *condition*

THEN *conclusion*

An example of a rule in the present context is given below:

IF *baseline* = *ascending* AND *pressure* = *heavy*

THEN *behavior* = *Optimistic and More Emotional*

The "IF" followed by the precondition part is referred to as the rule *antecedent*. Next comes the "THEN" followed by the rule *consequent* part. The precondition part usually composes of either a single condition check or the logical AND-ing of attributes checked against specific values (e.g., *baseline = ascending* AND *pressure = heavy*). The conclusion involves a specific class value to be assigned to the discerning attribute, which appears as the prediction of the class in the rule's *consequent* portion. The above rule can also be written as,

((baseline = ascending) ^ (pressure = heavy)) => (behavior = Optimistic and More Emotional)

The rule is said to 'cover' an input tuple, if for that specific tuple the condition part, or *antecedent*, logically satisfies the true value.

With this pocketbook knowledge to hand, the more ambitious can now delve into the details of the methodologies employed in the study.

4.4 Methodology

This section elaborates the technical details of the work done. In the process, it also provides the descriptions of the type of data utilized as well as the probable output from the system. The impact of a tool depends mainly on the outcome obtained from experiments. The outcome can be considered as a function of the inputs and the proper implementation of technologies employed on those inputs.

Fig. 4.1 is a schematic representation of the overall system discussed in this work:

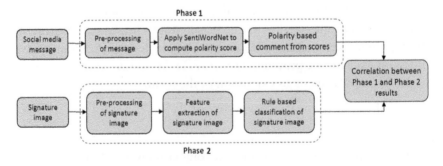

Figure 4.1 Schematic Diagram of the System.

4.4.1 Raw-data collection
4.4.1.1 Phase 1: data collection of social-media messages

Given the private nature of WhatsApp, this study's first challenge is to extract a message dataset from a WhatsApp Group while ensuring its users' privacy. The pertinent group is created to this end and a few persons from a known circle are added into the group. The participants' general demographic information – such as their age, gender, place of residence, and educational background – are also collected.

The participants are presented with some relevant topics for sharing their views and opinions. The purpose is to observe emotional trends while they interact with each other freely in addition to discussing the topic. The only restriction imposed is that the whole interaction has to be conducted strictly in English. However, as is naturally to be foreseen, there are quite a few occasions when the restriction is overlooked by the participants. The researchers have to eliminate all such multi-lingual entries rigorously at the very beginning. Participant recruitment is all the more challenging due to this restriction and the researchers end up with only 14 such, mostly amongst the student community – 4 female and 10 male, all being young adults between 20 and 28 years of age.

The option "Export chat" available in the group-level activity of WhatsApp is used to extract the individual messages from the selected Chat sessions. As mentioned earlier, only the text portions in English are extracted and stored separately, omitting all kinds of media files. This preserved text file served as the ultimate collected raw dataset for Phase 1 of the program.

4.4.1.2 Phase 2: data collection of signature images

First, all writers are asked to inscribe their handwritten signatures within 5 cm × 1.5 cm rectangular boxes marked on plain paper. They are provided with black signing pens with a fine nib size to achieve standard effects. Subsequently, the grayscale signature images are obtained by using scanners set typically at 600 dpi resolution. As expected, signatures pertain to the same group of people who participate in the previous phase.

4.4.2 Phase 1: text-message analysis
4.4.2.1 Data pre-processing

Here, the necessary data pre-processing and cleaning steps are performed on the collected message dataset – these involve the processes mentioned in Fig. 4.2 and described in detail subsequently.

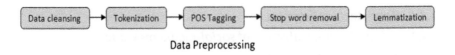

Data Preprocessing

Figure 4.2 Pre-processing of Phase 1 Message Text.

Data Cleansing

The term 'Cleansing' when associated with 'Data' indicates eradication of inadequacies lying therein – mainly through corrections such as replacements and modifications of erroneous parts, or incorporating missing parts, or by removing irrelevant parts within it. Here in this dataset, all emojis and non-English words are removed. Some common abbreviated words like "etc", "sms" are detected and replaced by their synonyms, if available, or removed otherwise.

Tokenization

Tokens are the atoms within a text document or sequence of characters, and **Tokenization** is the process of producing these tokens from the text under consideration. The tokens may be words or numbers and the task is performed by locating word boundaries. The task is also known as **Word Segmentation**.

POS Tagging

Here POS stands for 'Part-Of-Speech' and Tagging is a term used to grammatically associate each word with a category in this context. Two more popular synonyms for the process are 'grammatical tagging' and 'word-category disambiguation'. The process is heavily dependent on the semantic meaning and position of the word within the piece of text under consideration, relative to other words in that text. All these evolve from primary-school experience of being taught to identify a word as a valid part-of-speech according to the grammatical norms of a human language.

Stop-word removal

Stop words are generally thought to be a "single set of common words" that are not useful within a certain context. Usually, it is not desired that these words take up space in a dataset. Using NLTK and its readily available "Stop Word Dictionary", the stop words in the present dataset are removed.

Lemmatization

The term lemma means a heading indicative of the subject of a literary composition. Thus, in the context of NLP, lemmatization of a word indicates finding the root word shredded of all its garnished inflections, but retaining its original meaning in the text under consideration.

4.4.2.2 Applying lexical analysis

After data pre-processing, a set of tokens are obtained for each participant. The lexical resource, SentiWordNet is available in text-file format. First, a separate dictionary-type data structure is created for SentiWordNet. Given a word, this structure would provide a polarity score of that word accordingly. If any word is not present in the dictionary, then the word is considered to be neutral with a polarity score of zero.

Algorithm#1: Apply SentiWordNet for polarity-score list

Input:

1. Social-media messages

2. Lexical resource: SentiWordNet

Output:

List of polarity scores for each participant

Main_Method:

1. Begin

2. Call Method-1

3. Call Method-2

4. End

Method-1:

1. Begin

2. For each sentence s_i in social-media messages

3. p_i=sender of s_i

4. a_i=after data cleansing of s_i

5. b_i=tokenization of a_i

6. c_i=POS tagging of b_i

7. d_i=remove stop words from c_i

8. e_i=lemmatization of d_i

9.   tokenized[p_i]= tokenized[p_i]+e_i

10. End

Method-2:

1. Begin

2. Open source file of SentiWordNet

3. Create dictionary-type data structure d_r

4. For each participant p_i

5.   Set s_r = an empty list

6.   For each token t_j of tokenized[p_i]

7.   x = $d_r[t_j]$

8.   Add x at the end of the list s_r

9.   score$_r$[p_i] = s_r

10. Return score

11. End

4.4.2.3 Generating mood-oriented comments

The ultimate goal of this phase is to generate alerting comments for each participant based on the extent of polarity sentiment displayed by their captured text messages. The actual polarity scores obtained from the previous module are utilized here to be recorded in graphs and tables, which enables further calculation of different ratios − viz. that involving overall negative to positive sentiment over the whole content for each participant, negative to positive ratios for their average outstanding sentiment values, as well as the individual counts of those outstanding occurrences.

The standard deviation of each of these ratio values provides a measure for the extent of normalcy in the output for an individual. The output is taken to be 'Normal' if the participant's deviation from the average lies within the standard-deviation range in the bell curve. It generates an 'Alert' comment if it is outside this range, yet lies within twice the standard deviation range. For values exceeding this limit the comment generated is 'Alarm'. The comments appear as highlighted signals if the associated sentiment is of excessive negative polarity (see Table 4.4).

Algorithm#2: Polarity-based comment from scores

Input: List of polarity scores for each participant (score$_r$)

Output:

1. Sentiment-Value Ratios for participants – Negative: Positive
2. Alerting Comments for each participant based on the ratios

Steps:

1. Set all_score = an empty list
2. For each participant p$_i$
3. For each polarity score x in score$_r$[p$_i$]
4. Add x at the end of the list all_score
5. Set q1 = 1st quartile of all_score
6. Set q2 = 2nd quartile of all_score
7. Set q3 = 3rd quartile of all_score
8. Set IQR = q3 – q1
9. Set high_limit = q3 + (1.5 * IQR)
10. Set low_limit = q1 - (1.5 * IQR)
11. For each participant p$_i$
12.   Plot the polarity values in score$_r$[p$_i$] with respect to time axis
13.   Set a1 = Area above the time axis
14.   Set a2 = Area below the time axis
15.   Set b1 = and b2 as empty list
15.   For each polarity score x in score$_r$[p$_i$]
16.   if x > high_limit, then
                Add x at the end of the list b1
17.   if x < low_limit, then
                Add x at the end of the list b2
18.   Set c1 = Number of elements in b1
19.   Set c2 = Number of elements in b2
20.   Set d1 = Average of b1
21.   Set d2 = Average of b2

22. $ratio_1[p_i] = a2 \ / \ a1$

23. $ratio_2[p_i] = c2 \ / \ c1$

24. $ratio_3[p_i] = d2 \ / \ d1$

25. Set m_1, s_1 = Mean and Standard deviation of $ratio_1$

26. Set m_2, s_2 = Mean and Standard deviation of $ratio_2$

27. Set m_3, s_3 = Mean and Standard deviation of $ratio_3$

28. For each participant p_j

29.   For ith ratio

30.   if $| \, ratio_i - m_i \, | \, < s_i$ then
$$Remark_i[p_j] = \text{“Normal”}$$

31.   else if $| \, ratio_i - m_i \, | \, < 2 * s_i$ then
$$Remark_i[p_j] = \text{“Alert”}$$

32.   else
$$Remark_i[p_j] = \text{“Alarm”}$$

33. Return Remark

4.4.3 Phase 2: signature image analysis

In Phase 2, the analysis is based on the outputs of some algorithms computed on the pre-processed signature images. All the algorithms are implemented using Python 3.7.3. The actual packages used are *scikit-image* and *matplotlib*. The next few subsections describe each of the procedures in detail.

4.4.3.1 Pre-processing: handwritten digitized signatures

Prior to feature extraction, the raw images of the signatures need to be pre-processed extensively using the following standard techniques:

Image Binarization

The process of binarizing a digital image involves converting the grayscale image to a black-and-white one. Here, a clustering technique determines a discriminating threshold value of gray, beyond which darker shades would be treated as black and lighter ones as white.

Noise Reduction

An agglomeration of black pixels around a solitary white one, or the reverse, are treated as noise instances within an image. Such noise is usually removed during the pre-processing steps using a simple 3×3 mask template, which checks for a non-matching central pixel of the mask with the remaining 8 surrounding pixels. If the non-match count is substantial, the color of the central pixel needs to be reversed.

Minimal Area Cropping

Cropping of an image involves removal of irrelevant portions from the border. Here, the image, after noise removal, is subject to a tight-fitting border-sensing algorithm, which retains only the minimal rectangular bounding box of each signature.

Width Normalization

The pure width of a signature image is the width of the minimal rectangular bounding box of that image as obtained above. The average value of the pure width of all image instances in the dataset is first calculated. Next, the width of each instance image is scaled up or down with respect to the average pure width, while maintaining the aspect ratio of the original images in terms of their heights as well. All further processing is done on these width-normalized image sets.

4.4.3.2 Feature-extraction algorithms from signature images

A. Baseline Detection

A baseline is an imaginary line at the bottom that helps to form the handwritten signature better – these may be ascending, descending or relatively horizontal in nature.

Figure 4.3 A signature image with a descending baseline.

Fig. 4.3 depicts a typical baseline drawn using technology to decipher the tilt of a signature. The angle of inclination of the line between the initial and final points of the image is calculated here [20].

Algorithm#3: Baseline Detection

Input: Cropped Signature Image (IMG)

Output: Signature Image Baseline Slant: "Ascending"/ "Descending" / "Horizontal"

Steps:

1. Begin

2. totalSlope:= 0

3. for every image in a folder, Do

4.   imgBin:= binarization (IMG)

5.   Find the lowest and highest points along both the x-axis and y-axis

6.   height:= (highest point of y-axis) − (lowest point of the y-axis)

7.   width:= (highest point of x-axis) − (lowest point of the x-axis)

8.   referenceWidthDistance:= 5% of the width

9.   descenderHeight:= 10% of the height

10.   locate the lowest point of the y-axis from the lowest point of the x-axis up to the length of *referenceWidthDistance*, in order to find the x and y values of the start baseline point, provided the y value is above *descenderHeight*

11.   locate the lowest point of the y-axis from the highest point of the x-axis up to the length of *referenceWidthDistance* backwards, in order to find the x and y values of the end baseline point, provided the y value is above *descenderHeight*

12.   draw a line from start baseline point to end baseline point

13.   calculate *slope* of above line using arctan() value on ratio of the y-axis difference to the x-axis difference between start and end points of baseline

14.   totalSlope:= totalSlope + slope

15. avgSlope = totalSlope / total number of images in the folder

16. if avgSlope > 0.015

17. then

18. baseline = "Ascending"

19. else

20.   if avgSlope < -0.015

21.   then

22.   baseline = "Descending"

23.   else

24.   baseline = "Horizontal"

25. End

N.B. In the above algorithm the binarization() function returns the binary image that takes a grayscale image as input. During testing, it is observed that baselines with slopes in the range $(-0.015, 0.015)$ appear almost horizontal and hence are classified as such.

B. Writing-Pressure Detection

A modified version of the Writing-Pressure Measurement algorithm [26] helps to detect the Pressure value for each signature image by calculating a threshold average with respect to the standard deviation over all points on the image.

Algorithm#4: Writing-Pressure Detection

Input: Cropped signature images

Output: Classification of each writer according to pressure: "Heavy" / "Light"

Steps:

1. Begin

2. for folder in directory,

3. Do

4.   total_sd:= 0

5.   m:= 0

6.   pressure:= 0

7.   for IMG:= image in folder, Do

8.   BW:= binarization(IMG)

9.   r:= number of rows in BW

10.   c:= number of columns in BW

11.   n:= 1

```
12.        for i:= 1 to r do
13.            for j:= 1 to c do
14.                if(BW(i, j) != 1)
15.                    Image(n):= IMG(i, j)
16.                    n:= n + 1
17.        pressure:= pressure + standard_deviation(Image)
18. // End of for IMG
19. sd_pressure(m):= pressure / total number of images in the folder
20. total_sd:= total_sd + sd_pressure(m)
21. m:= m + 1
22. // End of for folder
23. threshold_value = total_sd / m
24. for i:= 0 to (m -1) Do
25.        if( sd_pressure(i) > threshold_value)
26.        pressure(i) = "Heavy"
27.        else
28.        pressure(i) = "Light"
29. end if
30. // End of for i
31. End
```

4.4.3.3 Applying rule-based classifiers

In the final system, the algorithmically extracted graphological features have been set up as the inputs to a rule-based classifier, where they serve as the antecedents (ref. Fig. 4.1. System Architecture: Phase 2). The characteristic traits for each such feature, extracted by applying graphology rules declared in Table 4.2, are obtained as the output in the form of the corresponding consequent part of the classifier, designed with the algorithm presented hereafter.

Phase 2: Algorithm#5: Rule-Based Classification

Input:

(1) Signature Image Baseline Slant

(2) Class value denoting Signature Pressure

Output: Behavioral traits of the signatory

1. Begin

2. if (baseline=Descending and pressure=Light)

3. then

4.   write "Pessimistic and Less Emotional"

5. else if (baseline=Ascending and pressure=Light)

6.   then

7.   write "Optimistic and Less Emotional"

8.   else if (baseline= Horizontal and pressure=Light)

9.   then

10.   write "Neutral and Less Emotional"

11.   else if (baseline=Descending and pressure=Heavy)

12.   then

13.   write "Pessimistic and More Emotional"

14.   else if (baseline=Ascending and pressure=Heavy)

15.   then

16.   write "Optimistic and More Emotional"

17.   else if (baseline=Horizontal and pressure=Heavy)

18.   then

19.   write "Neutral and More Emotional"

20. end if

21. End

N.B. In the above algorithm, 'Neutral' ≡ '*Neither Pessimistic nor Optimistic*'.

However, in order to develop an actual system, which should be guided to track the mood swings affecting the mental equilibrium of a person, the phase 2 modules have to suggest the degree of surveillance through a second

Table 4.2 Rules for Classification of Human Behavior.

Rule Antecedent	=>	Consequents
(baseline=Descending) and (pressure=Light)	=>	Pessimistic and Less Emotional
(baseline=Descending) and (pressure=Heavy)	=>	Pessimistic and More Emotional
(baseline=Ascending) and (pressure= Light)	=>	Optimistic and Less Emotional
(baseline=Ascending) and (pressure=Heavy)	=>	Optimistic and More Emotional
(baseline=Horizontal) and (pressure=Light)	=>	Neutral and Less Emotional
(baseline= Horizontal) and (pressure=Heavy)	=>	Neutral and More Emotional

set of rules, as indicated in Table 4.3. This clearly indicates the requirement for another simple rule-based classifier that takes in the graphology-based characteristic traits produced by the earlier classifier as antecedents and produces the surveillance suggestions as the desired output or consequents. The elementary nature of such a classifier eliminates the necessity to accommodate the algorithms to design it.

Table 4.3 Rule Set for Degree of Surveillance.

Rule Antecedent	=>	Consequents
Pessimistic	=>	Most Stringent
Neutral and More Emotional	=>	Most Stringent
Neutral and Less Emotional	=>	More Stringent
Optimistic and More Emotional	=>	More Stringent
Optimistic and Less Emotional	=>	Less Stringent

Finally, the results from the two phases are correlated in Table 4.6 to analyze the performance of the system.

4.5 Result and performance analysis

4.5.1 Phase 1: computerized analysis results on message dataset

4.5.1.1 Sample score graphs for Participants #1, and #11 to #14

Figs. 4.4 and 4.5 depict participants who are far more voluble than the participants following them, as is evident from the graphs in Fig. 4.6, and Figs. 4.7 and 4.8. Obviously, Participant#11 (Fig. 4.5) tops the list in this respect. The diamond dots on the graphs mark the negative outliers, while the square ones depict the positive outliers calculated on the basis of the five-number summary [28] on the distribution of the whole set of sentiment scores.

The ratio of negativity to positivity of these outliers for each participant, both with respect to the average value as well as the numerosity count are taken into account while building up the table following the graphs. The total volume of negative and positive aspects of the messages are also reflected in the deviation columns of Table 4.4.

In Table 4.4, the highlighted comment 'Alarm' for Participant #1 indicates the most excessive negative sentiments in this group, and thus a cause

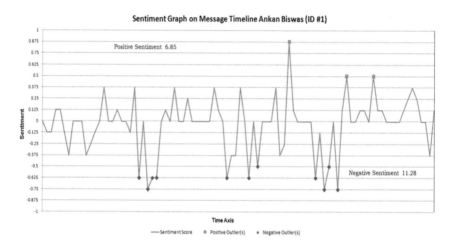

Figure 4.4 Sentiment Scores plotted for Participant #1.

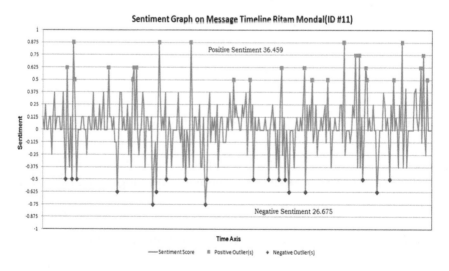

Figure 4.5 Sentiment Scores plotted for Participant #11.

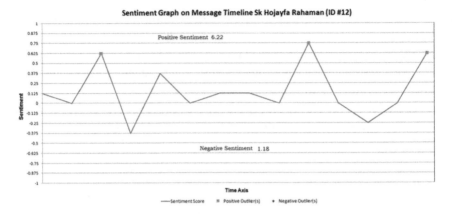

Figure 4.6 Sentiment Scores plotted for Participant #12.

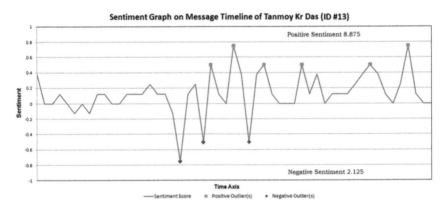

Figure 4.7 Sentiment Scores plotted for Participant #13.

for grave concern. While most of the rest remain in the normal range, participants #12 and #14 both attain 'Alarm's and 'Alert's, respectively, in two of the ratio heads, and participant #13 attained only one 'Alert'. However, all three are found to be in the excess positive score range, and hence their comments are not highlighted.

4.5.2 Phase 2: computerized analysis results on signature dataset

See Table 4.5.

Table 4.4 Summary Table for Sentiment-Ratio Deviation Rates.

Participant ID #	Overall Sentiment Value Ratio (-ve: +ve)	Average Outlier Sentiment Ratios (-ve +ve)	Outlier # Ratios (-ve: +ve)	Deviation of Sentiment Ratios		
				Overall Values	Outlier Average	Outlier Number
1	1.6467	1.018	3.6667	**Alarm**	Normal	**Alarm**
2	0.3786	1.1282	0.25	Normal	Normal	Normal
3	0.7435	0.6154	1	Normal	Normal	Normal
4	0.7142	0.5563	0.36	Normal	Normal	Normal
5	0.838	1	1	Normal	Normal	Normal
6	0.644	0.8749	1	Normal	Normal	Normal
7	0.7641	0.8295	1	Normal	Normal	Normal
8	0.7053	0.9722	0.6	Normal	Normal	Normal
9	0.5567	0.9515	0.6	Normal	Normal	Normal
10	0.5746	0.8535	0.4375	Normal	Normal	Normal
11	0.7316	0.867	0.76	Normal	Normal	Normal
12	0.1897	0	0	**Alert**	**Alarm**	Normal
13	0.2394	1	0.5	**Alert**	Normal	Normal
14	0.1087	0	0	**Alert**	**Alarm**	Normal
Average	0.631079	0.791179	0.798157			
SD	0.360644	0.342493	0.864251			

Range up to SD: Normal
Range up to 2*SD: Alert
Range Beyond: Alarm

Table 4.5 Machine-Predicted Behavior for Signature Dataset.

ID	Signature	Predicted Behavior	Surveillance
1		Neutral, More Emotional	Most Stringent
2		Neutral, Less Emotional	More Stringent
3		Optimistic, Less Emotional	Less Stringent
4		Neutral, More Emotional	Most Stringent
5		Optimistic, More Emotional	More Stringent
6		Neutral Less Emotional	More Stringent
7		Neutral, More Emotional	Most Stringent
8		Optimistic, Less Emotional	Less Stringent
9		Optimistic, Less Emotional	Less Stringent
10		Neutral, Less Emotional	More Stringent
11		Neutral, More Emotional	Most Stringent
12		Neutral, More Emotional	Most Stringent
13		Neutral, More Emotional	Most Stringent
14		Neutral, More Emotional	Most Stringent

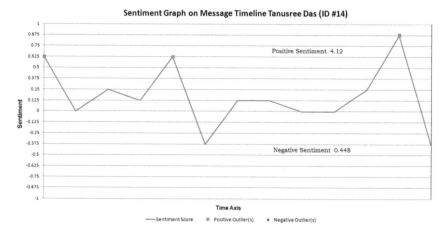

Figure 4.8 Sentiment Scores plotted for Participant #14.

4.5.3 Final output

It may be noted from the Final Output in Table 4.6 that 50% of the cases have been safely correlated. The remaining 50% are false-positive cases in the context of this particular message session, i.e., none amongst the rest have any abnormal mood swings detected in the first phase, indicating stable mental conditions throughout. In fact, all participants with Alarms and Alerts generated due to mood swings in the first phase have been successfully detected as requiring Most Stringent vigilance in the second phase too, depending on graphology features captured from their signatures. Thus it can be safely inferred that none of the negative personalities are missed by the system, which in itself is assumed as a 100% success rate within this small study group.

The experiments carried out are further augmented by manual corroboration at both phases with full authentication of the mechanized versions made by human annotators having intimate knowledge of the participants' psychological states during the study period.

4.6 Conclusion and future scope

The first-phase experiments yield some fair attributes for detecting maladjustment qualities within the small student circle surveyed. In the case of the first candidate, it actually proves helpful in providing appropriate and timely support based on the analytical results obtained from the chat ses-

Table 4.6 Profitability of Machine-Prediction Correlation.

Participant	Phase 1 Deviations	Phase 2 Vigilance	Remarks on Safe Correlation
1	2 Highlighted Alarms	Most Stringent	Safely Correlated
2	All Normal	More Stringent	Not applicable in present context
3	All Normal	Less Stringent	Safely Correlated
4	All Normal	Most Stringent	Not applicable in present context
5	All Normal	More Stringent	Not applicable in present context
6	All Normal	More Stringent	Not applicable in present context
7	All Normal	Most Stringent	Not applicable in present context
8	All Normal	Less Stringent	Safely Correlated
9	All Normal	Less Stringent	Safely Correlated
10	All Normal	More Stringent	Not applicable in present context
11	All Normal	Most Stringent	Not applicable in present context
12	1 Alarm, 1 Alert	Most Stringent	Safely Correlated
13	1 Alert, 2 Normal	Most Stringent	Safely Correlated
14	1 Alarm, 1 Alert	Most Stringent	Safely Correlated

sions. Most of the others also benefit to varied extents since it serves as an ideal space to vent one's spleen without any fear of retribution. The messages also succeed in reducing negativity within oneself by 'getting it out of the system' or at least 'ridding it of its bitterest tastes'! Hence, not only does it aid in discovering personality kinks, but it also helps to abate the issues to a certain measure. In addition to all its other advantages, this system further offers to maintain safe distance monitoring of mental health under the prevailing pandemic conditions.

In the second phase, the Baseline Detection Algorithm matches with the manual process of checking it with 100% accuracy for the used dataset, whereas the Writing-Pressure Algorithm performs with an average of 90% match. In the instances of mismatch, it is felt that greater reliance may be reposed on the computerized techniques, as they are based on statistical information derived from digitized images directly, rather than biased opinions of human viewers. Furthermore, the tedium and delay associated with manual inspection of each specimen signature is also an added justification for using the mechanized system, especially when more than one specimen is utilized per person to diminish chances of prevarication,

Finally, since the participants all belong to the close student community acquainted with the present researchers, the predicted behavior trends have been found to be perfectly satisfactory in each case under consideration. However, the researchers are acutely aware of the fact that the size of the dataset is too meager to base any decisive claim on the excellence of the algorithms with the presented result. The restrictions in collecting signatures and using more sophisticated tools, augmented by the general feeling of unrest amongst the student community, has detrimentally affected studies in this troubled time. Under more favorable conditions the system can be checked with a larger population, and a higher number of samples per participant, to substantiate the conclusions more strongly.

Future enhancements can be affected in the first phase by employing trained psychoanalysts to introduce proper probe topics to unfurl the dark thoughts within more successfully. The metrics employed may also be tuned more finely with better tools suggested by expert statisticians. For the second phase, what have been probed here are only two of the easiest detectable features of writing. These mark only the tip of the iceberg. A plethora of promising avenues remain open to explore for new entrants into this arena, including other writing-style idiosyncrasies exhibited not only in signatures, but also within text paragraphs, as indicated by some of the papers surveyed in this context.

Acknowledgments

With a heavy heart we acknowledge our deep gratitude to the late Ms. Chhanda Roy for her invaluable contributions to the original project that preceded the present work. Her sudden demise about a year ago was an irreparable loss, but we still feel her presence and everlasting motivating spirit all around us in each new venture. We also appreciate the sincere assistance lent by all participants of the current proceedings and the kind cooperation of the editorial team of this publication who made it all possible. Last but not the least, we would like to thank Jadavpur University for providing us with the perfect research environment needed for carrying out our experimental endeavors.

References

[1] C. Roy, R. Dey, C. Chaudhuri, D. Das, Emotion predictor using social media text and graphology, in: IEEE 9th International Conference on Advanced Computing (IACC), Tiruchirappalli, 2019.

[2] B. Pang, L. Lee, Opinion mining and sentiment analysis, Journal Foundation and Trends in Information Retrieval 2 (1–2) (2008) 1–135.

[3] P. Ekman, An argument for basic emotions, Cognition and Emotion 6 (3/4) (1992) 169–200.

[4] G. Miner, D. Delen, J. Elder, A. Fast, T. Hill, R. Nisbet, The seven practice areas of text analytics, in: Practical Text Mining and Statistical Analysis for Non-Structured Text Data Applications, Elsevier, 2012, pp. 30–41, Chapter 2.

[5] V.R. Lokhande, B.W. Gawali, Analysis of signature for the prediction of personality trait, in: 1st International Conference on Intelligent Systems and Information Management (ICISIM), Aurangabad, 2017, pp. 44–49, https://doi.org/10.1109/ICISIM.2017.8122145.

[6] A. Venkatesh, A. Bhanpurawala, S. Chowdhury, D.R. Kalbande, Demonstration of signature analysis using intelligent systems, in: S. Unnikrishnan, S. Surve, D. Bhoir (Eds.), Advances in Computing, Communication, and Control, ICAC3, in: Communications in Computer and Information Science, vol. 361, Springer, Berlin, Heidelberg, 2013.

[7] I. Marks, P. Vossen, A lexicon model for deep sentiment analysis and opinion mining applications, Decision Support Systems 53 (4) (2012) 680–688.

[8] A. Hogenboom, P. Van Iterson, B. Heerschop, F. Frasincar, U. Kaymak, Determining negation scope and strength in sentiment analysis, in: IEEE International Conference on Systems, Man, and Cybernetics, 2011.

[9] M. Dadvar, C. Hauff, F.D. Jong, Scope of negation detection in sentiment analysis, in: Dutch-Belgian Information Retrieval Workshop, 2011.

[10] R. Xia, C. Zong, S. Li, Ensemble of feature sets and classification algorithms for sentiment classification, Information Sciences 181 (2011) 1138–1152.

[11] R. Parikh, M. Movassate, Sentiment Analysis of User-Generated Twitter Updates using Various Classification Techniques, CS224N Final Report, 2009.

[12] P. Gamallo, M. Garcia, Citius: a naive-Bayes strategy for sentiment analysis on English tweets, in: Proceedings of the 8th International Workshop on Semantic Evaluation (SemEval 2014), 2014, pp. 171–175.

[13] R. Plamondon, G. Lorette, Automatic signature verification and writer identification the state of the art, Pattern Recognition 22 (2) (1989) 107–131.

[14] H. Ketabdar, J. Richiardi, A. Drygajlo, Global feature selection for on-line signature verification, in: Proc. 12th Internat. Graphonomics Society Conference, 2005.

[15] M.C. Fairhurst, E. Kaplani, Strategies for Exploiting Signature Verification Based on Complexity Estimates, University of Kent, Canterbury, 1998.

[16] A. Jain, F. Griess, S. Connell, On-line signature verification, Pattern Recognition 35 (12) (2002) 2963–2972.

[17] V.S. Nalwa, Automatic on-line signature verification, Proceedings of the IEEE 85 (2) (February 1997).

[18] S. Madabusi, V. Srinivas, S. Bhaskaran, M. Balasubramanian, On-line and off-line signature verification using relative slope algorithm, in: Measurement Systems for Homeland Security, Contraband Detection and Personal Safety Workshop, (IMS 2005), Proceedings of the IEEE International Workshop on, 2005, pp. 11–15.

[19] Qu Tong, A. El Saddik, A. Adler, A stroke based algorithm for dynamic signature verification, in: Electrical and Computer Engineering, Canadian Conference on, vol. 1, 2–5 May 2004, 2004, pp. 461–464.

[20] Azlinah Hj Mohamed, Rohayu Yusof, Shuzlina Abdul Rahman, Sofianita Mutalib, Baseline extraction algorithm for online signature recognition, WSEAS Transactions on Systems Archive 8 (2009) 491–500.

[21] Luiz S. Oliveira, Edson Justino, Cinthia Freitas, Robert Sabourin, The graphology applied to signature verification, in: 12th Conference of the International Graphonomics Society, 2005.

[22] Prachi Joshi, Aayushi Agarwal, Ajinkya Dhavle, Rajani Suryavanshi, Shreya Kodalikar, Handwriting analysis for detection of personality traits using machine learning approach, International Journal of Computer Applications (2015).

[23] Seema Kedar, Vaishnavi Nair, Shweta Kulkarni, Personality identification through handwriting analysis: a review, International Journal of Advanced Research in Computer Science and Software Engineering (2015).

[24] Bin Zhang, Sargur N. Srihari, Analysis of Handwriting Individuality Using Word Feature, State University of New York at Buffalo, Buffalo, NY, 2003.

[25] Somayeh Hashemi, Benrouz Vasegni, Fatemah Torgheh, Graphology for Farsi handwriting using image processing techniques, IOSR Journal of Electronics and Communication Engineering (2015).

[26] Hastuti Fatimah, Esmeralda C. Djamal, Ridwan Ilyas, Fazia Renaldi, Personality features identification from handwriting using convolutional neural networks, in: International Conference on Information Technology, Informational Systems and Electrical Engineering, 2019.

[27] R.C. Gonzalez, R.E. Woods, S.L. Eddins, Digital Image Processing Using MATLAB, 2nd ed., Tata McGraw-Hill, 2010.

[28] Jiawei Han, Micheline Kamber, Jian Pei, Data Mining Concepts and Techniques, third edition, Morgan Kaufmann, ISBN 9780123814791, 2011.

CHAPTER 5

Online social-network sensing models

Subhayan Bhattacharya, Sankhamita Sinha, Paramita Dey, Anindita Saha, Chandrayee Chowdhury, and Sarbani Roy

Department of Computer Science and Engineering, Jadavpur University, Kolkata, West Bengal, India

5.1 Introduction

With the advent of Online Social Networks (OSNs) and their plethora of features, the engagement and active screen-time of users have also increased, making it an indispensable part of life. This provides a range of interesting and rudimentary research problems, which includes, but is not restricted to, study of network properties and growth, study of multimedia and textual content publicly available on the OSNs to analyze individual and group behavior, and to study the addiction and extent of engagement of users and its effect in their real life [4].

The first recognizable online social network was started in the year 1997. The first OSN had minimalist features like the ability to add pictures and to connect with other users. Over the next two decades, the number of OSNs has increased to a few hundred, and more than half the world's population are active on some OSN, irrespective of their demographic or internet access.

With such a huge variety of people actively participating in OSNs, it is a gold-mine of data. The high velocity, variety, and volume of data that is produced and archived on OSNs on a daily basis allows researchers the opportunity to cultivate and explore endless insights. However, the same velocity, volume, and variety of data possess certain problems in processing this data, such as data-storage management, big-data processing, and information representation on such a huge scale.

This chapter gives an overview of:

- Network Properties and Information Propagation – the atomic phenomenon that contributes towards the growth and behavior of a network.

Computational Intelligence Applications for Text and Sentiment Data Analysis
https://doi.org/10.1016/B978-0-32-390535-0.00010-0

- Text Analysis in OSN data — The fundamental content analysis for OSN data that looks beyond the network structure and details the attributes of the participants/users of OSNs.
- Addiction and Cognitive Absorption — The study of engagement of half the world's population and the effects and inferences of it.

The rest of the chapter is organized as follows: Section 5.2 gives an overview of why sensing in online social networks is important. Section 5.3 provides a comprehensive overview of Network Properties and Information Propagation, Text Analysis in OSN data, and Addiction and Cognitive Absorption in OSNs. The applications of these studies is highlighted in Section 5.4 and Section 5.5 concludes the chapter.

5.2 Importance of sensing in online social networks

5.2.1 Why social sensing

Social Sensing has evolved as a multi-faceted research and development domain from both the academic as well as the industrial perspective. Social Sensing leads to an ever-growing data base that is rich in information about daily interactions, activities, preferences, choices, and other such details of individuals and communities that is not available otherwise. People can both contribute to the growth of this data base as well as use it to infer insights and heuristics about functional and behavioral patterns of stakeholders. Some of the prime facilitators of this unprecedented growth of social sensing are:

- flexibility of Online Platforms such as Online Social Networks;
- the information richness of the collected data;
- graph-theoretic approaches and algorithms simplifying modeling and processing data;
- evolution of smartphone technology;
- capability of storing and processing big data;
- addiction of the average netizen to Online Social Networks.

5.2.2 Areas of applications

There are many benefits and applications of sensing in online social networks beyond the obvious networking/community building activities. Some of the known applications of social sensing include:

- Social Awareness — The data publishing and subscription model of online social networks allows users to be aware of the cultural, socio-economic, political, and other aspects of the society. Without the online social networks, the reach of this awareness was very limited but social sensing allows a social awareness without boundaries.

- Mental Health – Identifying mood trends and sentiment of online social network posts of individuals over a period of time can give an insight into their mental health.
- Targeted Marketing – Inferring valuable insights such as buying patterns of individuals, preferred eating destinations, and so on can help in targeted marketing.
- Trajectory Projection – Identifying the physical movement of individuals can also be done using smartphone sensing, and to a certain extent, through their online activity as well.

5.3 Sensing modalities

5.3.1 Network analysis

5.3.1.1 Network properties

The network properties covered in this section are listed in Table 5.1.

5.3.1.1.1 Density, distance, diameter

Density: Network density is the ratio of the number of actual links to the possible or potential links of a network. A potential or possible link is a connection that exists potentially between two nodes [34]. The number of possible links of an undirected network is:

$$\mu = \frac{N * (N - 1)}{2} \tag{5.1}$$

and that of a directed network is:

$$\mu = N * (N - 1) \tag{5.2}$$

The network density is the Actual number of links/Possible number of links. Thus for an undirected network the network density can be represented as

$$D_{net} = \frac{2E}{N * (N - 1)} \tag{5.3}$$

and for directed networks the network density can be represented as

$$D_{net} = \frac{E}{N * (N - 1)} \tag{5.4}$$

Table 5.1 Network Properties.

Properties	Formula
Density	$D_{net} = \begin{cases} \frac{2E}{N*(N-1)}, & \text{if undirected} \\ \frac{E}{N*(N-1)}, & \text{directed} \end{cases}$
Distance	$\rho(i,j)$
Diameter	$max(\rho(i,j)\forall i,j)$
Power-law Exponent	$\gamma = 1 + n(\sum_{u \in V} \ln \frac{d(u)}{d_{min}})$
Global Clustering Coefficient	$gcc(c_i) = 1 + n(\sum_{u \in V} \ln \frac{d(u)}{d_{min}})$
Local Clustering Coefficient	$D_{net} = \begin{cases} lcc(c_i) = \frac{2e_i}{k_i(k_i-1)}, & \text{if undirected} \\ lcc(c_i) = \frac{e_i}{k_i(k_i-1)}, & \text{directed} \end{cases}$
Average Local Clustering Coefficient	$c_i = \frac{\sum_i \frac{e_i}{k_i(k_i-1)}}{N}$
Closeness Centrality	$c(i) = \frac{N-1}{\sum_{\forall(i \neq j)} \rho(i,j)}$
Betweenness Centrality	$bc(i) = \sum_{j,k \in V} \frac{s_{jk}(i)}{s_{jk}}$
Eigenvector Centrality	$e(i) = \frac{1}{\lambda} \sum_j g_{ij} e(j)$
Katz Centrality	$kc(i) = \alpha \sum_{j=1}^{n} g_{ij} kc(j) + \beta$
Page-rank Centrality	$prank(n) = \frac{1-d}{|V|} + d \sum_{v:(v,n) \in E} \frac{prank(u)}{|\{v:(v,u) \in E\}|}$
Homophily	$h_s^t = \begin{cases} 1, & \text{if } s = t \\ 0, & \text{otherwise} \end{cases}$
Assortativity	$r = \frac{\sum_{jk}(e_{jk} - q_j q_k)}{\sigma_q^2}$

A high value of density represents that the network is more dense and nodes are more cohesive. On the other hand, a low density value represents a less connected (sparse) network. In a dense network, the information can flow easily and faster than in a sparse network.

Distance: $\rho(i,j)$ represents the shortest path between a pair of nodes i and j. It calculates how far a node is from other nodes. The graph distance effectively quantifies the structural difference between complex networks [43].

Diameter: $max(\rho(i,j)\forall i,j)$, is the longest of all the calculated path lengths or the distance [34]. A larger diameter signifies that information propagation will have higher latency.

5.3.1.1.2 Degree distribution

The degree of a node in a network is the number of links connected with other nodes [34]. Thus the degree sequence of a network is represented as a vector $\{d(v1), d(v2), d(v3), ..., d(vn)\}$, where $d(V)$ holds the degree information of vertices $V = \{v1, v2, v3, ...vn\}$ of the network. The total number of connections or edges e is expressed as the sum of the degree of each node. Thus the total degree of the nodes is equal to

$$d(V) = \frac{\sum_{i=1}^{n} d(v_i)}{2} \qquad (5.5)$$

where v_i is the degree centrality of the ith node. The average degree of the network is $d(V)/n$, where n is the number of nodes or vertices. The heavy-tailed or power-law degree distribution follows the following degree distribution

$$p(k) = ck^{-\gamma} \qquad (5.6)$$

where c is the constant, γ is the power-law exponent, and k is the degree of nodes [31]. Sometimes, an exponential cut-off [31] is required to neglect some outliers. The degree distribution is then represented as

$$\gamma(x = k) \propto e^{\frac{-k}{\kappa}} k^{-\gamma} \qquad (5.7)$$

where $e^{\frac{-k}{\kappa}}$ is the exponential cut-off factor, k is the degree, and γ is the power-law exponent [31]. In addition, it gives an idea of whether the most nodes have very similar degrees or very different degrees, which can provide us with much information [15]. For instance, if some of the nodes have eight links or everybody has one or two links, then it is different kind of network. This different kind of network has different properties like a diffusion property, path links, and other attributes. In 1969, Price saw that the distribution of degrees in a citation network tend to have a fat tail [17]. That means there are too few articles that have lots of citation and too many that have very few citations. In the late 1990s, Albert and Barabasi looked at the World Wide Web link network whose log–log plot is almost linear and explained the concept of scale-free distribution that follows the power law [6]:

$$p(k) \sim k^{-\gamma} \qquad (5.8)$$

where, γ is the power-law exponent and $p(k)$ is the probability that a node in the network is connected to k other nodes. If the network is directed, two degree distributions are possible: in-degree, i.e., the number of links incoming to a node and out-degree, i.e., the number of links outgoing from a node [39].

5.3.1.1.3 Power-law exponent

Node degree refers to the number of links of a node. All nodes in a network do not have the same number of links. The degree distribution is used to characterize the node degrees by a probability distribution function [8]. It explains the probability to select the node with degree k randomly. The random graphs (Erdos–Renyi) [19] are generated by a set of disconnected nodes initially with a uniform probability, which follow a Poisson distribution, whereas Watts and Strogatz [46] proposed a model where the connections between the nodes of a regular network are attached with a certain probability. In both models, the probability of degree distribution $p(k)$ is bounded [2]. The real-world networks like the World Wide Web [1], the Co-author network [17], etc., follow the power law. This is represented by

$$p(k) \sim k^{-\gamma} \tag{5.9}$$

where γ is the power-law exponent. The power-law exponent describes the distribution of node degrees in a network. The scale-free properties of networks depend on the degree exponent. The difference between the random graph and a scale-free network comes in the tail of the degree distribution [7]. For a directed network, the in-degree distribution and out-degree distribution are calculated. It has been observed that the value of γ is more accurate when some nodes of degrees lower than a threshold (d_{min}) are ignored. The power-law exponent is computed from the degree distribution of a network using the following formula

$$\gamma = 1 + n\left(\sum_{u \in V} \ln \frac{d(u)}{d_{min}}\right) \tag{5.10}$$

where V = Set of vertices.
$d(u)$ = Degree of node u.
d_{min} = Minimum degree.

For Online Social Networks, the value of γ generally lies between 2 to 3 whatever the size of the network. A higher value of γ makes the curve of degree distribution steeper.

5.3.1.1.4 Clustering coefficient

The clustering coefficient is used to explain the network connectivity. It is a metric of the degree to find the nodes in a network that cluster together. There are two ways to represent the measure of clustering coefficient: global clustering coefficient and local clustering coefficient. The global cluster-ing coefficient calculates the overall connectivity of nodes in a network, whereas the local clustering coefficient finds the closeness of a single node to its neighbor locally.

5.3.1.2 Global clustering coefficient

The global clustering coefficient measures how the nodes are globally con-nected in a network. The global clustering coefficient $gcc(c_i)$ is the fraction of the number of closed triplets (triangles) and the sum of all open and closed triplets in a network [34]

$$gcc(c_i) = \frac{3 * tr}{3 * tr + otr} \tag{5.11}$$

where $tr = \#\_of\_triangles$.
$otr = \#\_of\_open\_triplets$.

5.3.1.3 Local clustering coefficient

The local clustering coefficient of a node represents the fraction of exist-ing links of the neighbors of each pair of the node and the number of all possible connections of neighbors of the node. If a node i has k_i neigh-bors/friends, then all possible connections among neighbors' pairs of the nodes in an undirected network are $\frac{k_i(k_i-1)}{2}$. Similarly, if a node i in a di-rected network has k_i neighbors, then all possible connections among the neighbors' pairs of the node are $k_i(k_i - 1)$. If e_i is the number of existing connections among the neighbors of node i in a network, then the local clustering coefficient $lcc(c_i)$ of node i is defined as

$$lcc(c_i) = \frac{2e_i}{k_i(k_i - 1)} \tag{5.12}$$

for undirected networks and

$$lcc(c_i) = \frac{e_i}{k_i(k_i - 1)} \tag{5.13}$$

for directed networks [42].

5.3.1.4 Average local clustering coefficient

The average local clustering coefficient C_i gives the clustering level of the overall network [46]. This is the average of the local clustering coefficient of N number of nodes and is defined as

$$c_i = \frac{\sum_i \frac{e_i}{k_i(k_i-1)}}{N} \tag{5.14}$$

for directed networks [42]. A higher average local clustering coefficient indicates that the network has densely connected groups or clusters. A lower average local clustering coefficient indicates the lack of such densely connected groups or clusters.

5.3.1.4.1 Centrality

The idea of centrality is applied in a communication network by Bavelas in 1948 (A Mathematical Model for Group Structures). It is an important structural property of an actor that helps to clarify the interrelationship between the actors. It identifies the most influential actors and the major active information channels in the communication network. Basically, this matrix is used to measure the importance of nodes in a network. There are seven kinds of centrality measures that are described: Degree centrality, Closeness centrality, Betweenness centrality, Page-rank centrality, Eigenvector centrality, Katz Prestige, and Bonacich centrality based on network topology.

Degree Centrality Degree centrality measures the number of links or degree of a node, in general, which node maintains the majority of connections, which is important in a network. From the Social Network point of view, which node has many neighbors is the important node of a network. Mathematically, it is defined as $d(i)$, where $d(i)$ is the degree of node i. For a directed network, there are two versions of measure: in-degree is the number of in-coming connections and out-degree is the number of out-going connections. A higher degree centrality generally signifies importance and is generally referred to as a hub. The probability of information propagation is higher through a high-degree node.

Closeness Centrality Closeness centrality, $c(i)$ of a node i is the reciprocal of the sum of the shortest distances from i to j, where $j \in (N - 1)$. It focuses on the relative distances of a node to all other nodes, whereas degree centrality states the connectedness of a node with other nodes. According to the closeness principle, a central node has minimum path distances from all other nodes in the network [40],

$$c(i) = \frac{1}{\sum_{\forall_{(i \neq j)}} \rho(i,j)} \tag{5.15}$$

Here, $\rho(i,j)$ denotes the distance of the shortest path from i to j in the network. Since the sum of distances depends on the number of nodes in the network, closeness is normalized by the sum of minimum possible distances $(N-1)$. A high closeness centrality signifies that the vertex is well connected to all other vertices in the network. Thus it can be a key node for information propagation.

$$c(i) = \frac{N-1}{\sum_{\forall(i\neq j)} \rho(i,j)} \qquad (5.16)$$

Betweenness Centrality Betweenness centrality is a metric to measure the strength of the betweenness of a node between other pair of nodes in a network. It is measured by

$$bc(i) = \sum_{j,k\in V} \frac{\varsigma_{jk}(i)}{\varsigma_{jk}} \qquad (5.17)$$

which is the number of shortest paths (between any pair of nodes say j and K in the network) that passes through the target node i (denoted by $\varsigma_{jk}(i)$) and the total number of shortest paths existing between any pair of nodes (say j and K) of the network (denoted by ς_{jk}). The higher betweenness value means the flow of information that passes through that node is high. Therefore, in social-network analysis, it is used to find the influential nodes that participate to flow the information rapidly.

Eigenvector Centrality In social-network analysis, eigenvector centrality is used to measure the influence of a node and determine the most peripheral node in a network. It could help to identify the most crucial node to the function of a group too [34]. It is special version of degree centrality. Degree centrality counts the high-degree node with similar priority, whereas eigenvector centrality does not give importance to all the connections. Generally, it focuses on the highly influential (degree) neighbors rather than the less influential (degree) neighbors of a node [46]. The eigenvector centrality $e(i)$ of vertex i, then $e(i)$ is proportional to the average of the centralities of i's network neighbors:

$$e(i) = \frac{1}{\lambda}\sum_{j} g_{ij}e(j) \qquad (5.18)$$

where λ is a proportionality constant and the adjacency matrix g_{ij} is the NXN symmetric matrix. Another formation of the above equation is:

$$g_{ij}.X = \lambda.X \qquad (5.19)$$

where $X = (x1, x2, x3, ..)$, X is an eigenvector of the adjacency matrix with corresponding non-negative (by the Perron–Frobenius theorem) largest eigenvalue λ. A high eigenvector centrality means the node is connected to a high number of important or hub nodes, and thus can be crucial for information propagation. For closeness centrality and eigenvector centrality, the average value for the whole network has been considered. The average value can be calculated as $\frac{\sum c(i)}{N}$, where $c(i)$ is the centrality measure for vertex i and N is the number of vertices in the network.

Katz Centrality In 1953, Leo Katz introduced Katz Centrality to find the relative influence of a node within a social network. For a directed network, when a node with outgoing edges belongs to a directed acyclic graph specifically, the eigenvector centrality becomes zero, although this node is connected with many edges. To overcome this problem, Katz centrality adds a bias term b to all the nodes irrespective of the network topology. The formula of Katz centrality is

$$kc(i) = \alpha \sum_{j=1}^{n} g_{ij} kc(j) + \beta \qquad (5.20)$$

where g_{ij} is the NXN adjacency matrix. The 1st term of the equation is the eigenvector centrality. α is the controller of the effect of the eigenvector centrality. The 2nd term β helps to avoid the zero eigenvector centrality value. In general, $\alpha < 1/\lambda$, where λ is the highest eigenvalue of g_{ij}.

Page-rank Centrality PageRank [36] is a link analysis algorithm and it assigns a numerical weighting to each node in a graph, with the purpose of measuring its relative importance within the set. It was named after Larry Page, one of the founders of Google. The PageRank of a node $n \in V$ is defined as

$$prank(n) = \frac{1-d}{|V|} + d \sum_{v:(v,n)\in E} \frac{prank(u)}{|\{v : (v, u) \in E\}|} \qquad (5.21)$$

where d is a dampening factor.

5.3.1.4.2 Homophily

When the online social media is represented as a graph, the users of social-network sites are considered as nodes and their relationships depict the links between them. These links can be built based on different structural-parameter values of nodes and relationships. As users tend to have most interaction with similar individuals: this concept is called homophily. The observable characteristics like race, age, income, education, work place, etc., can be considered as a similar tendency. If the s and t are two groups of a network, then the level of homophily of those two groups can be defined as [34]

$$\hbar_s^t = \begin{cases} 1, & \text{if } s = t \\ P, & \text{otherwise} \end{cases}$$

where the value of $\hbar$ varies from 0 to 1. If $\hbar = 0$, then the groups are homophilic, which means a node of group s does not connect through a link with a node of group t. In this scenario, the nodes are connected within their own groups, so that, $s \neq t$. $\hbar = P$ refers to the value of probability of connections between the nodes within similar groups to connections between the nodes belonging to dissimilar groups [24]. If $\hbar = P = 1$ this represents that the nodes are not homophilic in nature. The average homophily of the whole network is calculated as

$$h_{avg} = \frac{\sigma h_g}{c}, \quad \text{where } c \text{ is the number of non-zero } h_g$$

A network with high homophily value indicates that in the network similar nodes (for this chapter, nodes with similar degree) are connected and dissimilar nodes are disconnected. To calculate the homophily of the network, a clustering algorithm proposed by Faith et al. [42] that clusters nodes into groups depending on local clustering coefficients has been considered. After the clustering, the nodes in the same clusters are assumed to be of the same group. From the preferential attachment rule [6], [42], we obtain the probability Π_i that an existing node i with degree d_i connects a new link to a new node: $\Pi_i = \frac{d_i}{\sum_{j \in V} d_j}$, where V is a set of nodes of the network. In this case, if we introduce the homophily property, the probability Π_i^{st} of a new node of group t is linked to node i of group s is [24]:

$$\Pi_i^{st} = \frac{d_i^s \hbar_s^t}{\sigma_{j \in V} d_j^\theta \hbar_\theta^t} \tag{5.22}$$

where d_s^i = Degree of node i of group s.

h_s^t = Fraction of homophily between the group t of the new node and the group s of node i.

V = Set of nodes of the existing network.

A normalizing value is needed if the preference of a new node is to connect to an existing node i of group s. The normalizing factor is defined as the sum of the preferences of node j of group θ to connect the new node in group t [24]. If the preferential attachment rule is fitted on between existing nodes of the network, then the current nodes are attached to each other with a probability value. This value is proportional to the multiplication of the degree of existing nodes [7]. Therefore, $\Pi_{ij} = \frac{d_i d_j}{\sum_z \sum_{m>z\in V} d_z d_m}$ that refers the probability of the connection of node i with degree d_i and node j with degree d_j. In this situation, if we apply the homophily nature between the groups s and t, the normalized probability Π_{ij}^{st} of an existing node i of group s that is connected to another existing node j of group t, is defined as [24]:

$$\Pi_{ij}^{st} = \frac{d_i^s d_j^t h_s^t}{\sum_{j\in V} \sum_{j>z\in V} d_z^\theta d_m^B h_\theta^B} \tag{5.23}$$

where d_s^i = Degree of existing node i of group s.

d_j^t = Degree of another existing node j of group t.

V = Set of existing nodes.

h_s^t = The homophily level between groups s and t.

The denominator is the sum of product degrees of node $z \in V$ and $m \in V$, which belong to groups θ and B, respectively.

5.3.1.4.3 Assortativity

The concept of assortativity says that nodes with similar degrees tend to connect with each other [33]. The assortativity r for directed networks can be calculated in terms of in-degree (rin) and out-degree (rout). An assortative network is one in which nodes with similar degrees tend to connect with each other and nodes with dissimilar degrees are disconnected. On the other hand, the disassortative network indicates that high–degree nodes tend to connect to low-degree nodes and nodes with similar degrees are disconnected. To compute the assortativity of a network, the degree coefficient r is defined as [33], [32],

$$r = \frac{\sum_{jk}(e_{jk} - q_j q_k)}{\sigma_q^2} \tag{5.24}$$

where

$$\sigma^2 = \sum_k k^2 q_k - [\sum_k k^2 q_k]^2 \tag{5.25}$$

If $r > 0$, then the network is assortative.

$r = 0$, then the network is neutral.

$r < 0$, then the network is disassortative.

In assortative networks, therefore, the tendency would be to have groups or clusters of nodes with similar degrees. On the other hand, for disassortative networks, the tendency would be to form stars rather than clusters, with a high degree node at the center of the star and many low degree nodes at the periphery.

An interesting study in this field is represented in Fig. 5.1 [10]. The figure depicts the observed centrality values for multiple open sourced real-life online social networks. In this figure, CC means Clustering Coefficient. Facebook, YouTube, and the Email network are represented as undirected graphs and Twitter and Google+ as directed graphs. For directed graphs, the number of components have two values, the first one being weakly connected and the second one strongly connected. Also, the power-law exponent, average local clustering coefficient, diameter, homophily, and assortativity have 2 values each, for an in-degree network and an out-degree network, respectively.

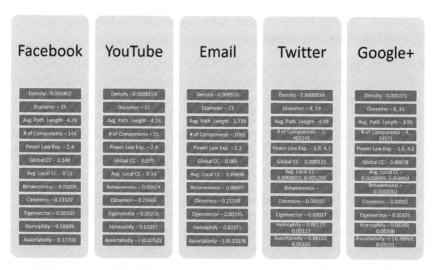

Figure 5.1 Centrality Values of Real-Life Online Social Networks.

5.3.1.5 Propagation models

The maximum information propagation is an important criterion for the social-network user. Users at the time of information propagation always intend to reach a maximum number of people through the content. An information-propagation simulator is discussed in this subsection.

Breadth first search Breadth first search (BFS) is a graph-search technique that was proposed by E.F. Moore in 1958. C.Y. Lee also proposed a similar algorithm in 1961 for wire routing. BFS works by discovering the graph as a tree, starting at a root, and iteratively exploring the nodes at shortest distance i, where i ranges between 1 and the diameter of the graph. The drawback of BFS is that it might become stuck at local maxima. The nodes that have a higher degree are discovered more often in the network compared to nodes with lower degree, displaying an inherent bias. Nevertheless, BFS is quite popular and is commonly used in OSNs for finding user-behavior patterns, measurement, and topological characterization of a social network.

Forest Fire Forest Fire is an information-propagation technique that works with a grid-like method. Nodes are arranged in a d-dimensional plane, where adjacent nodes are placed in adjacent grids. A node can be empty, occupied, or burning. Initially only the seed nodes are burning. A burning node turns into an empty grid. A burning node can ignite its neighboring node with a probability p. A node with no burning neighbors might also start burning with a probability s.

Random Walk Random walk is a mathematical concept extrapolated to information propagation in online social networks. Starting from the seed nodes, random walk chooses a neighboring node with a probability p randomly, and continues the walk. The walk stops either when the whole network has been traversed or at a pre-determined walk length. Markov chains or Markov models or Markov processes and random walks are closely associated, with other possible applications as well.

SI Model This epidemic model is a basic model with two states – susceptible and infectious. A node without immunity power/unhealthy is susceptible from birth and is equally likely to be transmitted the disease through contact with an infected node. If it is infected without treatment, it stays infected throughout its life. Let $S(t) > 0$ be the population of susceptible and $I(t) > 0$ at discrete tth time. The S becomes I at time, i.e., $S \to I$, then the total population is $S(t) + I(t) = N$, which is constant. Now, the equation of infection is:

$$S(t+1) = S(t)[1 - \chi \frac{\Delta t}{N} I(t)]$$

$$I(t+1) = I(t)[1 + \chi \frac{\Delta t}{N} S(t)]$$

where Δt <the average time required for transmission is the fixed time step, $\chi > 0$ is infection/contact rate, i.e., number of nodes with which an infectious node makes sufficient contact.

SIS Model In a susceptible–infectious–susceptible (SIS) epidemic model, the infected nodes are recovered and return to the susceptible state because the disease confers no immunity against reinfection. Let $S(t)$ be the number of susceptible individuals, and let $I(t)$ be the number of infected individuals. The SIS model in discrete time is:

$$S(t+1) = S(t)[1 - \chi \frac{\Delta t}{N} I(t)] + \vartheta \Delta t I(t)$$

$$I(t+1) = I(t)[1 - \vartheta \Delta t I(t) + \chi \frac{\Delta t}{N} S(t)]$$

where, the total population is $S(t) + I(t) = N$, which is constant, $\vartheta \Delta t \leq 1$ and $\chi \Delta t < (1 + \sqrt{\vartheta} \Delta t)^2$. The reproductive rate of this model is $\frac{\chi}{\vartheta}$.

SIR Model The Susceptible–Infected–Removed model is another epidemic model that is used in information propagation. The three types of nodes in the SIR model are Susceptible, Infected, and Removed. Initially, the seed nodes are infected and all other nodes are susceptible. An infected node can spread the infection to susceptible nodes with a probability p. A susceptible node moves to the removed state when it is either immune or deceased (that is, no longer active). Removed nodes can no longer participate in the propagation.

Diffusion model The diffusion model [37] is based on the decision-making activities. The fundamental component of this model is the decision process, that is represented by the rate of accumulation and the settings of the boundaries (Threshold value). The representation of decision making is as follows: 1. Sensory-evidence detection 2. Sensory-evidence integration, because the evidence is noisy 3. Checking the boundaries whether the conditions are satisfied [38]. The diffusion model is dependent on four parameters. The fist parameter is the drift rate, which determines the rate and direction at which information propagation is facilitated.

Linear threshold model The Linear threshold model [16] focuses on the threshold behavior in influencing propagation. A non–negative weight value or 0 is assigned for each edge, where the sum of weight is less than or equal to 1. For each node, a threshold value is assigned that is chosen uniformly at random in the range [0, 1]. A node (v) becomes active if the sum of the weight of the active neighbors is greater than the threshold value of v. Influence maximization is NP-hard under the linear threshold model.

Independent Cascade model In the Information Cascade model [16], an individual makes a decision based on other observations without regard to his own private information. This model assigns a weight for each edge. When a node becomes activated it has one chance to activate each neighbor with probability p. Influence maximization is NP-hard under the Information Cascade model.

5.3.2 Text analysis

5.3.2.1 Collection of information

Twitter is a popular microblogging website and each tweet is 280 characters in length. The Twitter dataset contains 50 million tweets 240+ million active users and 500 million tweets are generated everyday. As Twitter data is shared in the public domain, data can be retrieved using Twitter API.

5.3.2.2 Information retrieval

After the collection of text data from OSN, information are pre-processed in the following manner:

- Sentence segmentation: The main purpose of this step is to break a long text or paragraph into small sections of sentences. As working with small sentences is much easier to understand for not only humans but also the analyzer, it helps the system to adopt and understand the text.
- Word tokenization: After obtaining the small sentences, further sentences are broken into even smaller sections, i.e., into words. Words have a huge role to play in this project because in the case of the matching process of a text with the news it is matched to a few key words and also the sentiments to make the process more accurate.
- Predicting parts of speech of each token: This helps in grammatically understanding a language in a better way.
- Identifying stop words: Stop words are basically less important words in a sentence for analysis because they mainly work with keywords.

5.3.2.3 Text-mining

Lexical analyzer One of the primary methods of Text Mining is Lexical Analysis, This comprises two kinds of analysis – Semantic and Syntactic. Both these types of analysis are required to process the data collected from online social networks.

- Semantic analysis: Semantic analysis refers to the study of opinion-expressing words and emoticons that are commonly present in texts and excerpts. Semantic analysis is an integral part of sentiment-classification tasks, and is used to identify strong, negative, and positive opinion words (e.g., terrible, robust, untrustworthy, etc.). Using semantic analysis, the individual perspectives of users can be identified, which may reflect strong emotions.

  There are many indicators of emotional status or personal points of view that can be extracted from textual content. For example, the use of profanities, or the use of phrases like "I believe", "We demand" and so on indicate the degree of engagement of the user with the content. The use of emoticons also help in semantic analysis to identify the emotions of the user.

- Syntactic analysis: There are certain key identifiers of emotions and perspectives expressed through textual content that can be exploited for syntactic analysis. For example, use of punctuation such as exclamation(!), interrogation(?) or the use of part-of-speech tags help in obtaining insights such as identifying personal viewpoints of the user or the use of adjectives and interjections for sentiment analysis. Interjections are mostly used to convey the emotions of users. This in turn can be indicative of expressions that are present in the information. Similarly, adjectives can indicate expressions or recommendations of the user. The common point between these two is that they both indicate personal belief.

Classification of sentiment Textual data is often associated with some sentiment. The broad classification sentiment is in three classes – positive, negative, and neutral. Positive and Negative can be further divided into subclasses such as happy, excited, and so on for positive, sad, disappointed, and so on for negative. There are multiple supervised and unsupervised models, e.g., [11], [44]. A single text could be associated with multiple sentiments as well. Some texts can have an apparent sentiment with a different undertone, as in the case of sarcastic comments. Identifying such sentiments pose exciting research problems. The identified sentiment, and the trend of sentiment over time for both an individual as well as for a community, can help in identifying mental state and related mental-health issues.

Bursty Term Analysis Text collected over time exhibits certain patterns in terms of frequency of keywords. The general keywords, that have a low and steady frequency over the whole length of the text are not very indicative of their association with a particular event or emotion. Similarly, keywords with a constant high frequency, although apparently more informative than low-frequency keywords, are not very indicative of events or emotions either. However, keywords that have bursty frequencies, that is, sudden fluctuations in frequency with unevenly distributed frequency spikes, are often associated with contents showing strong emotion or some form of event.

Skewness of information distribution The distribution pattern of information over time is also indicative of the nature of the information. For planned and periodic events, the information follows a normal or gaussian distribution. Thus there is a build-up to the actual event, with a peak in the distribution, and the information distribution then eventually flattens out at 0. However, for unplanned events, or for short-lived rumors, there is generally a skewness in the information distribution.

User Identities Identifying the nature of users in information diffusion plays an important role to classify a content as potential rumor. The criteria for identification of potential rumor are:
- Controversiality: indicative of the users' followers;
- Originality: indicative of the originality of the content;
- Credibility: The credibility of a user is measured by whether the user's account has been verified by Twitter or not;
- Influence: potential positive or negative impact of the information shared;
- Role: whether the user plays a passive or active role in the propagation;
- Engagement: overall degree of activity of the user.

5.3.2.4 Sentence clustering

Once the individual's tokens in a sentence have been processed, the next step is clustering sentences. The first step is to take an average of the weights of individual tokens in the sentence and use it as the sentence weight. The second step is to identify the top k sentences with respect to their weights based on some predefined or learned value of k. These top k sentences can then be considered as the centers of k clusters. Finally, using a clustering algorithm such as K-means, all the sentences are defined into clusters around the initial k centers.

5.3.2.5 Sentiment analysis

There are multiple aspects of sentiment analysis. One such aspect is feeling examination, which is a study of the perspective or assumptions of the author towards a particular topic, which can be nonpartisan, certain or negative. Feeling examination utilizes standard text-analysis methodologies including text investigation, computational etymology, and language preparing. Another such direction of sentiment analysis is opinion examination that is a similar kind of study but from the reader/consumer point of view.

The origin of estimation examination can be followed to the 1950s, when conclusion investigation was essentially utilized on composed paper records. Today, in any case, feeling investigation is broadly used to mine emotional data from content on the Internet, including writings, tweets, web journals, online life, news stories, audits, and remarks. This is finished by utilizing a wide range of procedures, including NLP, measurements, and AI techniques. Associations at that point utilize the data mined to recognize new chances and better direct their message toward their objective socio-economics.

Types of Sentiment Analysis Estimations allude to mentalities, feelings, and opinion. As it were, they are emotional impressions rather than target realities. Various sorts of slant examination utilize various systems and strategies to recognize the notions contained in a specific book. There are two primary sorts of assessment examination: subjectivity/objectivity distinguishing proof and highlight/perspective-based supposition investigation.

Subjectivity/Objectivity Identification: Subjectivity/objectivity distinguishing proof involves arranging a sentence or a section of text into one of two classifications: emotional or objectivity. However, it ought to be noted that there are difficulties with regards to directing this sort of examination. The fundamental test is that the significance of the word or even an expression is frequently dependent upon its specific situation.

Feature/Aspect-Based Identification: Highlight/perspective distinguishing proof takes into account the assurance of various feelings or opinions (highlights) according to various parts of an element. In contrast to subjectivity/objectivity distinguishing proof, highlight/viewpoint-based

ID takes into account a significantly more nuanced outline of assessments and sentiments.

5.3.3 Smartphone-sensor data analysis

In the last decade, Smartphones have become increasingly popular among individuals irrespective or age, gender or location. Smartphones pose an interesting combination of sensing, communication, and computation capabilities, paving the way to developing pervasive behavior-monitoring applications for its users. Almost all modern Smartphones are well equipped with sensors like Accelerometer and Gyroscopes that can sense data well on a par with specialized wearable devices. The sensor data collected from Smartphones, are sent to either a remote server or the cloud through the Internet. Sometimes, the data is also sent to an edge server for convenience, hence data analysis could be conducted either at the device itself (Smartphone) or at the edge server or even on the cloud. Smartphones provide a useful tool to measure Social-Networking behavior among users because they can measure the thoughts and feelings of the user via several means like surveys, tweets or replies, etc. In addition, with exceptional sensing and computational capabilities, Smartphones can capture social and behavioral data passively from real-time information, as users can interact with each other dynamically, in real time, which generates a huge amount of data depending on the duration of interactions. For example, Smartphone data can be used to understand the lifestyles of different categories of people based on their personal or group interactions. Such studies can be used to build classifiers that can successfully identify sets of patterns of lifestyle of a person based on the frequency of messaging, amount of messages, time of messages denoting activity hours of the person, and mobility patterns based on locations. The data can be utilized to understand the socializing pattern as well as the activity pattern of the users on a regular basis, as in [21]. Hence, incorporating Smartphone-sensor data to be an integral part of data analytics in social networking may be a smart step for the future.

5.3.3.1 Addiction

For over a decade now, Smartphones have been the key reason that enables individuals to communicate with each other and exchange information anytime and anywhere. However, the convenience brought about by them is not devoid of manifold issues affecting users at different levels. A few of them may be the excessive use of Smartphones on a regular basis, spending more time on them than usual, texting while driving, which may result in fatal consequences, or even lack of sleep or low academic performance. In particular, with the recent surge of Social Networking, most young adults spend considerable amounts of time on Facebook, Instagram, and Twitter, through Smartphones, as depicted by the authors of [20]. Research has revealed that around 70–80% of social-networking activities are carried over Smartphone devices and that has emerged as the most threatening problem in the form of addiction that has prominent physiological and psychological effects on users. In recent decades Social-Networking sites have witnessed a huge increase in popularity and studies have revealed that individuals are subscribed to more than one social platform in general, which has been facilitated by the easy availability of Smartphones at finger tips. A few reasons for this addiction pertain to other factors like free or low cost Internet access on Smartphones, constant development of devices for computational and communicational ease, and the convenience of carrying a Smartphone all the time, unlike laptops or desktops. This authenticates the theory of addiction to social media and a few studies have been conducted to investigate psychometric scales capable of measuring the amount of time spent on Social Networks [35]. There are several negative effects of addiction to Social Networking via Smartphones that include change in social and psychological behavioral attitude among individuals [13]. Mostly youngsters use Smartphones to access Social Networks at night, which leads to impaired quality and quantity of sleep that often creates health issues. Studies have shown that adolescents with Smartphones and adequate data, are more prone to social media than users with an ordinary phone. This also incorporates sleep disturbance and eventually depressive symptoms in users as observed by [26]. Studies reveal that individuals who are addicted to social media via a Smartphone have their anxiety levels increased when kept separated from it for hours. Another concept of Fear Of Missing Out is prevalent among Users, which leads them to adhere to social-networking sites so that constant updates of daily activities are received and furnished without missing out a single instance. This propels them to use their phones while driving or even during academic hours. This can usher young adults and students towards a lethal future, which is catastrophic and hence undesirable, as depicted by the authors of [14].

5.3.3.2 Cognitive absorption

Being one of the most common phenomena found in users addicted to Social Network, CA may be defined as the state of deep involvement with technology. It may be expressed through five dimensions such as temporal dissociation (state of inability of a user to register passage of time while interacting with technology), focused immersion (experience of being engrossed thoroughly into technology ignoring other demands), heightened enjoyment (captures the moments of pleasure while interacting with technology and is the key factor of CA), control (the extent to which users can control themselves) and curiosity (the level to which the interaction with technology arouses the sensory and cognitive curiosity of a user) [9]. These authors argue that users with high addiction to Smartphones and Social-Networking usage habits experience a high level of CA as that indicates their high level of involvement and hence experience these five factors at their maximum levels. They claim that while interacting with social media through Smartphones the individuals lose the sense of temporal flow and the surroundings lose their significance, thus CA influences their beliefs and intentions to the greatest extent possible [22]. Studies also reveal that through CA, users experience a pleasurable experience and immense satisfaction that in turn motivates them to re-experience it repeatedly. Since CA is related to individual perceptions, users with positive CA will experience perceived usefulness, increased satisfaction towards the service, and intend to re-use their service with greater involvement. The correlation between visibility on Social-Networking platforms and addiction to Smartphone is found to be directly proportional to the amount of CA experienced by users. However, this high level of CA is an indicator of damaged behavioral and social attitude among individuals, which might result in sensitive consequences, especially among young adults and students [45].

5.4 Applications

5.4.1 Link prediction

Link Prediction is one of the primary applications of OSN network property analysis. Link Prediction determines the growth pattern of a network by preemptively finding probable edges between nodes in the network. [29] provides one such novel link prediction algorithm based on network structure. Fig. 5.2 depicts an example of link prediction in OSN.

5.4.2 Event prediction

Online Social Networks have played a pivotal role in free expression of opinions. Through text analysis and by studying the growth of the network and the frequency of communication, the OSN data can be used to predict

Figure 5.2 Link Prediction in Online Social Networks.

events such as elections [12]. Predicting election results from trends and surveys in online social networks has proven to be effective as well [25]. Fig. 5.3 shows an example flow of how event prediction works in OSNs.

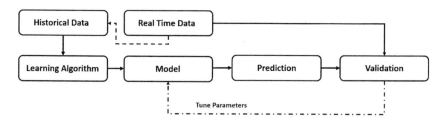

Figure 5.3 Flow Diagram of Event Prediction in OSN.

5.4.3 Marketing

Targeted Marketing is a primary application area for Network Analysis. The authors of [30] provided an approach to influencer identification for influencer-based marketing on OSNs that utilizes both network analysis as well as textual data analysis [25]. Fig. 5.4 shows the generic steps involved in targeted marketing through online social networks.

5.4.4 Influence maximization

Only identifying influencers may not be enough from the influence maximization perspective. The idea is to utilize network structural properties and information-propagation techniques to maximize the sustainability and reach of information within a network, which has been studied in [27].

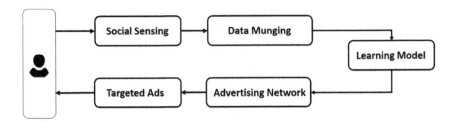

Figure 5.4 Digital Marketing Model Schematic Representation.

5.4.5 Rumor blocking

Identifying fake content or potentially offensive content is equally important as maximizing information reach. The authors of [23] helped to identify fake reviews for products on Amazon using sentiment analysis on review text, highlighting the importance of text analysis on OSNs.

5.4.6 Mental health

One of the up and coming research domains with severe impact on the lives of OSN users is the study of mental health through the addiction level and online behavior of the participants of OSN. One such study is covered in [18] that explores the mental-health scenario of students before and during the COVID-19 situation. The authors of [28] explored the link between the participation pattern of OSN users and their likelihood of suffering from depressing and anxiety. Similarly, [41] explored the likelihood of an OSN user having suffered from childhood trauma based on their online behavior, especially on OSNs. Fig. 5.5 highlights some of the key aspects of mental-health study through OSNs.

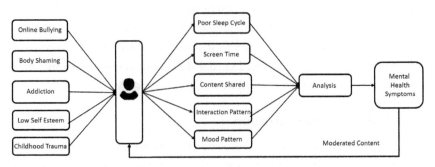

Figure 5.5 Aspects of Mental-Health Study through OSNs.

5.4.7 Social awareness

With such a huge reach amongst people of different demographics and from different geographical locations, OSN provides the best platform for spreading awareness. This awareness can be towards issues of the OSN itself, such as privacy risk on OSN, which was studied in [3], or some real-life social issues such as the municipal election in Spain and the mobilization of the public [5].

5.5 Conclusion

This chapter is an extensive and comprehensive collection of what social sensing is and how it is currently being utilized in different contemporary research studies. The chapter highlights the different sensing modalities with respect to online social networks. The perceived effects of online social networks, both in the online world as well as the real life has been captured in this chapter. The network-analysis aspect of the sensing modality explores the effect of different network properties and information propagation in an OSN and how it can help in determining the growth and behavioral characteristics of different OSNs. The text-analysis aspect of OSN helps identify the sentiment and semantics of online communication and correlates with the real-life mental-health attributes of OSN users. The sensor-data analysis aspect highlights how currently every smartphone owner is a potential vault of information, and how the high dependence on smartphones and OSNs can affect the users. Thus all the three aspects of sensing modalities have been covered in this chapter.

The chapter highlights the various applications of the different aspects of sensing modalities. The key application areas have been pointed out for each of the three different aspects and recent developments and contributions in these and related relevant fields have been explained. The use of sensing modalities with respect to modalities not only enriches the research literature but also finds a number of real-life applications that works towards the betterment of the user experience in OSNs, the users' understanding of how OSNs work, and the short- and long-term effects of addictive smartphone and OSN usage on average social-network participants.

References

[1] A.L. Barabasi, Network Science Degree Computing, Research Repository, arXivelation, Cambridge University Press, 2015.

[2] A.L. Barabasi, R. Albert, Topology of evolving networks: local events and universality, Physical Review Letters 85 (2000) 5234–5237.

[3] José Alemany, Elena del Val, J. Alberola, Ana García-Fornes, Enhancing the privacy risk awareness of teenagers in online social networks through soft-paternalism mechanisms, International Journal of Human-Computer Studies 129 (2019) 27–40.

[4] Tim Althoff, Pranav Jindal, Jure Leskovec, Online actions with offline impact: how online social networks influence online and offline user behavior, in: Proceedings of the Tenth ACM International Conference on Web Search and Data Mining, 2017, pp. 537–546.

[5] Eva Anduiza, Camilo Cristancho, José M. Sabucedo, Mobilization through online social networks: the political protest of the indignados in Spain, Information, Communication & Society 17 (6) (2014) 750–764.

[6] R. Albert, A.L. Barabasi, Emergence of scaling in random networks, Science 286 (1999) 509–512.

[7] Albert-Laszlo Barabási, Hawoong Jeong, Zoltan Néda, Erzsebet Ravasz, Andras Schubert, Tamas Vicsek, Evolution of the social network of scientific collaborations, Physica A: Statistical Mechanics and its Applications 311 (3–4) (2002) 590–614.

[8] M. Posfai, A.L. Barabasi, Network Science, Cambridge University Press, 2016.

[9] Stuart J. Barnes, Andrew D. Pressey, Eusebio Scornavacca, Mobile ubiquity: understanding the relationship between cognitive absorption, smartphone addiction and social network services, Computers in Human Behavior 90 (2019) 246–258.

[10] Subhayan Bhattacharya, Sankhamita Sinha, Sarbani Roy, Impact of structural properties on network structure for online social networks, Procedia Computer Science 167 (2020) 1200–1209.

[11] Danushka Bollegala, Tingting Mu, John Yannis Goulermas, Cross-domain sentiment classification using sentiment sensitive embeddings, IEEE Transactions on Knowledge and Data Engineering 28 (2) (2015) 398–410.

[12] Michael P. Cameron, Patrick Barrett, Bob Stewardson, Can social media predict election results? Evidence from New Zealand, Journal of Political Marketing 15 (4) (2016) 416–432.

[13] Lütfiye Can, Nihat Kaya, Social networking sites addiction and the effect of attitude towards social network advertising, Procedia – Social and Behavioral Sciences 235 (2016) 484–492.

[14] Seong-Soo Cha, Bo-Kyung Seo, Smartphone use and smartphone addiction in middle school students in Korea: prevalence, social networking service, and game use, Health Psychology Open 5 (1) (2018) 2055102918755046.

[15] A. Tavoni, S. Currarini, C. Marchiori, Network economics and the environment: insights and perspectives, Environmental & Resource Economics 65 (2016) 159–189, Springer.

[16] David Kempe, Jon Kleinberg, Éva Tardos, Maximizing the spread of influence through a social network, Theory of Computing 4 (2003) 137–146.

[17] D.J.D.S. Price, Network of scientific papers, Science 149 (1965) 510–515.

[18] Timon Elmer, Kieran Mepham, Christoph Stadtfeld, Students under lockdown: comparisons of students' social networks and mental health before and during the Covid-19 crisis in Switzerland, PLoS ONE 15 (7) (2020) e0236337.

[19] A. Renyi, P. Erdos, On the evaluation of random network, Publication of the Mathematical Institute of the Hungarian Academy of Sciences, 1960, pp. 17–61.

[20] Deniz Mertkan Gezgin, Özlem Çakır, Analysis of nomofobic behaviors of adolescents regarding various factors, Journal of Human Sciences 13 (2) (2016) 2504–2519.

[21] Gabriella M. Harari, Nicholas D. Lane, Rui Wang, Benjamin S. Crosier, Andrew T. Campbell, Samuel D. Gosling, Using smartphones to collect behavioral data in psychological science: opportunities, practical considerations, and challenges, Perspectives on Psychological Science 11 (6) (2016) 838–854.

[22] Ibrahim A. Jumaan, Noor Hazarina Hashim, Basheer M. Al-Ghazali, The role of cognitive absorption in predicting mobile Internet users' continuance intention: an extension of the expectation-confirmation model, Technology in Society 63 (2020) 101355.

[23] Erick Kauffmann, Jesús Peral, David Gil, Antonio Ferrández, Ricardo Sellers, Higinio Mora, A framework for big data analytics in commercial social networks: a case study on sentiment analysis and fake review detection for marketing decision-making, Industrial Marketing Management 90 (2020) 523–537.

[24] J. Altmann, K. Kim, Effect of homophily on network formation, Communications in Nonlinear Science and Numerical Simulation 44 (2017) 482–494, Elsevier.

[25] Debra Leiter, Andreas Murr, Ericka Rascón Ramírez, Mary Stegmaier, Social networks and citizen election forecasting: the more friends the better, International Journal of Forecasting 34 (2) (2018) 235–248.

[26] Sakari Lemola, Nadine Perkinson-Gloor, Serge Brand, Julia F. Dewald-Kaufmann, Alexander Grob, Adolescents' electronic media use at night, sleep disturbance, and depressive symptoms in the smartphone age, Journal of Youth and Adolescence 44 (2) (2015) 405–418.

[27] Jianxin Li, Taotao Cai, Ke Deng, Xinjue Wang, Timos Sellis, Feng Xia, Community-diversified influence maximization in social networks, Information Systems 92 (2020) 101522.

[28] Shikang Liu, David Hachen, Omar Lizardo, Christian Poellabauer, Aaron Striegel, Tijana Milenković, The power of dynamic social networks to predict individuals' mental health, in: Pac Symp Biocomput, vol. 25, World Scientific, 2020, pp. 635–646.

[29] Amin Mahmoudi, Mohd Ridzwan Yaakub, Azuraliza Abu Bakar, A new real-time link prediction method based on user community changes in online social networks, Computer Journal 63 (3) (2019) 448–459.

[30] Rakesh R. Mallipeddi, Subodha Kumar, Chelliah Sriskandarajah, Yunxia Zhu, A framework for analyzing influencer marketing in social networks: selection and scheduling of influencers, Management Science 68 (1) (2022) 75–104.

[31] C. Faloutsos, M. McGlohon, L. Akoglu, Statistical properties of social networks, in: Social Network Data Analytics, 2011, pp. 17–42.

[32] M.E.J. Newman, Assortative mixing patterns in networks, Physical Review Letters 89 (2002) 208701.

[33] M.E.J. Newman, Mixing patterns in networks, Physical Review E 67 (2003) 026126.

[34] M.E.J. Newman, The structure and function of complex networks, Society of Industrial and Applied Mathematics Review 45 (2003) 167–256.

[35] Yunusa Olufadi, Social networking time use scale (SONTUS): a new instrument for measuring the time spent on the social networking sites, Telematics and Informatics 33 (2) (2016) 452–471.

[36] Lawrence Page, Sergey Brin, Rajeev Motwani, Terry Winograd, The pagerank citation ranking: Bringing order to the web, Technical report, Stanford InfoLab, 1999.

[37] R. Ratcliff, A theory of memory retrieval, Psychological Review 85 (1978) 59–108.

[38] G. McKoon, R. Ratcliff, The diffusion decision model: theory and data for two-choice decision tasks, Neural Computation 20 (4) (2008) 873–922.

[39] D. Kundu, S. Roy, P. Dey, Social network analysis of cricket community using a composite distributed framework: from implementation viewpoint, IEEE Transactions on Computational Social Systems 5 (2018) 64–81.

[40] H.D. Swart, M. Grabisch, A. Rusinowska, R. Berghammer, Social networks: prestige, centrality, and influence, in: H. de Swart (Ed.), Relational and Algebraic Methods in Computer Science, in: Lecture Notes in Computer Science, Springer, 2011, pp. 22–39.

[41] F. David Schneider, Cynthia A. Loveland Cook, Joanne Salas, Jeffrey Scherrer, Ivy N. Cleveland, Sandra K. Burge, Residency Research Network of Texas Investigators, Childhood trauma, social networks, and the mental health of adult survivors, Journal of Interpersonal Violence 35 (5–6) (2020) 1492–1514.

[42] N. Agarwal, S. Tokdemir, R. Kasprzyk, F. Sen, R. Wigand, Focal structure analysis: identifying influential sets of individuals in a social network, Social Network Analysis and Mining 6 (2016) 17.

[43] T. Ikeguchi, K. Aihara, Y. Shimada, Y. Hirata, Graph distance for complex networks, Scientific Reports 6 (2016) 34944.

[44] Huifeng Tang, Songbo Tan, Xueqi Cheng, A survey on sentiment detection of reviews, Expert Systems with Applications 36 (7) (2009) 10760–10773.

[45] Öznur Tanrıverdi, Feride Karaca, Investigating the relationships between adolescents' levels of cognitive absorption and cyberloafing activities according to demographic characteristics, ADDICTA: The Turkish Journal On Addictions 5 (2) (2018) 285–315.

[46] S.H. Strogatz, D.J. Watts, Collective dynamics of small-world networks, Nature 393 (1998) 440–442.

CHAPTER 6

Learning sentiment analysis with word embeddings

Mounika Marreddy and Radhika Mamidi
IIIT Hyderabad, LTRC, Hyderabad, India

6.1 Introduction

Sentiment Analysis is one of the most successful and well-studied fields in Natural Language Processing [1–3]. Traditional approaches mainly focus on designing a set of features such as bag-of-words, a sentiment lexicon to train a classifier for sentiment classification [4]. However, feature engineering is labor intensive and almost reaches its performance bottleneck. Moreover, due to the increasing information on the web, like writing reviews on review sites and social media, opinions influence human behavior and help organizations or individuals make decisions. With the huge success of deep-learning techniques, some researchers have designed effective neural networks to generate low-dimensional contextual representations and yielded promising results on sentiment analysis [5,14,15].

Since the work of [16], the NLP community is focusing on improving the feature representation of sentences/documents with continuous development in a neural word embedding. Word2Vec embedding was the first powerful technique to achieve semantic similarity between words, but it failed to capture the meaning of a word based on context [17]. As an improvement to Word2Vec, [18] introduced GloVe embeddings, primarily focusing on the global co-occurrence count for generating word embeddings. Using Word2Vec and GloVe, it was easy to train with application in question-answering tasks [19], sentiment analysis [20], automatic summarization [21], word analogy, word similarity, and named entity-recognition tasks [22]. However, the main challenge with GloVe and Word2Vec is the inability to differentiate the word used in a different context. The authors of [23] introduced a deep LSTM (long short-term memory) encoder from an attentional sequence-to-sequence model trained for machine translation (MT) to contextualize word vectors (MT-LSTM/CoVe). The main limitation with CoVe vectors was that it uses zero vectors for unknown words (out of vocabulary words).

Computational Intelligence Applications for Text and Sentiment Data Analysis
https://doi.org/10.1016/B978-0-32-390535-0.00011-2

ELMo (Embeddings from Language Models) [24] and BERT (Bidirectional Encoder Representations from Transformers) [25] embeddings are two recent popular techniques that outperform many of the NLP tasks and achieved huge success in neural embedding techniques that represent the context in features due to the attention-based mechanism. ELMo embedding is a character-based embedding, which allows the model to capture out of vocabulary words, and deep contextualized word representation can capture syntax and semantic features of words and outperforms in problems like sentiment analysis [26] and named entity recognition [27]. In advancement to contextual embedding, BERT embedding is a breakthrough in neural embedding techniques and built upon transformers, including the self-attention mechanism. It can represent features with the relationship between all words in a sentence. BERT outperforms state-of-the-art feature representation for a task like question answering with SQuAD [28], language modeling/sentiment classification.

In recent years, the use of neural word embeddings provides better vector representations of semantic information, although there has been relatively little work on direct evaluations of these models. There has been previous work to evaluate various word-embedding techniques [29] on a specific task like word similarity or analogy, named-entity recognition [30], and evaluate it based on the obtained performance metric.

In this chapter, we evaluate four successful pre-trained neural word embeddings: Word2Vec, GloVe, ELMo, and BERT on sentiment analysis task in two steps: (i) propose a mixture of classification experts (MoCE) model for the sentiment classification task, (ii) compare and improve the classification accuracies by combining the popular word embedding as the first level of features and pass it to the cascade model inspired by gcForest. The underlying mechanism of the MoCE model is that it has great potential to discriminate positive and negative examples for sentiment-classification tasks on Amazon product-review data.

In the first step, a mixture of classification experts uses a combination of the simpler learner to improve predictions. Each learner divides the dataset into several different regions based on the relationship between input and output. In our case, it will divide the region with different polarities using the help of a probabilistic gating network. The underlying mechanism of the MoCE model is that it has great potential to discriminate between positive and negative examples for sentiment-classification tasks on Amazon product-review data. In the second step, we validated and improved the classification accuracy by combining the four embedding vectors and passed this to cascaded gcForest for better feature representation. The gcForest model with combined word embeddings can perform better with the sentiment-analysis task. The following sections discuss the word-embedding representations, contextual word representations, proposed MoCE approach, cascading gcForest, and observations.

6.2 Word-embedding representations

Word-embedding methods allow machine-learning algorithms to understand words with similar meanings. Moreover, these distributed word representations capture many precise syntactic and semantic word relationships. In this section, we describe different word embeddings, such as Word2Vec [17], and GloVe [18].

6.2.1 Word2Vec

6.2.1.0.1 Contributions of Word2Vec

- Word2Vec [17] introduced techniques that can be used for learning high-quality word vectors from huge datasets with billions and millions of words in the vocabulary.
- In Word2Vec, the word representations are dense and have reduced dimension (depending on the number of hidden neurons).
- Try to maximize the accuracy of word-vector operations by developing new model architectures that preserve the linear regularities among words.
- Design a new comprehensive test set for measuring syntactic and semantic regularities and show that many such regularities can be learned with high accuracy.
- Proposed two new model architectures for learning distributed representations of words that try to minimize computational complexity.

6.2.1.0.2 Model architectures

Word2Vec is not a single algorithm but a combination of two techniques – CBOW (Continuous bag of words) and SG (Skip-gram) model. These are shallow neural networks that map word(s) to the target variable, which is also a word(s). Both of these techniques learn weights that act as word-vector representations.

- The objective of CBOW is to predict the current word based on neighboring words.

- The objective of SG is to predict the neighboring words based on a window size given the current word.

The Skip-gram model architecture is shown in Fig. 6.1. From Fig. 6.1, the training objective of the Skip-Gram model is to find word representations that are useful for predicting neighboring words in a sentence or document.

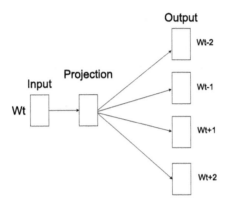

Figure 6.1 Word2Vec architecture.

Let w_1, w_2, w_3, ..., w_T represent the sequence of training words. The objective of SG is to maximize the log probability and is given by the equation:

$$\frac{1}{T}\sum_{t=1}^{T}\sum_{-c\leq j\leq c, j\neq 0} log\, p(\frac{w_{t+j}}{w_j}) \qquad (6.1)$$

where c is the training context size. The SG formulation defines $p(w_{t+j}/w_j)$ using the softmax function:

$$p(w_O/w_I) = \frac{\exp(v'^{T}_{w_O} v_{w_I})}{\sum_{(w=1)}^{W} \exp(v'_{w}^{T} v_{w_I})} \qquad (6.2)$$

where v_w and v'_w are the "input" and "output" representations of w, and W is the number of words in the vocabulary.

Pros
- Learning semantics and grammar information, taking into account the context of the words.
- Arithmetic operations can easily be done on word-embedding vectors to find semantic analogies.

- The resulting word-vector dimension is small, needs little pre-processing, and requires less memory.
- The embeddings from Word2Vec improved performance on NLP tasks.

Cons

- Learning out-of-vocabulary/unknown word representations is absent.
- Unable to understand the context, thus gives the same embedding representation for a word that occurs in different places.
- Training is slow if we use a softmax function.
- Words and vectors are one-to-one relationships that do not solve the problem of polysemous words.

6.2.2 GloVe

Another well-known model that learns vectors or words from their co-occurrence information, i.e., how frequently they appear together in large text corpora, is Global Vectors (GloVe) [18]. While Word2Vec is a predictive model – a feed-forward neural network that learns vectors to improve the predictive ability, GloVe is a count-based model.

6.2.2.0.1 Contributions

- The main idea of GloVe [18] is to utilize the statistics of the whole corpus.
- GloVe takes global information into account while learning the dimensions of meaning.
- GloVe model efficiently uses statistical information by training on a word–word co-occurrence matrix rather than the entire sparse matrix or individual context windows in a large corpus.

6.2.2.0.2 Model architecture

GloVe predicts surrounding words by maximizing the probability of a context word occurring given a center word by performing a dynamic logistic regression. The main intuition underlying the model is the simple observation that ratios of word–word co-occurrence probabilities can encode some form of meaning.

Given that i and j are two words that co-occur, we can optimize a word vector by minimizing the difference between the dot product of the word vectors for i, j and the log of the number of times i and j co-occur, squared.

This equation gives the objective function of the glove:

$$\hat{J} = \sum_{i,j}^{W} f(X_{i,j})(w_i^T \tilde{w}_j - \log X_{ij})^2 \qquad (6.3)$$

where $\hat{J}$ is the objective function, W is the size of vocabulary, $w_i^T w_j$ is the dot product of vectors w_i and w_j, X_{ij} is the count of the number of times i and j co-occur. Here, $f(X_{ij})$ is the weighing function to avoid an undefined value of the objective function when i and j never co-occur ($X_{ij} = 0$ and log 0 is undefined). $f(X_{ij})$ has a few properties. First, $f(X_{ij}) = 0$ when $X_{ij} = 0$. This means that when i and j do not co-occur, we do not need to calculate $(uiTvj - \log Pij)^2$, we can just stop at $f(X_{ij})$. Secondly, $f(X_{ij})$ helps counteract the problem of balancing the weight of very common or very uncommon words.

Pros
- GloVe Word vectors capture sub-linear relationships in the vector space. Thus it performs better than Word2Vec in the word-analogy tasks.
- Glove adds more practical meaning into word vectors by considering the relationships between word pair and word pair rather than word and word.
- GloVe takes care of stop words by giving lower weight for highly frequent word pairs.

Cons
- GloVe is trained on the co-occurrence matrix of words, which takes a lot of memory for storage. In particular, if you change the hyperparameters related to the co-occurrence matrix, you have to reconstruct the matrix again, which is very time and memory consuming.
- Learning representations of out of vocabulary is absent.
- It is unable to understand the context, thus gives the same embedding representation for a word that occurs in different places.

6.3 Contextual word representations

6.3.1 ELMo (deep contextualized word representations)

ELMo (Embeddings from Language Model) [24] overcomes the limitations of traditional word-embedding methods by learning contextualized word embeddings from the language model.

6.3.1.0.1 Contributions of ELMo

- Embeddings from Language Models (ELMos) use language models to obtain embeddings for individual words while taking the entire sentence or paragraph into account.
- Concretely, ELMos use a pre-trained, multi-layer, bidirectional, LSTM-based language model and extract the hidden state of each layer for the input sequence of words. Then, they compute a weighted sum of those hidden states to obtain an embedding for each word.
- ELMo improves the performance of models across a wide range of tasks, spanning from question answering and sentiment analysis to named-entity recognition.

6.3.1.0.2 ELMo model architecture

The Language Model architecture is shown in Fig. 6.2. Without labeling data we can train vast amounts of running text. Given a sequence of N tokens, $(t_1, t_1, ..., t_N)$, the forward language model computes the probability of a sequence by modeling the probability of token t_k given the history $(t_1, t_1, ..., t_{k-1})$:

$$p(t_1, t_2, ..., t_N) = \prod_{k=1}^{N} p(t_k|t_1, t_2, .., t_{k-1}) \qquad (6.4)$$

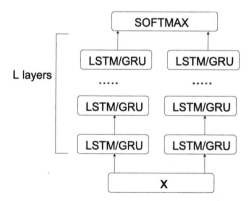

Figure 6.2 ELMo Architecture.

The backward language model predicts the previous token given the future context and is given by the equation:

$$p(t_1, t_2, ..., t_N) = \prod_{k=1}^{N} p(t_k|t_{k+1}, t_{K+2}, .., t_N) \qquad (6.5)$$

A biLM combines both forward and backward language models. The objective function is to maximize the log likelihood of the forward and backward language models and is given by the equation:

$$\sum_{k=1}^{N}(\log p(tk|t_1, .., t_{k-1}; \Theta_x, \overrightarrow{\Theta_{LSTM}}, \Theta_s)$$

$$+ \log p(tk|t_{k+1}, .., t_N; \Theta_x, \overleftarrow{\Theta_{LSTM}}, \Theta_s)) \qquad (6.6)$$

where Θ_x, Θ_s are the token representation and softmax layer parameters. The ELMo equation for task-specific representation is given by the equation:

$$ELMo_k^{task} = \gamma^{task} \sum_{j=0}^{L} s_j^{task} h_{k,j}^{LM} \qquad (6.7)$$

where γ is of practical importance to aid the optimization process and γ^{task} allows the task model to scale the entire ELMo vector, s_j^{task} are softmax normalized weights, and $h_{k,j}^{LM}$ are top-layer biLSTM outputs.

The training process of ELMo is as follows:

1. First, we built a vocabulary file that contains all the unique words along with three extra tokens <S>, </S>, </UNK>.
2. The vocabulary file is in the descending order with the most frequently occurring word at the top.
3. A data file containing all the sentences in the corpus with one sentence per line.
4. We split the data into different files in which 70% of the data we considered for training, the remaining data are held back for testing.
5. A configuration file consists of the vocabulary size, a number of tokens to train the ELMo model, and the output dimension of each token.
6. Each embedding is of dimension 1024.

Pros

- ELMo generates context-aware embeddings.
- ELMo uses character-level representations, so the network learns embeddings for out of vocabulary words.
- ELMo is built for sentence-level embeddings, but it can generate embeddings for characters, words, and sentences.

Cons

- ELMo, which uses a bidirectional LSTM, concatenated the left-to-right and right-to-left information, meaning that the representation could not take advantage of both left and right contexts simultaneously.

6.3.2 BERT (pre-training of deep bidirectional transformers for language understanding)

BERT [25] is a deep-learning model that has given state-of-the-art results on a wide variety of natural language processing tasks. It stands for Bidirectional Encoder Representations for Transformers.

6.3.2.0.1 Problem with previous methods

Language models only use left or right contexts, but language understanding is bidirectional. The feature-based approach, such as ELMo [24], uses task-specific architectures that include the pre-trained representations as additional features. The fine-tuning approach introduces minimal task-specific parameters and is trained on the downstream tasks by simply fine tuning all pre-trained parameters. The major limitation of these techniques is that standard language models are unidirectional, limiting the choice of architectures that can be used during pre-training.

6.3.2.0.2 Contributions of BERT

- BERT uses masked language models to enable pre-trained deep bidirectional representations. In masked language modeling, a percentage of input tokens is masked at random instead of predicting every next token, and only those masked tokens are predicted.
- BERT is also trained on a next sentence prediction task to better handle tasks that require reasoning about the relationship between two sentences (e.g., question answering).
- BERT is the first fine-tuning-based representation model that achieves state-of-the-art performance on a large suite of sentence- and token-level tasks, outperforming many task-specific architectures.

6.3.2.0.3 BERT model architecture

There are two steps in the BERT framework: pre-training and fine tuning. During pre-training, the model is trained on unlabeled data over different pre-training tasks. For fine tuning, the BERT model is first initialized with the pre-trained parameters, and all of the parameters are fine tuned using labeled data for the downstream tasks.

BERT uses the Transformer architecture (the attention mechanism that learns contextual relationships between words in a text) for its underlying model shown in Fig. 6.3. A basic Transformer consists of an encoder to read the text input and a decoder to produce a prediction for the task. Since the BERT goal is to generate a language-representation model, it only needs the encoder part. The input to the encoder for BERT is a sequence of tokens, which are first converted into vectors and then processed in the neural network.

There are four types of pre-trained versions of BERT depending on the scale of the model architecture: BERT-Base: 12-layer, 768-hidden-nodes, 12-attention-heads, 110M parameters BERT-Large: 24-layer, 1024-hidden-nodes, 16-attention-heads, 340M parameters.

6.3.2.0.4 Input/output representations

- Token embeddings: A [CLS] token is added to the input word tokens at the beginning of the first sentence, and a [SEP] token is inserted at the end of each sentence.
- Segment embeddings: A marker indicating Sentence A or Sentence B is added to each token. This allows the encoder to distinguish between sentences.
- Positional embeddings: A positional embedding is added to each token to indicate its position in the sentence.

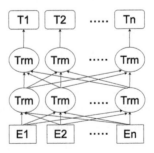

Figure 6.3 BERT Architecture.

Pros
- BERT's bidirectional approach (MLM) converges slower than left-to-right approaches (because only 15% of words are predicted in each

batch), but bidirectional training still outperforms left-to-right training after a small number of pre-training steps.

- Model size matters, even at a huge scale. BERT_large, with 345 million parameters, is the largest model of its kind. It is demonstrably superior on small-scale tasks to BERT_base, which uses the same architecture with "only" 110 million parameters.

Cons

- BERT is limited to handling sentences of a maximum length (smaller length sentences are padded).
- [MASK] token exists in the training phase, while it does not exist in the prediction phase of masked language modeling.

6.4 Sentiment-analysis definition

Sentiment analysis is one of the most successful tasks in NLP. It helps in identifying and analyzing the subject information present in a user–written text [6,7,10–12]. Moreover, it is a well-established task in many business applications like movie reviews that can enhance or damage the revenue of the movie, and product reviews that can praise the quality of a product or damage the product sales. In the literature, sentiment analysis performed on either sentence level or document level provides personal information to a user about his/her opinion [8,9,12,13]. Further, recent developments of efficient deep-feature representations yield better accuracy. For sentiment analysis, the model should automatically predict the sentiment of a sentence as "positive", "negative", or "neutral".

6.5 Model architecture

We use a mixture of an expert-based model whose architecture is inspired from [31]. The mixture of expert architectures is composed of a gating network and several expert networks, each of which solves a function approximation problem over a local region of the input space. The detailed overview of our model is shown in Fig. 6.4 where the input is a text vector extracted from recently successful neural embeddings such as Word2Vec, GloVe, ELMo, and BERT. These input features pass through both the gating network and two experts. The gating network uses a probabilistic model to choose the best expert for a given input text vector.

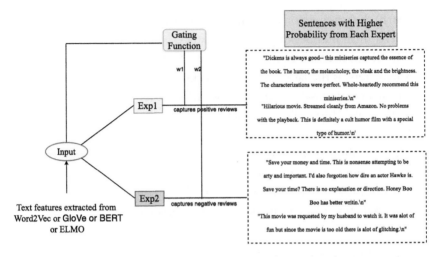

Figure 6.4 Proposed Mixture of Classification Experts (MoCE) model. Here, Expert1 captures positive reviews and Expert2 captures negative reviews.

6.5.1 MoCE architecture

Given an input feature vector $\mathbf{x}$ from one of the neural word-embedding methods, we model its posterior probabilities as a mixture of posteriors produced by each expert model trained on $\mathbf{x}$,

$$p(\mathbf{y}|\mathbf{x}) = \sum_{j=1}^{K} P(S_j|\mathbf{x}, \theta_0) p(\mathbf{y}|\mathbf{x}, S_{\theta_j})$$

$$= \sum_{j=1}^{K} g_{S_j}(\mathbf{x}, \theta_0) p(\mathbf{y}|\mathbf{x}, S_{\theta_j}) \qquad (6.8)$$

Here, $P(S_j|\mathbf{x}, \theta_0) = g_{S_j}(\mathbf{x}, \theta_0)$ is the probability of choosing the S_jth expert for given input $\mathbf{x}$. Note that $\sum_{j=1}^{K} g_{S_j}(\mathbf{x}, \theta_0) = 1$ and $g_{S_j}(\mathbf{x}, \theta_0) \geq 0$, $\forall j \in [K]$. $g_{S_j}(\mathbf{x}, \theta_0)$ is also called a gating function and is parameterized by θ_0.

Since the class labels $\{\mathbf{y}_1, \mathbf{y}_2, ..., \mathbf{y}_n\}$ are independent and identically distributed samples of outcome variables from a population modeled by a K-component finite mixture model, the outcome variable is discrete (positive or negative sentiment). Due to this, in this chapter, we choose $p(\mathbf{y}|\mathbf{x}, S_{\theta_j})$ as a Gaussian probability density for each of the experts, denoted by:

$$p(\mathbf{y}|\mathbf{x}, S_{\theta_j}) = \frac{1}{(|\sigma_j|2\pi)^{1/2}} \exp\left(-\frac{1}{2\sigma_j^2}(\mathbf{y} - W_j\mathbf{x})^T(\mathbf{y} - W_j\mathbf{x})\right) \qquad (6.9)$$

where $S_{\theta_j} \in \mathbb{R}^{m \times n}$ is the weight matrix associated with the S_jth expert. Thus $S_{\theta_j} = \{W_j\}$. We use the softmax function for the gating variable $g_{S_j}(\mathbf{x}, \theta_0)$,

$$g_{S_j}(\mathbf{x}, \theta_0) = \frac{\exp\left(\mathbf{v}_j^T\mathbf{x}\right)}{\sum_{i=1}^{K} \exp\left(\mathbf{v}_i^T\mathbf{x}\right)} \qquad (6.10)$$

where $\mathbf{v}_j \in \mathbb{R}^n$, $\forall j \in [K]$. Thus $\theta_0 = \{\mathbf{v}_1, \ldots, \mathbf{v}_K\}$. Let Θ be the set of all the parameters involved for the K-experts. Thus $\Theta = \{\theta_0, (W_1), \ldots, (W_K)\}$. We train the MoCE model and update the weights iteratively using the expectation-maximization (EM) algorithm.

6.5.2 Multigrained gcForest architecture

In order to improve the classification performance of each dataset, we passed the input feature vector to a multigrain gcForest model for better feature representation. The gcForest model we use is from [32], and the cascade structure is illustrated in Fig. 6.5, where each cascading level receives an input from the primary level, and the processed result is passed to the next level.

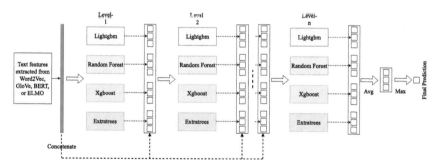

Figure 6.5 Cascading gcForest Architecture.

The raw input feature vector is given to gcForest with different dimensions associated with pre-trained embeddings. Each cascading level contains different ensemble-based forest models, i.e., an ensemble of ensembles yields the diversity in feature construction. Each forest produces a class distribution for each instance and finally estimates the average of all class distributions across the ensemble-based forests, giving an output vector. The output vector is concatenated with the original feature vector and passed to the next cascading level. In order to avoid the risk of overfitting, each forest uses K-fold cross-validation to produce the class vector. Moreover, the complexity of a model can be controlled by checking the training error and validation error to terminate the process when the training is adequate.

6.6 Experimental setup

In order to evaluate the word embeddings, we choose the sentiment-analysis task to perform the experiments. Here, we briefly describe the Amazon Product-Reviews dataset.

6.6.1 Dataset description

Amazon-product domains: This corpus is a collection of 20 product reviews derived from Task-1 of ESWC Semantic Challenge-2019. The 20 different Amazon-product domain names are mentioned here,[1] and this corpus belongs to the sentiment-analysis task. The data for Task-1 will consist of 50k reviews for each domain, of which 25k reviews are positive and 25k reviews are negative. The evaluation metrics for evaluation are precision, recall, and macro F1-score.

6.6.2 Feature extraction

In this chapter, we mainly focus on four successful pre-trained word embeddings such as: Word2Vec (embeddings are of 300 dimensions) [17], GloVe (embeddings are of 300 dimensions) [18], BERT (embeddings are 768 dimensions each) [25], and ELMo (embeddings are 1024 dimensions each) [24].

6.6.3 Training strategy

Using the approach discussed in Section 6.2, we trained a separate mixture of classification experts models (MoCE) for the Amazon Product-Reviews dataset with the associated task sentiment analysis using the above embeddings. The input to the MoCE model is a text vector, and the output is

---

[1] http://www.maurodragoni.com/research/opinionmining/events/challenge-2019/.

the corresponding classes based on a specific task. Here, we select the number of experts based on the number of output classes. The gating function selects one of the experts with a higher probability score for the corresponding input. The selected expert predicts the target label using that particular expert weight. Expert and gating parameters are updated using the iterative expectation-maximization (EM) algorithm. The training model is validated by the K-fold approach in which the model is repeatedly trained on K-1 folds, and the remaining one fold is used for validation. The proposed model is trained until the model reaches convergence with a lower bound of $1e^{-5}$ or a maximum of 100 iterations.

6.7 Results & discussion

Here, we conducted the experiments in two steps. In the first step, we evaluated the four word embeddings using the MoCE model and the second step describes better feature representation using cascading gcForest. This proposed model outperforms the state-of-the-art results on Amazon-product review datasets.

6.7.1 Evaluation of embeddings using MoCE

Experiments are conducted on the 20 Amazon-product domains dataset by passing input as text vector extracted from recent successful neural word embeddings and output as corresponding target classes positive or negative. We split the dataset into 40000 reviews in training and 10 000 reviews in testing. The MoCE model performance was evaluated by training and testing the different subsets of the 50000 reviews in a 5-fold cross-validation scheme.

Table 6.2 presents the performance results of each embedding scheme where the two experts discriminate both positive and negative examples. From Table 6.2, we can observe that both GloVe and Word2Vec embeddings have better discrimination where one expert captures the majority of positive-sentiment examples as the other expert captures more negative-sentiment examples. Here, we use a test dataset of 10000 examples, of which 5000 samples are positive, and 5000 samples are negative. For example, from Table 6.2 consider the shoe-domain dataset for the GloVe Embedding: expert1 captures 92% positive-sentiment samples, and expert2 captures 86% negative-sentiment samples, showing better discrimination and similarly with the Word2Vec and ELMo. Word embeddings like Word2Vec and GloVe embedding feature as input, the MoCE model isolate the positive and negative examples by two experts. On the contrary, for the domains Baby, Electronics, Office_Products, and Patio (here expert1 only captures all the positive and negative samples), this is mainly because expressing the opinion in reviews is similar in both classes. However, in the case of BERT and ELMo embedding: both experts isolate the samples for all the domains to capture context-sensitive information.

6.7.2 Polarity identification using gcForest

Using the MoCE results described in Table 6.2, we can observe the better feature representation of each pre-trained word-embedding model based on the experts who discriminate the positive or negative samples. In order to validate and improve the classification performance, we also built the cascading gcForest classification model described in Section 6.5.2. We use four ensemble forest models such as LightGBM [33], XGboost [34], Random Forest, and Extra Trees classifier in each cascading layer. The configuration of the gcForest model is shown in Table 6.1. Here, we use a 5-fold cross-validation method to avoid the overfitting problem. With this method, the model outperforms the state-of-the-art models mentioned in [35] for different combination features such as GloVe, Word2Vec, ELMo, and BERT as shown in Table 6.3. We also improve the classification performance of each domain dataset by using the above-mentioned four embeddings, since gcForest does not require more hyper-parameters and deeper layers to achieve good performance and is very fast to train.

Table 6.1 Model Parameters of Cascading gcForest.

Model	Parameters
XGB	n_folds: 5 n_estimators: 100 max_depth: 5 learning_rate: 0.1
LGBM	n_folds: 5 n_estimators: 100 max_depth: 5 learning_rate: 0.1
RF	n_folds: 5 n_estimators: 100
ET	n_folds: 5 n_estimators: 100

Table 6.2 Comparison of word-embedding results of 20 domains of Dranziera dataset with our MoCE Model. The values in the table indicate the percentage of positive reviews captured by Expert1 and the percentage of negative reviews captured by Expert2.

Domain	Word2Vec		GloVe		BERT		ELMo	
	Expert1	Expert2	Expert1	Expert2	Expert1	Expert2	Expert1	Expert2
Amazon_Instant_Video	0.81	0.36	0.81	0.86	0.54	0.55	0.71	0.72
Automotive	0.81	0.35	0.85	0.82	0.54	0.55	0.72	0.72
Baby	0.73	0.37	0.97	0.05	0.61	0.67	0.77	0.72
Beauty	0.02	0.98	0.86	0.82	0.55	0.54	0.68	0.71
Books	0.82	0.83	0.84	0.83	0.57	0.57	0.75	0.68
Clothing_Accessories	0.90	0.79	0.85	0.88	0.66	0.74	0.78	0.73
Electronics	0.98	0.04	0.85	0.81	0.56	0.55	0.73	0.75
Health	0.80	0.83	0.81	0.84	0.59	0.55	0.71	0.73
Home_Kitchen	0.81	0.87	0.88	0.83	0.59	0.59	0.69	0.73
Movies_TV	0.85	0.80	0.03	0.97	0.54	0.57	0.72	0.76
Music	0.80	0.86	0.85	0.80	0.64	0.62	0.78	0.79
Office_Products	0.99	0.02	0.87	0.80	0.65	0.64	0.80	0.82
Patio	0.03	0.59	0.99	0.04	0.31	0.55	0.69	0.67
Pet_Supplies	0.82	0.80	0.82	0.80	0.54	0.56	0.71	0.73
Shoes	0.92	0.84	0.92	0.86	0.60	0.65	0.77	0.75
Software	0.82	0.84	0.87	0.71	0.55	0.55	0.71	0.73
Sports_Outdoors	0.78	0.87	0.79	0.87	0.58	0.59	0.69	0.73
Tools_Home_Improvement	0.85	0.78	0.85	0.79	0.55	0.54	0.70	0.77
Toys_Games	0.88	0.85	0.87	0.85	0.45	0.43	0.75	0.73
Video_Games	0.81	0.83	0.04	0.99	0.43	0.39	0.71	0.73

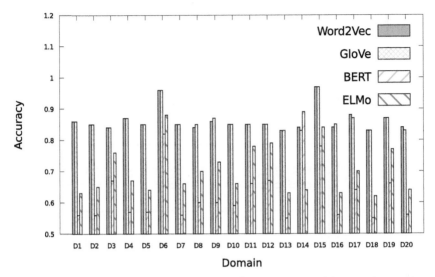

Figure 6.6 Figure presents the accuracy of amazon 20 products using gcForest on four word embeddings Word2Vec, GloVe, BERT, and ELMo.

Fig. 6.6 illustrates each domain results for all the pre-trained embeddings with an evaluation metric accuracy. From Fig. 6.6, we can observe that Word2Vec, GloVe, and ELMo methods perform better when compared to BERT embeddings in terms of accuracy and similar comparison we observed in Table 6.2 using an evaluation metric F1-score. One of the main reasons BERT and ELMo do not perform better than Word2Vec and GloVe is that fine-tuned language models (LMs) like BERT/ELMo for a specific dataset training for a few epochs achieve better results instead of simply using pre-trained embeddings. In Table 6.3, we describe the comparison between previous state-of-the-art methods and using gcForest. The combination of word-embedding results in comparison we observed in Table 6.3, and it outperforms the state-of-the-art results.

6.8 Conclusion

Neural word embeddings have delivered impressive results in many Natural Language Processing tasks. However, choosing the right set of word embeddings for a given dataset is a major challenging task for enhancing the results. In this chapter, we have evaluated four neural word-embedding methods such as Word2Vec, GloVe, ELMo, and BERT on sentiment-analysis task in two steps (i) a mixture of classification experts (MoCE)

Table 6.3 Detailed results of domains (Dom) of Amazon product-reviews dataset by the Baselines, existing method results and by passing combinations of word embeddings to gcForest.

Dom	Tested System (Macro F1-Score)							
	SVM	ME	DBP	DDP	CNN	GWE	NS	gcF
(1)	0.70	0.70	0.72	0.71	0.80	0.80	0.80	**0.87**
(2)	0.72	0.71	0.72	0.70	0.73	0.79	0.85	**0.87**
(3)	0.69	0.72	0.71	0.69	0.84	0.79	0.85	**0.86**
(4)	0.69	0.72	0.74	0.73	0.82	0.81	0.85	**0.88**
(5)	0.69	0.69	0.69	0.69	0.78	0.75	0.79	**0.86**
(6)	0.69	0.72	0.80	0.78	0.77	0.81	0.86	**0.97**
(7)	0.68	0.69	0.73	0.70	0.79	0.77	0.86	**0.87**
(8)	0.67	0.66	0.69	0.69	0.78	0.79	0.86	**0.86**
(9)	0.72	0.69	0.71	0.69	0.75	0.82	0.87	**0.88**
(10)	0.73	0.72	0.70	0.71	0.75	0.79	0.80	**0.86**
(11)	0.69	0.65	0.71	0.72	0.76	0.77	0.80	**0.86**
(12)	0.73	0.73	0.72	0.70	0.79	0.80	0.87	**0.87**
(13)	0.69	0.71	0.70	0.69	0.86	0.80	0.86	**0.86**
(14)	0.68	0.73	0.67	0.66	0.82	0.79	0.84	**0.85**
(15)	0.67	0.73	0.83	0.81	0.81	0.84	0.86	**0.97**
(16)	0.74	0.69	0.72	0.71	0.79	0.76	0.85	**0.86**
(17)	0.67	0.73	0.71	0.71	0.76	0.81	0.87	**0.89**
(18)	0.73	0.73	0.68	0.69	0.79	0.79	0.85	**0.85**
(19)	0.66	0.69	0.74	0.71	0.77	0.84	0.86	**0.88**
(20)	0.69	0.70	0.70	0.70	0.72	0.78	0.82	**0.84**

SVM (Support Vector Machines), ME (Maximum Entropy), DBP (Domain Belonging Polarity), NS (NeuroSent), DDP (Domain Detection Polarity), gcF (gcForest), CNN (Convolutional Neural Networks), GWE (Google Word Embeddings)

model for the sentiment–classification task, (ii) to compare and improve the classification accuracy by different combinations of word embedding as the first level of features and pass it to the cascade model inspired by gcForest for extracting various features.

References

[1] Yohan Jo, Alice H. Oh, Aspect and sentiment unification model for online review analysis, in: Proceedings of the Fourth ACM International Conference on Web Search and Data Mining, ACM, 2011, pp. 815–824.

[2] Erik Cambria, Bebo White, Jumping NLP curves: a review of natural language processing research, IEEE Computational Intelligence Magazine 9 (2) (2014) 48–57.

[3] Long Jiang, Mo Yu, Ming Zhou, Xiaohua Liu, Tiejun Zhao, Target-dependent Twitter sentiment classification, in: Proceedings of the 49th Annual Meeting of the Association for Computational Linguistics: Human Language Technologies-Volume 1, Association for Computational Linguistics, 2011, pp. 151–160.

[4] Bo Pang, Lillian Lee, Shivakumar Vaithyanathan, Thumbs up? Sentiment classification using machine learning techniques, in: Proceedings of the ACL-02 Conference on Empirical Methods in Natural Language Processing-Volume 10, Association for Computational Linguistics, 2002, pp. 79–86.

[5] Li Dong, Furu Wei, Chuanqi Tan, Duyu Tang, Ming Zhou, Ke Xu, Adaptive recursive neural network for target-dependent Twitter sentiment classification, in: Proceedings of the 52nd Annual Meeting of the Association for Computational Linguistics (Volume 2: Short Papers), vol. 2, 2014, pp. 49–54.

[6] Z. Chen, N. Ma, B. Liu, Lifelong learning for sentiment classification, arXiv preprint, arXiv:1801.02808, 2018.

[7] L.C. Yu, J. Wang, K.R. Lai, X. Zhang, Refining word embeddings for sentiment analysis, in: Proceedings of the 2017 Conference on Empirical Methods in Natural Language Processing, 2017, pp. 534–539.

[8] A. Yessenalina, Y. Yue, C. Cardie, Multi-level structured models for document-level sentiment classification, in: Proceedings of the 2010 Conference on Empirical Methods in Natural Language Processing, Association for Computational Linguistics, 2010, pp. 1046–1056.

[9] D. Tang, B. Qin, T. Liu, Document modeling with gated recurrent neural network for sentiment classification, in: Proceedings of the 2015 Conference on Empirical Methods in Natural Language Processing, 2015, pp. 1422–1432.

[10] R. Sharma, A. Somani, L. Kumar, P. Bhattacharyya, Sentiment intensity ranking among adjectives using sentiment bearing word embeddings, in: Proceedings of the 2017 Conference on Empirical Methods in Natural Language Processing, 2017, pp. 547–552.

[11] B. Pang, L. Lee, Seeing stars: exploiting class relationships for sentiment categorization with respect to rating scales, in: Proceedings of ACL, 2005, pp. 115–124.

[12] Qiao Qian, Minlie Huang, Jinhao Lei, Xiaoyan Zhu, Linguistically regularized LSTM for sentiment classification, arXiv preprint, arXiv:1611.03949, 2016.

[13] Madhuri Tummalapalli, Manoj Chinnakotla, Radhika Mamidi, Towards better sentence classification for morphologically rich languages, 2018.

[14] Yoon Kim, Convolutional neural networks for sentence classification, arXiv preprint, arXiv:1408.5882, 2014.

[15] Duy-Tin Vo, Yue Zhang, Target-dependent Twitter sentiment classification with rich automatic features, in: Twenty-Fourth International Joint Conference on Artificial Intelligence, 2015.

[16] Yoshua Bengio, Réjean Ducharme, Pascal Vincent, Christian Jauvin, A neural probabilistic language model, Journal of Machine Learning Research 3 (Feb 2003) 1137–1155.

[17] Tomas Mikolov, Ilya Sutskever, Kai Chen, Greg S. Corrado, Jeff Dean, Distributed representations of words and phrases and their compositionality, in: Advances in Neural Information Processing Systems, 2013, pp. 3111–3119.

[18] Jeffrey Pennington, Richard Socher, Christopher D. Manning, GloVe: global vectors for word representation, in: Empirical Methods in Natural Language Processing (EMNLP), 2014, pp. 1532–1543, http://www.aclweb.org/anthology/D14-1162.

[19] Caiming Xiong, Stephen Merity, Richard Socher, Dynamic memory networks for visual and textual question answering, in: International Conference on Machine Learning, 2016, pp. 2397–2406.

[20] Richard Socher, Alex Perelygin, Jean Wu, Jason Chuang, Christopher D. Manning, Andrew Ng, Christopher Potts, Recursive deep models for semantic compositionality over a sentiment treebank, in: Proceedings of the 2013 Conference on Empirical Methods in Natural Language Processing, 2013, pp. 1631–1642.

[21] Tom Kenter, Maarten De Rijke, Short text similarity with word embeddings, in: Proceedings of the 24th ACM International on Conference on Information and Knowledge Management, ACM, 2015, pp. 1411–1420.

[22] Jason P.C. Chiu, Eric Nichols, Named entity recognition with bidirectional LSTM-CNNs, Transactions of the Association for Computational Linguistics 4 (2016) 357–370.

[23] Bryan McCann, James Bradbury, Caiming Xiong, Richard Socher, Learned in translation: contextualized word vectors, in: Advances in Neural Information Processing Systems, 2017, pp. 6294–6305.

[24] Matthew E. Peters, Mark Neumann, Mohit Iyyer, Matt Gardner, Christopher Clark, Kenton Lee, Luke Zettlemoyer, Deep contextualized word representations, arXiv preprint, arXiv:1802.05365, 2018.

[25] Jacob Devlin, Ming-Wei Chang, Kenton Lee, Kristina Toutanova, BERT: pre-training of deep bidirectional transformers for language understanding, arXiv preprint, arXiv: 1810.04805, 2018.

[26] Jorge A. Balazs, Edison Marrese-Taylor, Yutaka Matsuo, IIIDYT at IEST 2018: implicit emotion classification with deep contextualized word representations, arXiv preprint, arXiv:1808.08672, 2018.

[27] Changki Lee, Yi-Gyu Hwang, Hyo-Jung Oh, Soojong Lim, Jeong Heo, Chung-Hee Lee, Hyeon-Jin Kim, Ji-Hyun Wang, Myung-Gil Jang, Fine-grained named entity recognition using conditional random fields for question answering, in: Asia Information Retrieval Symposium, Springer, 2006, pp. 581–587.

[28] Wei Yang, Yuqing Xie, Aileen Lin, Xingyu Li, Luchen Tan, Kun Xiong, Ming Li, Jimmy Lin, End-to-end open-domain question answering with BERTserini, arXiv preprint, arXiv:1902.01718, 2019.

[29] Sahar Ghannay, Benoit Favre, Yannick Esteve, Nathalie Camelin, Word embedding evaluation and combination, in: LREC, 2016, pp. 300–305.

[30] Mengnan Zhao, Aaron J. Masino, Christopher C. Yang, A framework for developing and evaluating word embeddings of drug-named entity, in: Proceedings of the BioNLP 2018 Workshop, 2018 , pp. 156–160.

[31] Michael I. Jordan, Lei Xu, Convergence results for the EM approach to mixtures of experts architectures, Neural Networks 8 (9) (1995) 1409–1431.

[32] Zhi-Hua Zhou, Ji Feng, Deep forest: towards an alternative to deep neural networks, arXiv preprint, arXiv:1702.08835, 2017.

[33] Guolin Ke, Qi Meng, Thomas Finley, Taifeng Wang, Wei Chen, Weidong Ma, Qiwei Ye, Tie-Yan Liu, LightGBM: a highly efficient gradient boosting decision tree, in: Advances in Neural Information Processing Systems, 2017, pp. 3146–3154.

[34] Tianqi Chen, Carlos Guestrin, XGboost: a scalable tree boosting system, in: Proceedings of the 22nd ACM SIGKDD International Conference on Knowledge Discovery and Data Mining, ACM, 2016, pp. 785–794.

[35] Mauro Dragoni, Giulio Petrucci, A neural word embeddings approach for multi-domain sentiment analysis, IEEE Transactions on Affective Computing 8 (4) (2017) 457–470.

CHAPTER 7

An annotation system of a medical corpus using sentiment-based models for summarization applications

Anupam Mondal[a], Erik Cambria[b], and Monalisa Dey[a]
[a]Institute of Engineering and Management, Kolkata, India
[b]Nanyang Technological University, Singapore, Singapore

7.1 Introduction

In health care, an annotation system is important to understand the large amount of daily produced healthcare information such as medical reports, discharge summaries, and medical prescriptions [12,13]. Nowadays, collected online information is mainly represented in the form of unstructured data. Hence, one of the emerging research areas is the conversion of unstructured to a structured corpus that could help to recognize the knowledge-based information from the corpus [2,15,18]. Primarily, the information contains medical concepts and their categories and sentiments. In order to identify this information an automated annotation system is essential.

To address these issues, researchers have developed various annotation systems, namely, GENIA[1] and PennBioIE[2] that are able to annotate medical concepts in various forms. However, researchers are still facing difficulties while annotating unstructured corpus text as medical concepts and their sentiments. In the current work, we have designed a medical annotation system to identify and assign medical concepts and their sentiments. As an addition to the work, we have also designed a preliminary version of a sentiment-based summarization system that helps to extract relevant information or a corpus related to a medical query. This will help to effortlessly derive important concepts related to that specific query. This annotated

---

[1] http://www.nactem.ac.uk/GENIA/tagger/.
[2] https://catalog.ldc.upenn.edu/LDC2008T21.

Computational Intelligence Applications for Text and Sentiment Data Analysis
https://doi.org/10.1016/B978-0-32-390535-0.00012-4
163

corpus can assist in developing multiple applications like a recommendation system, a relationship-extraction system, etc., in healthcare [9,11].

We have split this task into two sub-tasks; namely a medical annotation system and a sentiment-based summarization system. In the first sub-task, we have annotated medical concepts and their sentiments from unstructured corpora. On the other hand, the second subtask has been presented as a summarization system using the developed annotated corpus.

The challenges that we had observed while we tried to design an annotated medical corpus and summarize it are: First, how to identify a medical concept from the corpus accurately and separate it from the general concepts? Secondly, how to identify the text spans accurately? Thirdly, how to map the sentiments to the medical concepts? Fourthly, how accurately a sentiment-based query-specific summarization system can be designed? Finally, how to prepare and validate both of the developed systems?

In order to address these challenges, we have designed two systems; namely Lexicon-based and supervised for the first part of the work that identifies medical concepts and sentiments. The Lexicon-based method uses a domain-specific lexicon (WME 3.0) and linguistic rule-based approach. The supervised approach used feature extraction along with machine-learning classifiers ([3]). Finally, we have used the TF-IDF method and sentiment-based approaches to design the baseline summarization system [4].

Dataset preparation was also a major challenge in this work. Hence, we have prepared an experimental dataset by collecting 11 854 medical contexts (as sentences) from the MedicineNet website.[3] Fig. 7.1 presents the overall flow diagram of the annotation and sentiment-identification systems.

The rest of the chapter is organized as follows: Section 7.2 illustrates related work; Section 7.3 describes the preparation process of the experimental dataset; Section 7.4 discusses the development steps of the annotation system in the form of medical-concept identification and sentiment extraction; thereafter, Section 7.5 presents a baseline summarization system in healthcare; Section 7.6 discusses the evaluation processes for both of the developed systems; and finally, concluding remarks are given in Section 7.7.

---

[3] http://www.medicinenet.com/script/main/hp.asp.

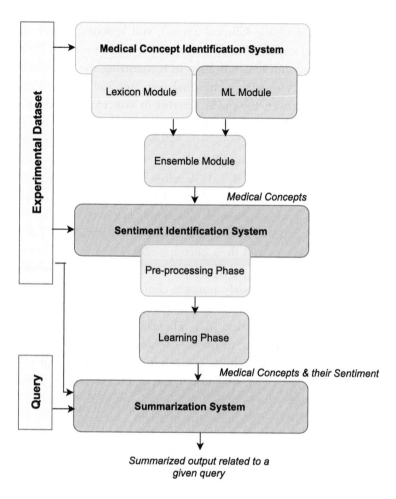

Figure 7.1 Flow diagram of the proposed systems.

7.2 Background work

The research on biomedical information extraction is demanding to extract medical concepts and their sentiments from the daily produced large number of unstructured and semi-structured medical corpora. In order to present a structured corpus and extract subjective information from corpora, we have perceived that the medical-domain-related ontologies and lexicons are essential [1,17]. Hence, researchers have developed various ontologies; namely UMLS (Unified Medical Language System), GATE (General Architecture for Text Engineering) and SNOMED-CT (Systematized

Nomenclature of Medicine-Clinical Terms), and lexicons; namely MEN (Medical WordNet) and WME (WordNet of Medical Event) [10,19,27].

These ontologies and lexicons assist in recognizing the relevant information from the corpus, such as medical concepts and their sentiments, and categories. Moreover, the medical terms or concepts extraction from a clinical corpus are treated as an ambiguous task [14,28]. A group of researchers introduced a sense selection and pruning strategies to expand the ontology in the medical domain [29].

In addition, Pakhomov et al. [21] developed a system that helps to annotate clinical corpus labeled with Parts-Of-Speech (POS) and anaphoric relations [21,26]. Also, Roberts et al. [24] designed the Clinical E-Science Framework (CLEF) that is an annotated corpus with medical attributes such as medical concepts and their corresponding relations, co-references and modifiers [24,25]. Their primary aim was to capture and present clinical information from the publicly available clinical corpus.

On the other-hand, Pal and Saha proposed a summarization approach using a simplified Lesk algorithm [22]. Thereafter, they have arranged the sentences in descending order to obtain the summarized output. This algorithm is simple and each sentence is taken individually for evaluation.

Ferreira et al. developed an extractive text summarization based on sentence-scoring approaches [5]. Word-, graph-, and sentence-based scoring techniques are combined to obtain weights. The summarized output has been evaluated by ROUGE where they have counted the number of system-selected sentences that matches with a gold-standard human summary. The primary datasets that were used in this work are news, articles, and blogs, although they have observed that this sentence-scoring method is not providing adequate accuracy for the input posts.

Jayashree et al. proposed a keyword-based summarization approach by combining two approaches for extracting keywords namely IDF methods along with TF and GSS coefficients [8]. Thereafter, they selected sentences with the highest weights for generating the final summary, which has not given promising results.

The background provides an idea of how a lexicon helps to design an automated annotation system in healthcare. It also provides an overview related to the applied techniques for building a summarization application using a sentiment-based annotation system in healthcare. In addition, these observations motivated development of a sentiment-based medical-annotation system that addressed the summarization task.

7.3 Dataset preparation

This section describes how we have collected and prepared our experimental dataset to build and validate the proposed medical annotation system and sentiment-based summarization system. The dataset has been collected from a well-known medical website, namely MedicineNet.[4] This website provides detailed information about diseases, conditions, medications, and general health. This resource was launched by William Shiel in October 1996. MedicineNet is a network of U.S. Board-Certified Physicians and Allied Health Professionals working together to provide the public with current, comprehensive medical information, written in easy to understand language.[5] We have obtained a large number of medical terms related to diseases, conditions, and medications and their related medical contexts. To acquire this data, we have used two Python-based packages; Beautiful Soup and Scrapy.

In order to build the experimental dataset, we have performed data cleansing using various open-source tools like NLTK, stemming, etc. In data cleansing, we have removed the stop words and stemmed the concept words. Finally, we have collected 11 854 unique medical contexts as an experimental dataset. Each sentence of the medical corpus is presented in the form of its medical context in this research.

Then, the experimental dataset has been divided into two different parts of 70% and 30%. 70% of the experimental dataset (8298) is taken as the training data and 30% of the experimental dataset (3556) is taken as the test data. The training dataset has been used for building both of the systems, whereas the test dataset helps to validate the same. The detailed distributions of the instances are shown in Table 7.1.

In that time we have taken help from a group of medical practitioners (medical students) to annotate the medical contexts with two different labels such as, medical concepts and their sentiments. Also, these practitioners helped us to validate the output of the summarization system that we have described in Section 7.6. Fig. 7.2 shows an annotated output of the proposed Medical annotation system, which assists in developing the summarization application.

---

[4] http://www.medicinenet.com/script/main/hp.asp.
[5] https://www.hon.ch/HONcode/Conduct.html?HONConduct594277.

Table 7.1 [Color online] Detailed statistics of the experimental dataset.

Datasets	No. of Contexts	
Experimental dataset	11 854	
Statistics of the labeled dataset		
	Training	Test
No. of Unique Contexts	8298	3556
No. of Unique Concepts	24 851	10 949
Medical Concepts — uni-gram	12 584	4987
Medical Concepts — bi-gram	6092	3459
Medical Concepts — tri-gram	4748	1912
Medical Concepts — more than tri-gram	1427	591
Sentiments — Positive	6958	1951
Sentiments — Negative	17 298	8612
Sentiments — Neutral	595	386

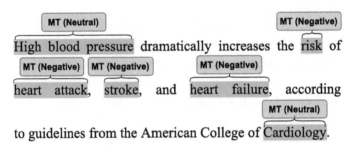

Figure 7.2 A sample annotated output.

7.4 Proposed annotation system

7.4.1 Medical-concept identification

Medical concepts are basically the key terms or phrases that carry the information of medical entities in a context. In order to recognize medical concepts from the contexts, in this chapter we have developed a medical-concept identification system by combining a lexicon-based module along with a supervised machine-learning module. The Lexicon-based module has been designed taking help from a pre-defined lexicon (WME 3.0), additionally, the supervised module has been developed using a feature-oriented classification technique. Finally, we have combined both the modules to recognize the medical concepts from the corpus.

Lexicon-based module

For recognizing medical concepts from their contexts, a domain-specific lexicon namely WordNet of Medical Event (WME) has been employed. Due to the lack of availability of medical-domain-specific lexicons we have selected WME, which helps to identify medical concepts and their related features from our experimental dataset. The WME lexicon is presented with three different versions based on the number of medical concepts and their features.

Initially, WME provides 6415 medical concepts and their features such as gloss, Parts-of-Speech (POS), sentiment, and polarity score [16]. In this version (WME 1.0), the descriptive attribute is presented as gloss and the linguistic attribute is represented as POS, whereas sentiment contains the sentiment-based groups as positive, negative, and neutral and finally the polarity score refers to their corresponding strength (+1) and weakness (-1) score.

The next version of WME (WME 2.0) is presented with additional three features, namely affinity score, gravity score, and Similar–Sentiment Words (SSW) with the same number of medical concepts [19]. The strength of a medical concept is represented by its affinity score that uses the probability scores of its corresponding SSWs. The SSW refers to the set of medical concepts that have common sentiment properties. In addition, the gravity score assists in recognizing the sentiment-based relations between a medical concept and its corresponding glosses.

Thereafter, Mondal et al. designed the next version of WME (WME 3.0) with a number of medical concepts and category features [20]. This version contains 10 186 unique medical concepts along with their POS, categories, polarity scores, sentiments, affinity and gravity scores, and similar-sentiment words (SSW). We have employed this version due to its better coverage of medical concepts and its three different classes of sentiments.

First, we have designed a set of rules from our training dataset to identify the words or phrases. In order to identify those words or phrases we have used TF-IDF (Term Frequency-Inverse Document Frequency) and Parts-of-Speech. Secondly, to identify the medical concepts from the recognized words or phrases, we have compared with the medical concepts of WME 3.0 lexicon.

We have observed that due to a lack of medical concepts in WME over our experimental dataset we have designed another version of a medical-concept identification system as a supervised module.

Supervised module

For building this module we have extracted various features of all concepts of the context. The features extracted using WME 3.0 lexicon are POS, SSW, polarity score, and sentiment. In addition, capital letter, punctuation, n-grams, term frequency (TF) along with previous and next words of the target words features have been extracted as context-level features for this experiment. Finally, those features are applied on two machine-learning classifiers Naïve Bayes and Decision tree. We have tagged the concepts with two labels, namely Medical Terms (MT) and Non Medical Terms (NMT). To learn the supervised modules, we have used the above-mentioned features and their corresponding labels of the training dataset.

Thereafter, to enhance the performance of this system we have combined both the above-mentioned modules and built an ensemble module. The ensemble module provides better accuracy in terms of identifying medical concepts in higher lexicon scopes.

Ensemble module

The ensemble module has been designed by combining prior-mentioned lexicon-based and supervised modules. The aim of the module is to identify the medical concepts having the highest lexical scope. The following steps describe the method briefly.

I refers to the number of applied techniques such as lexicon, Naïve Bayes, and Decision tree (1-N) where N = 3

$I' = I + 1$

J refers to the number of lexical scopes of medical concepts (1-L) where L presents 4 n-grams (such as uni-, bi-, tri- and more than tri-).

$J' = J + 1$

    if $C_I \neq C_{I'}$ **then**

        if $M_J == M_{J'}$ **then**

            $MC_{EN} = C_I M_J / C_{I'} M_{J'}$

        end

        else

            $MC_{EN} = C_{I'} M_{J'} \, when J' > J$ *or*

            $MC_{EN} = C_I M_J \, when J > J'$

        end

    end

Here, C_I and $C_{I'}$ indicate each applied technique of both modules individually. M_J and $M_{J'}$ refer to each assigned lexical scope for both medical and non-medical concepts. MC_{EN} presents the final output of this ensemble system.

Thereafter, to build a sentiment-based annotation system on the top of the identified medical concepts, we present the following subsection.

7.4.2 Sentiment identification

In order to recognize the sentiments of the identified medical concepts, we have proposed two different modules, namely lexicon based and machine learning. Both modules have been processed through two different phases such as pre-processing and learning phases.

Pre-processing phase

In this phase, we have concentrated to prepare noise-free and structured data from our experimental dataset. This structured data assists in annotating the sentiments of identified medical concepts. Additionally, it helps to extract the sentiments of medical contexts. We have followed data cleansing and formatting as part of the pre-processing steps. Hence, we have used various open-source tools like NLTK, stemming, lemmatization, and parsing. The data-cleansing part mainly considered removing stop words, stemming, and lemmatization. Also, identification of negation words along with classifying medical and non-medical concepts are taken care of by the data-cleansing step [7]. On the other hand, parsing techniques help to format the extracted medical concepts and their sentiment labels.

The formatted concept structure is represented as follows: <Concept (gastric), POS (noun), Semantics (abdominal breathing, visceral, intestinal, belly, duodenal, stomachic), Polarity Score (-0.5), Sentiment (Negative)>

The pre-processing output has been processed through two different learning mechanisms: first, lexicon-based learning using domain-specific lexicon, namely WME 3.0, and secondly, a machine-learning-based approach to annotate sentiment of the identified medical concepts. Finally, we have combined both of the mechanisms using a voting technique.

Learning phase

First, we have designed various rules to identify the sentiment of medical concepts using a polarity score. Thereafter, we have compared those rules with WME 3.0 and assigned the sentiment of medical concepts. Secondly, we have used the features and labels of medical concepts of our training dataset and processed through Naïve Bayes and Support Vector

Machine (SVM) classifiers to build the model. We have used the Naïve Bayes classifier to address the multi-class prediction problem and utilize the independence characteristics of the features. On the other hand, SVM has been used for dealing with the characteristics of pattern recognition by determining the decision boundary. Finally, we have applied the majority-voting technique on the above-mentioned mechanisms such as lexicon based, Naïve Bayes, and Support Vector Machine to produce the anno-tated output. All the mechanisms predicted the sentiments for all medical concepts and the final output prediction is the one that receives more than half of the votes.

Additionally, the sentiment for each of the contexts has been assigned using the following algorithm in the presence of our developed annotation system:

Step 1: The sentiments of all medical and non-medical concepts of the context are identified using their corresponding polarity score.

Step 2: In addition, we have handled the negation characteristics of the context. If we observe a negation word (like no, not, neither, etc.) then we toggle the sentiment of the next words or phrases of the context.

Step 3: Thereafter, the overall polarity of the medical context has been calculated using the following equation:

$$Context\ polarity = \sum_{n=-1}^{+1} Polarity_c$$

where c = number of concepts in the context and $Polarity_c$ indicates the polarity score of each concept.

Step 4: Finally, the context polarity decides the sentiment of the con-text.

Fig. 7.3 describes the development steps of the proposed sentiment-identification system.

In this chapter, we have utilized the developed sentiment annotated system and built a baseline summarization system in healthcare.

7.5 Sentiment-based summarization

In order to provide optimal care to patients, health practitioners need to efficiently interpret relevant information from multiple sources. Moreover, with the advent of the internet, a large amount of medical information is available online. Not only medical practitioners but also researchers in the

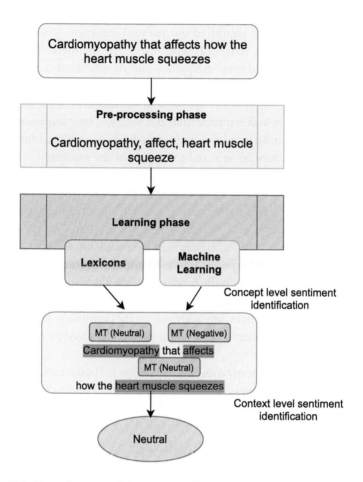

Figure 7.3 Flow diagram of the proposed systems.

biomedical domain need to go through this information. Any common user also when searching for a medical term, obtains much information as output from well-known online resources like MedicineNet. Hence, we are motivated to build a sentiment-based summarization system to summarize the output of a medical concept (query).

The proposed summarization system has been designed by the relevant sentiment score of medical concepts and their relevant contexts. Hence, we have used our acquired experimental dataset that mainly contains diseases, conditions, symptoms, and medicine-related information. The following steps describe the summarization process.

Step 1: First, we have identified the relevant sentences (contexts) from the extracted documents (corpora) with respect to the medical query using the standard weighted term-frequency and inverse sentence-frequency method.

Step 2: Sentence frequency is the number of sentences in the document that contain that term and is represented as a vector. These sentence vectors are then scored by similarity to the query (medical concept) and the highest scoring sentence vectors are selected to be part of the summary.

Step 3: To filter the summary and make it sentiment specific, we use our developed annotation system as described in Section 7.4. This annotation system assists in identifying the polarity score and sentiment for both the query and their contexts.

Step 4: Thereafter, we have prepared a ranked list for the extracted contexts of a query based on their obtained polarity scores.

Step 5: We have calculated the sentiment-based difference between the query phrase and the different extracted contexts. Finally, the n most important or related sentences are selected as the summary based on the difference of their sentiment scores. The value of n is user or application specific.

The developed summarization system helps to build various applications, like a question–answering and recommendation system in the healthcare domain. We have observed that the standard evaluation tools like ROUGE and BLEU are unable to evaluate the accuracy of the developed summarization system due to the lack of domain-specific knowledge [6,23]. To address this challenge, we have taken help from the domain experts to validate the summarization output.

7.6 Results analysis

In order to evaluate the proposed medical concept and their sentiment-identification system, we have used a part of the experimental dataset. Thereafter, we have applied an agreement analysis to validate the summarized output. The medical-concept identification system has been validated in terms of various n-grams. The validation matrices are precision, recall, and F-measure. Table 7.2 presents the result analysis for the medical-concept identification modules.

In addition, to validate the extracted sentiments of medical concepts, we have applied the experimental dataset on the Naïve Bayes and support vector machine supervised classifiers. Both of the classifiers have been pre-

Table 7.2 Detailed evaluation of the medical-concept identification system.

Distributions	Precision	Recall	F-Measure
Lexicon–based			
uni–gram medical concepts	0.98	0.98	0.98
bi–gram medical concepts	0.95	0.97	0.96
tri–gram medical concepts	0.97	0.89	0.93
more than tri–gram medical concepts	0.78	0.90	0.83
Supervised (Naïve Bayes/Decision Tree)			
uni–gram medical concepts	0.94/0.97	0.96/0.98	0.95/0.97
bi–gram medical concepts	0.95/0.95	0.97/0.98	0.96/0.96
tri–gram medical concepts	0.96/0.97	0.93/0.93	0.94/0.95
more than tri–gram medical concepts	0.81/0.83	0.91/0.92	0.86/0.87
Ensemble			
uni–gram medical concepts	0.97	0.98	0.97
bi–gram medical concepts	0.97	0.96	0.96
tri–gram medical concepts	0.89	0.91	0.90
more than tri–gram medical concepts	0.93	0.90	0.91

Table 7.3 Detailed evaluation of the sentiment-extraction system.

Distributions	Precision	Recall	F-Measure
Naïve Bayes			
Positive	0.85	0.87	0.86
Negative	0.86	0.88	0.87
Neutral	0.82	0.80	0.81
SVM			
Positive	0.87	0.87	0.87
Negative	0.88	0.90	0.89
Neutral	0.81	0.83	0.82

dicted three different type of outputs such as positive, negative, and neutral sentiment. These sentiments have been evaluated by precision, recall, and F-measure matrices. Table 7.3 gives the results analysis of the extracted sentiments for medical concepts.

Additionally, to validate the summarization system, we have used the agreement analysis technique in the presence of domain experts. The agreement analysis score proves the correctness of the summarized output of our system in the form of Yes and No. For this experiment we have used 3556 medical contexts that were collected for 298 medical concepts (query). The

Table 7.4 Detailed Agreement Analysis for the Summarization System.

No. of Samples: 298	Annotator 1		
	$\kappa = 0.68$	**Yes**	**No**
Annotator 2	**Yes**	231	13
	No	15	39

agreement score has been calculated using Cohen's Kappa coefficient score[6] (κ) that is described in Eq. (7.1). Table 7.4 shows the agreement analysis between two domain experts.

$$\kappa = \frac{Pr_a - Pr_e}{1 - Pr_e} \tag{7.1}$$

where Pr_a describes the observed proportion of the entire agreement between the annotators. Additionally, Pr_e presents the proportion expected by chance and shows a kind of random agreement between the annotators.

The annotators have provided the agreement score as number of yes (agreed) and number of no (disagreed). These scores help to calculate 0.68 κ scores using Eq. (7.1) that prove an almost perfect output for the experimental dataset.

7.7 Conclusions

The present chapter reported the development process of a sentiment-based annotation system in healthcare. The motivation of this work is supporting medical practitioners for enhancing their understanding of identifying important keywords and summarized output from the corpus. The developed annotation system is able to recognize medical concepts and their sentiments, whereas, the summarization system provides the relevant information related to a given query. Hence, we have proposed a combined model of lexicon-based and machine learning to build the annotation system. On the other hand, we have applied a TF–IDF-based approach along with a sentiment-based annotation system to assign the rank of the context. This rank assists in identifying the summarized output. Finally, we have prepared a dataset that helps to build and validate the systems. In the future, we will try to enhance the accuracy of the proposed annotation and summarization systems to build various applications in healthcare.

[6] https://en.wikipedia.org/wiki/Cohen's_kappa.

References

[1] A. Borthwick, J. Sterling, E. Agichtein, R. Grishman, Exploiting diverse knowledge sources via maximum entropy in named entity recognition, in: Proc. of the Sixth Workshop on Very Large Corpora, 1998, pp. 152–160.

[2] E. Cambria, A. Hussain, C. Eckl, Bridging the gap between structured and unstructured healthcare data through semantics and sentics, in: Proceedings of the ACM WebSci'11, 2011, pp. 1–4.

[3] I. Chaturvedi, E. Ragusa, P. Gastaldo, R. Zunino, E. Cambria, Bayesian network based extreme learning machine for subjectivity detection, Journal of the Franklin Institute 355 (2017) 1780–1797.

[4] M. Dey, A. Mondal, D. Das, NTCIR-12 MOBILECLICK: sense-based ranking and summarization of English queries, in: Proceedings of the 12th NTCIR Conference on Evaluation of Information Access Technologies, Tokyo, Japan, 2016, pp. 138–142.

[5] R. Ferreira, F. Freitas, L. de Souza Cabral, R.D. Lins, R. Lima, G. França, S.J. Simske, L. Favaro, A context based text summarization system, in: 2014 11th IAPR International Workshop on Document Analysis Systems, IEEE, 2014, pp. 66–70.

[6] T. He, J. Chen, L. Ma, Z. Gui, F. Li, W. Shao, Q. Wang, ROUGE-C: a fully automated evaluation method for multi-document summarization, in: 2008 IEEE International Conference on Granular Computing, IEEE, 2008, pp. 269–274.

[7] Y. Huang, H.J. Lowe, A novel hybrid approach to automated negation detection in clinical radiology reports, Journal of the American Medical Informatics Association 14 (2007) 304–311.

[8] R. Jayashree, M.K. Srikanta, B.S. Anami, Categorized text document summarization in the Kannada language by sentence ranking, in: 2012 12th International Conference on Intelligent Systems Design and Applications (ISDA), IEEE, 2012, pp. 776–781.

[9] J.E. Katz, R.E. Rice, Public views of mobile medical devices and services: a US national survey of consumer sentiments towards RFID healthcare technology, International Journal of Medical Informatics 78 (2009) 104–114.

[10] A. Kilgarriff, C. Fellbaum, WordNet: an electronic lexical database, JSTOR 76 (2000) 706–708.

[11] J.D. Kim, T. Ohta, Y. Tateisi, J. Tsujii, Genia corpus—a semantically annotated corpus for bio-textmining, Bioinformatics 19 (2003) i180–i182.

[12] Y. Kim, E. Riloff, J.F. Hurdle, A study of concept extraction across different types of clinical notes, in: AMIA Annual Symposium Proceedings, American Medical Informatics Association, 2015, p. 737.

[13] S. Kulick, A. Bies, M. Liberman, M. Mandel, R. McDonald, M. Palmer, A. Schein, L. Ungar, S. Winters, P. White, Integrated annotation for biomedical information extraction, in: HLT-NAACL 2004 Workshop: Linking Biological Literature, Ontologies and Databases, 2004, pp. 61–68.

[14] V.L. Mane, S.S. Panicker, V.B. Patil, Summarization and sentiment analysis from user health posts, in: 2015 International Conference on Pervasive Computing (ICPC), IEEE, 2015, pp. 1–4.

[15] A. Mondal, E. Cambria, D. Das, A. Hussain, S. Bandyopadhyay, Relation extraction of medical concepts using categorization and sentiment analysis, Cognitive Computation (2018) 1–16.

[16] A. Mondal, I. Chaturvedi, D. Das, R. Bajpai, S. Bandyopadhyay, Lexical resource for medical events: a polarity based approach, in: 2015 IEEE International Conference on Data Mining Workshop (ICDMW), IEEE, 2015, pp. 1302–1309.

[17] A. Mondal, D. Das, Ensemble approach for identifying medical concepts with special attention to lexical scope, Sādhanā 46 (2021) 1–12.

[18] A. Mondal, D. Das, S. Bandyopadhyay, Relationship extraction based on category of medical concepts from lexical contexts, in: Proceedings of 14th International Conference on Natural Language Processing (ICON), 2017, pp. 212–219.

[19] A. Mondal, D. Das, E. Cambria, S. Bandyopadhyay, WME: sense, polarity and affinity based concept resource for medical events, in: Proceedings of the Eighth Global WordNet Conference, 2016, pp. 242–246.

[20] A. Mondal, D. Das, E. Cambria, S. Bandyopadhyay, WME 3.0: an enhanced and validated lexicon of medical concepts, in: Proceedings of the Ninth Global WordNet Conference, 2018.

[21] S.V. Pakhomov, A. Coden, C.G. Chute, Developing a corpus of clinical notes manually annotated for part-of-speech, International Journal of Medical Informatics 75 (2006) 418–429.

[22] A.R. Pal, D. Saha, An approach to automatic text summarization using WordNet, in: 2014 IEEE International Advance Computing Conference (IACC), IEEE, 2014, pp. 1169–1173.

[23] K. Papineni, S. Roukos, T. Ward, W.J. Zhu, BLEU: a method for automatic evaluation of machine translation, in: Proceedings of the 40th Annual Meeting of the Association for Computational Linguistics, 2002, pp. 311–318.

[24] A. Roberts, R. Gaizauskas, M. Hepple, N. Davis, G. Demetriou, Y. Guo, J.S. Kola, I. Roberts, A. Setzer, A. Tapuria, et al., The CLEF corpus: semantic annotation of clinical text, in: AMIA Annual Symposium Proceedings, American Medical Informatics Association, 2007, p. 625.

[25] A. Roberts, R. Gaizauskas, M. Hepple, G. Demetriou, Y. Guo, I. Roberts, A. Setzer, Building a semantically annotated corpus of clinical texts, Journal of Biomedical Informatics 42 (2009) 950–966.

[26] G.K. Savova, W.W. Chapman, J. Zheng, R.S. Crowley, Anaphoric relations in the clinical narrative: corpus creation, Journal of the American Medical Informatics Association 18 (2011) 459–465.

[27] B. Smith, C. Fellbaum, Medical WordNet: a new methodology for the construction and validation of information resources for consumer health, in: Proceedings of the 20th International Conference on Computational Linguistics, Association for Computational Linguistics, 2004, p. 371.

[28] W.F. Styler IV, S. Bethard, S. Finan, M. Palmer, S. Pradhan, P.C. de Groen, B. Erickson, T. Miller, C. Lin, G. Savova, et al., Temporal annotation in the clinical domain, Transactions of the Association for Computational Linguistics 2 (2014) 143–154.

[29] D. Widdows, A. Toumouh, B. Dorow, A. Lehireche, et al., Ongoing developments in automatically adapting lexical resources to the biomedical domain, in: Fifth International Conference on Language Resources and Evaluation, LREC, Genoa, Italy, 2006, pp. 1039–1044.

CHAPTER 8

A comparative study of a novel approach with baseline attributes leading to sentiment analysis of Covid-19 tweets

Arunava Kumar Chakraborty[a] **and Sourav Das**[b]

[a]Department of Computer Science & Engineering, RCC Institute of Information Technology, Kolkata, India
[b]Maulana Abul Kalam Azad University of Technology, Kolkata, India

8.1 Introduction

The Covid-19 outbreak was initially reported on 31st December 2019 in Wuhan, Hubei Province, China and it started spreading rapidly throughout the world. Finally, on 11th March 2020 the WHO declared the Covid-19 outbreak as a pandemic at the time when the infection keeps on spreading [1]. Millions of people lost their lives due to the rapid spread of the virus in different countries around the world. More than 22.5 million active instances of Coronavirus were encountered in more than 188 nations and territories on 21st August 2020, resulting in over 792,000 deaths; Although 14.4 million people were declared to have recuperated.[1] Analyzing the lethal trend of this virus, different countries implemented strict lockdowns for different periods to prevent the spread of this epidemic [1]. Since the Covid-19 vaccine had not yet been discovered, maintaining social distance was the only way to reduce the spread of the virus [2]. We survey several previous research papers with different experiments to understand the overall situation all over the world. In this chapter, we discuss different approaches and their performance measures to compare their technical efficiency over real-time data. Different micro-blogging sites have played a large role in sharing information about this pandemic and Twitter is one of the most popular micro-blogging sites. During these lockdowns, many people used Twitter to share their expressions, which inspired us to use our

---

[1] https://gisanddata.maps.arcgis.com.

Computational Intelligence Applications for Text and Sentiment Data Analysis
https://doi.org/10.1016/B978-0-32-390535-0.00013-6
179

research to analyze the huge Twitter dataset to measure the global awareness regarding the pandemic [3].

Many people from all over the world use their native language instead of English to share their opinions on social-networking platforms so we faced many challenges in collecting exclusive English tweets from these multilingual tweets [3]. During the period April–June 2020, we collected 235k Covid-19-related English tweets to develop our dataset. The popular Covid-19-specific words were extracted from the dataset. Then n-gram model was used to identify the trend of tweets so that we can extract the most relevant grams for further computation. The sentiment polarities of the pre-processed tweets were evaluated to classify them into *positive*, *negative*, and *neutral* classes. Finally, the vectorized tweets along with the corresponding sentiment ratings were used to train the proposed deep Bidirectional LSTM network.

8.1.1 Motivation and objective

The motivation behind this work is to study the recent flow of studies on Covid-19 from a dedicated natural language research perspective and also to analyze the behavioral direction and nature of people throughout the world about such a pandemic. As a social-media platform, Twitter is one of the trendiest micro-blogging sites and can be considered as a repository of meaningful information [41]. In 2020, out of 320 million active Twitter users from all over the world, India has 18.9 million active Twitter users, i.e., currently the third-highest in the world.[2] The users tweet their expressions within the allotted 280 characters. During the lockdown phases due to this pandemic situation since many people have shared their feelings on Twitter, we were inspired to analyze the emotional tendencies of the public from time to time.

This particular pandemic has not only claimed millions of lives but has plunged the entire world economy into recession. Many people have lost their jobs in these difficult times and the unemployment rate is increasing day by day all over the world. We present a plethora of related Natural Language Processing-based Covid-19 analytical studies from recent times to study the respective proposals, methodologies, and research contributions. The main objective of this research work is to analyze the public sentiment to find the global sentiment trend about this pandemic. Finally, a Bidirec-

---

[2] www.statista.com.

tional long short-term network has been trained to predict the sentiment by analyzing correlations between words.

The organization of the chapter is as follows: Section 8.2 consists of several previous research studies on sentiment analysis from different aspects. The comparisons between different methodologies of recent NLP research works on Covid-19 are presented in Section 8.3. We present our proposed contributions from data collection to deep-learning-based sentiment prediction in Section 8.4. The benchmark comparisons between our proposed methodology and recent NLP research studies on Covid-19 are represented in Section 8.5. In Section 8.6, we present the overall discussion and prospects of our research work. Finally, we conclude our proposed experiment in Section 8.7.

8.2 Related study

8.2.1 Groundwork of sentiment analysis

Sentiment analysis is a process of computationally analyzing and identifying opinions and judgments from a piece of text, although the sentiment analysis can be implemented for different purposes, like Aspect-based, Document-level, and Sentence-level sentiment analysis. Aspect-based sentiment analysis is a type of textual analysis that can classify the text by aspects and determines the corresponding sentiment based on their association. The Document-level sentiment-analysis module analyzes a whole document containing a section of text to determine the sentiment of text, e.g., positive, negative, or neutral. Sentence-level sentiment analysis is one of the main directions in the sentiment-analysis area. Numerous research studies in this domain concentrated on recognizing the polarity of a sentence (e.g., *positive, neutral, negative*), according to the semantic information learned from the textual content of sentences.

In 2015, Bhatia, Ji, and Eisenstein [4] found that the Document-level sentiment analysis can be improved by using Rhetorical Structure Theory that describes the structure of a document in terms of text spans that form discourse units and the relations between them. From this research, it is evident that reweighting the discourse units based on their position in a dependency representation can improve lexical-based sentiment analysis. Finally, they proposed a recurrent neural network over their evaluated data to give further improvements in sentiment classification.

One research study demonstrates the machine translation of multilingual sentence-level sentiment analysis. In their experiment, the authors evaluated the sentiment prediction accuracy of 21 English sentiment-level methods on different datasets in 9 different languages [5]. As the result, they found that SO-CAL, Umigon, and Vader methods have performed well on different datasets based on the Macro-F1 score and Coverage.

Several researchers developed a three-stage statistical hybrid model to detect explicit and implicit polarity shifts from the reviews [7]. After elimination of the identified polarity shifts using the antonym-reversion method, the piece of text is divided into four subsets as polarity-unshifted text, eliminated negations, explicit contrasts, and sentiment inconsistency. Finally, they trained different base classifiers on these textual subsets and computed a weighted ensemble as the final layer of the sentiment classifier to decrease the polarity shifts.

Another research study by Mubarok, Adiwijaya, and Aldhi [8] gives an aspect-based sentiment analysis of the different product reviews. After the pre-processing of data using part-of-speech (POS) tagging the researchers used a Chi-Square probability distribution to extract highly relevant words from each opinion. Finally, the Naïve Bayes classifier was used for sentiment classification of the polarity ratings and as a result, their model achieved 78.21% of the highest F1-score.

A comparative study on document-based sentiment analysis using the clustering method presents the experimental result of several clustering techniques. During the study, Ma, Yuan, and Wu [9] found that considering the clustering accuracy K-means algorithms performed better on balanced datasets compared to unbalanced datasets. They also found some clustering models, like Agglo-WSlink, Slink, UPGMA, Spect-Sy, Spect-RW, PCA-Kmeans, and Spect-Un achieved better accuracy on unbalanced datasets than on balanced datasets. The BM25, DPH_DFR, and H_LM models performed better than traditional weighting models, like Binary, TF, and TF_IDF.

For polarity classification, the sentiment analysis using radical-level and character-level processing achieved a better result [10]. Research work on Chinese sentiment analysis claims that using Chinese radical-based hierarchical embeddings the proposed system achieved better accuracy over state-of-the-art textual and embedding features.

Some researchers proposed a deep Sentic-LSTM model for targeted aspect-based sentiment analysis to incorporate implicit and explicit pieces of knowledge [11]. The two-step attention model based on the sentiment aspects and polarity sequentially encodes the target expression. The target-level attention model achieved more accurate target representation as it attends to only the sentimental part of the sentence.

Another research study by Rintyarna, Sarno, and Fatichah [12] demonstrated the extraction of sentence-level features (SLF) and domain-sensitive features (DSF) from textual data. The researchers trained different machine-learning algorithms based on extracted features. They also compared the feature-selection method WEKA with baseline features. Finally, the supervised ML algorithm improves the 7.1%, 7.2%, and 7.4% performance for precision, recall, and F1-score, respectively, with the combined SLF-DSF features.

8.2.2 Sentiment analysis from the web and social media

In traditional media different forms of text are available, among which micro-blogging texts are short, noisy, and embedded with social relations. In order to manage networked texts in micro-blogging, some researchers developed a novel sociological technique (SANT) based on social theories [13]. They extracted sentimental relationships between tweets to model those relationships using the Laplacian graph. Furthermore, they used those relationships to classify the tweets into different sentiment categories. They developed a SANT optimization technique to achieve stable performance for various sizes of training data.

Semi-automated sentiment analysis was developed based on the online social network using the probability model. These authors proposed a model that analyzes sample texts from a train set and constructs a sentiment lexicon with a list of words that occurred in the texts and the likelihood that a text message having those words is positive [14]. The list of words in a message and sentiment lexicon is then used to calculate the positivity score of text messages in a test set. Depending on the threshold value determined using a training set, each message is classified as positive or negative.

Fornacciari, Mordonini, and Tomaiuolo [15] demonstrated a system for a possible combined approach between Social-Network Analysis and Sentiment Analysis, which can operate on Twitter data. They collected three types of data and used a classifier based on the Multinomial Naive Bayes algorithm to identify the tweets from different sentiment classes. They experimented with their approach on a couple of Twitter channels like the *SamSmith* channel during the Grammy Awards in 2015, and the #Ukraine channel during the crisis of 2014. They also mentioned a methodology and some guidelines for the automatic classification of Twitter content.

In 2016, a few researchers found that using Bidirectional LSTM with two-dimensional max-pooling improves text classification. They introduced two combinational models, i.e., BLSTM-2D Pooling and BLSTM-2DCNN, which can be used as an extension of the previous model [16]. They achieved 52.6% of highest accuracy with 2D filter and 2D max-pooling having sizes as (5,5).

Another research study describes the usage of a multimodal feature learning approach, using neural-network models such as Skip-gram and Denoising Autoencoders, to address sentiment analysis of micro-blogging content like tweets, which are composed of a short text and, possibly, an image. The authors developed a semi-supervised model CBOW-LR for learning concurrently vector representation [17]. By using a sentiment-polarity classifier, the model achieved better accuracy over a CBOW representation on the same quantity of tweets. For learning text and image representation, another unified model (CBOW-DA-LR) works in an unsupervised and semi-supervised manner, and obtained a higher classification accuracy compared to SentiBank, a state-of-the-art approach on a publicly available Twitter dataset.

Baziotis, Pelekis, and Doulkeridis [18] described the Topic-based and Message-level sentiment analysis using a deep LSTM architecture. They used the LSTM model associated with two types of attention techniques, on popular word embeddings that have been pre-trained on large-scale Twitter data.

In 2017, Yang and Eisenstein [19] proposed a new method for learning to overcome language variation, leveraging the tendency of socially proximate individuals to use language similarly. Their approach captured subtle shifts in meaning across the network by learning-based models that concentrate on various local regions of the social network. This model was developed by using a social-attention methodology to forecast the weighted combination of the fundamental model outputs, where each author has different importance based on their social popularity. Their model greatly outperforms the standard CNN model in terms of accuracy for sentiment prediction on Twitter and review data.

Some researchers proposed the LSTM hyperparameter optimization technique for the Emotion-Recognition framework based on artificial neural networks. During their experiment, they identified that the recognition rate of four-quadrant dimensional emotions can be improved by 14% through optimized LSTM hyperparameters [20]. Finally, the LSTM model along with the Differential Evolution algorithm achieved a 77.68% prediction accuracy.

A generative model HUB was created by Gong and Wang [21] to integrate two companion learning tasks, opinionated content modeling, and social-network structure modeling, to pair and cluster the learning tasks to reflect the homogeneity among users, while modeling each user as a mixture over the instances of paired tasks to analyze the user behavior by utilizing multiple types of user-generated data. In comparison to the corresponding baselines on two large collections of review datasets from Amazon and Yelp, the trained user-behavior models are interpretable and predictive to achieve greater accuracy in sentiment classification and item/friend recommendations.

Topic modeling was introduced to automatically extract the different subjects of discussion on climate change and sentiment analysis was used to classify tweets as positive, neutral, or negative. Dahal, Kumar, and Li [22] used the pooled Latent Dirichlet Allocation (LDA) model to train a topic model by looking at the word co-occurrences within collected tweets. Finally, their proposed pooled LDA model outperforms both LDA (unpooled) and the Biterm Topic Model (BTM) based on the average UMass coherence score.

Another research study by Dang, Moreno-García, and De la Prieta [23] describes the comparative study of different deep-learning models for sentiment analysis. During the survey, the authors found that it is better to combine deep CNN with word embedding than with TF-IDF when performing sentiment analysis.

There have been different research opportunities for sentiment analysis on public views from social media. A research paper by Chauhan, Sharma, and Sikka [24] demonstrates some sentiment-analysis techniques based on deep-learning and word-embedding methods from different state-of-the-art studies. In order to explore some critical research gaps, the researchers analyzed past research studies on election-result prediction in different countries and states, respectively.

8.2.3 Sentiment analysis in healthcare

Sentiment Analysis for textual classification can be used to measure the public concern about a disease outbreak. Ji, Chun, and Geller [25] presented an Epidemic Sentiment Monitoring System (ESMOS) to identify the progression and peaks of concern for a disease. In their experiments, Multinomial Naïve Bayes achieved overall the best results in classifying negative-sentiment tweets versus neutral tweets and took significantly less time to build the classifier than other methods.

In 2014, Coppersmith, Dredze, and Harman [26] from Johns Hopkins University analyzed the mental-health phenomena in publicly available Twitter data by using natural language processing. After gathering data for mental illnesses, they analyzed the data for finding symptoms of post-traumatic stress disorder (PTSD), depression, bipolar disorder, and seasonal affective disorder (SAD). They provide some insight into classifying the quantifiable linguistic information by examining correlations between the various analytics.

There are some commercial and non-commercial tools for analyzing the sentiment polarities (positive, negative, or neutral) of textual data. Some popular commercial tools are Semantria and TheySay and the non-commercial tools are WEKA and Google Prediction API. Another research study by Georgiou, MacFarlane, and Russell-Rose [27] demonstrates the difficulty of analyzing sentiment by using different tools in the healthcare domain and the comparative study of the ability of different tools over a large dataset. As a result of their experiment, they found that WEKA performed best on their data.

Another research study describes the sentiment-tracking methodology to detect the evidence of depression from tweets [28]. Then, the proposed system further checks whether the detected tweets contained a depressive symptom or not. The sentiment classifier classified the tweets having depressive symptoms into three sub-classes: depressed mood, disturbed sleep, fatigue, or loss of energy. Researchers found that different machine-learning approaches improved the precision of simple keywords for precisely detecting depressive symptoms and all their subtypes from the tweets.

In 2017, based on hybrid matrix-factorization methods, a group of researchers proposed a healthcare recommendation system named iDoctor [29]. They used the LDA model for topic modeling to extract the user's latent priority and doctor features can be extracted from user review comments on doctors, which are involved in matrix factorization integrated with two feature distributions for providing more accurate counseling [29].

A psychometric analyzer can be used for sentiment analysis and emotion recognition of a patient's health based on their previous medical history and recorded voice. Vij and Pruthi [30] proposed a method to analyze the intensity, emotion, polarity, and subjectivity of the tweets. The researchers implemented the Support Vector Regression (SVR) and Support Vector

Machine (SVM) for sentiment analysis and the Decision Tree for detecting emotions.

One group of researchers proposed a methodology for finding the trends of health information from social media to examine the public's opinions about health technology and identify their needs [31]. They used Senti-WordNet for the sentiment classification of the collected tweets based on the most frequent words from the corpus.

Sentiment analysis can be used in healthcare as large-scale information about healthcare is available online. In order to increase healthcare quality, it provides many benefits such as using medical information to achieve the best result [32]. In a comparative study of different research studies regarding sentiment analysis in healthcare the authors found that SVM with a Naïve Bayes classifier outperforms other similar supervised or corpus-based approaches.

8.2.4 Sentiment analysis on Covid-19

In order to predict the number of COVID-19 positive cases from different states of India, a Covid-19 trend–identification model was implemented by Arora, Kumar, and Panigrahi [33]. They proposed the LSTM model since it performs well on time-series predictions. Several LSTM models such as stacked, convolutional, and Bidirectional LSTM have been tested on the previous records, and Bi-LSTM achieved better results over other LSTM variants based on the absolute error metric.

Some researchers developed the evolutionary K-means clustering model on a huge number of Covid-19 tweets [34]. The tweet patterns have been analyzed by them using the n-gram architecture to find the associativity of the relevant words. Finally, they identified the dissimilarity between the popularities of the tokens from the corpus.

A deep CNN-based LSTM model was developed by Das and Kolya [35] for sentiment-accuracy evaluation on large-scale tweets on novel Coronavirus. Then, using Logistic regression, they build a data model for visualization and finally achieved 90.67% of overall accuracy. They performed Bayesian regression on the identified polar tweets for constant point-to-point predictability based on the prior and posterior conditional distribution on a common plane.

Kabir and Madria [36] developed an interactive web application for real-time tweet tracking on COVID-19 to analyze public behaviors during the pandemic situation. The popular words, as well as the bigrams, were extracted from the tweets. They extracted trending topics using the LDA model. Finally, they used the Sentiment-Intensity Analyzer from the NLTK library for finding the sentiment polarities of each tweet.

A group of researchers demonstrated the comparative performance analysis of four different machine-learning classifiers on Coronavirus Tweets data [37]. They observed that the Naïve Bayes classifier achieved 91% classification accuracy for short Tweets, while using the Logistic Regression classifier provides classification accuracy of 74% on the same number of tweets.

Another research study describes the application of NLP on sentiment evaluation using the deep–learning model. The researchers used the LDA model to detect the topics on Coronavirus-related issues from online healthcare forums [38]. During the experiment, their proposed deep LSTM model achieved 81.15% of prediction accuracy on COVID-19 comments for categorizing them into positive, neutral, and negative classes.

In 2020, Chimmula and Zhang [39] deployed a system for forecasting the trend of the Covid-19 pandemic in Canada using the long short-term memory model. Using the public datasets provided by Johns Hopkins University and the Canadian health authority they trained the deep LSTM network and obtained 93.40% and 92.67% accuracy for short-term and long-term predictions, respectively.

A hybrid artificial-intelligence (AI) model was proposed for predicting the worldwide Covid-19 trend. RoBERTa, the pre-trained model of the BERT model is used for textual-feature selection [40]. They developed an improved susceptible–infected (ISI) model with multiple parameters to identify the different infection rates for analyzing the transmission pattern of Coronavirus. The hybrid AI-based ISI model was developed based on the NLP module and the LSTM network so that the prediction results of the model will be highly consistent with actual epidemic cases.

8.3 Comparisons of methodology on recent Covid-19-based NLP research

The Covid-19 pandemic has not only claimed the lives of millions of people but also caused the global market to face a global recession. There has been much research on Covid-19 in various fields as well as in the NLP domain over the last year and a half. In the literature survey, we found several approaches and techniques to analyze the global sentiment trend of different events. In this section, we present a comparative survey on recent research experiments on Covid-19. Table 8.1 lists the proposed contributions of those research works concerning their methodologies.

8.4 Proposed contribution

8.4.1 Preparing Covid-19 dataset

We streamed live tweets from Twitter after the WHO declared Covid-19 as a pandemic.[3] Considering the enormity of this Covid-19 epidemic worldwide, we collected almost 10k English tweets every day, totaling about 235k tweets on Covid-19 from April 19 to June 20, 2020. The dataset we created contains significant data about the vast majority of the tweets as its features. Finally, 235,240 tweets have been collected containing different hash-tagged keywords, e.g., - #covid-19, #coronavirus, #covid, #covaccine, #lockdown, #homequarantine, #quarantinecenter, #socialdistancing, #stayhome, #staysafe, etc. Table 8.2 lists the data description of the collected Covid-19 data.

8.4.2 Data pre-processing

The collected tweets have been pre-processed by using a user-defined pre-processing function developed using the NLTK (Natural Language Toolkit) library that is a Python package mainly used for NLP-oriented tasks. It converts all of the tweets into lower case in the initial stage. Following that, it strips the tweets of any excess white spaces, numeral values, special characters, ASCII characters, URLs, punctuation, and stop words. Then, it converts all 'covid' words into 'covid19' as we already removed all numbers from the tweets. The tweets have been tokenized using the function to split the sentence into a smaller chunk of words. The pre-processing function reduced inflected words to their word stem using the stemming operation.

8.4.3 Attribute I: word-trend detection using n-gram

In the Natural Language Processing research domain, lexicon-based n-gram models are generally used for statistical analysis and composition-feature mapping. The n-gram model has been developed to analyze the tokenized word lexicon for identifying the popularity of tokens or a group of neighboring tokens. In this context, the probability chain rule has been used to

---

[3] https://www.who.int/westernpacific/emergencies/covid-19/news-covid-19.

Table 8.1 Comparative experimental study on Covid-19-based NLP research.

Year	Author	Model	Proposed Contribution
2020	Arora, Kumar and Panigrahi [33].	RNN-based Long Short-Term Network • Deep LSTM • Convolutional LSTM • Bidirectional LSTM	• Dataset – Covid-19 Positive cases from 32 states of India. • Covid-19 Trend prediction. • The Bi-LSTM model achieved better prediction accuracy.
2020	Arpaci et al. [34].	K-means clustering based on the n-gram Model	• Dataset – 43 million collected tweets. • Analyze tweet patterns using clustering on frequently occurred grams.
2021	Das and Kolya [35].	Convolutional Neural Network with *GloVe* Embedding Bayesian Regression	• Dataset – 600k collected tweets. • Gradient-scale comparison between the major affected countries. • Sentiment evaluation using deep CNN model with *GloVe* embedding layer. • Predictive analysis of Covid-19 Trend using Bayesian Regression.

continued on next page

Table 8.1 (*continued*)

Year	Author	Model	Proposed Contribution
2020	Kabir and Madria [36].	Latent Dirichlet Allocation (LDA)	• Dataset – CoronaVis Twitter dataset. • Extraction of frequent words and bigrams. • Topic modeling based on extracted features using the LDA model. • Sentiment analysis using NLTK–based sentiment analyzer.
2020	Samuel et al. [37].	• Naïve Bayes Classifier • Logistic Regression	• Dataset – 900k collected tweets. • Comparisons of different textual classifications for sentiment prediction. • Naïve Bayes classifier outperforms the Logistic Regression model based on classification accuracy.
2020	Jelodar et al. [38].	• Latent Dirichlet Allocation (LDA) • Deep LSTM Model	• Dataset – 563k collected comments from Reddit. • LDA for topic modeling and Gibbs sampling • Sentiment prediction using the deep LSTM model.
2020	Chimmula and Zhang [39].	Deep LSTM Network	• Dataset – Covid-19 dataset from Johns Hopkins University. • Covid-19 trend prediction in Canada.

continued on next page

Table 8.1 (*continued*)

Year	Author	Model	Proposed Contribution
2020	Zheng et al. [40].	Hybrid AI Model • Improved Susceptible-Infected (ISI) Model • LSTM Network	• Dataset – News data on Covid-19 from different provinces in China. • RoBERTa, pre-trained BERT model for textual-feature selection. • ISI model detects the infection rate. • LSTM is used to update the weights for infection rate.
2020	Chakraborty et al. [41].	Different Deep-Learning Classifiers with • Bag-of-Words Model • Doc2Vec Model • Gaussian Fuzzy logic	• Dataset – DATA_SET 1 and DATA_SET 2 consist of 227k and 315 million collected tweets, respectively. • Sentiment identification using Logistic Regression with trigrams under the Tf-Idf Vectorizer outperforms other classifiers on DATA_SET 1. • Sentiment prediction using SVM with Gaussian membership-function-based Fuzzy logic on DATA_SET 2.
2020	Al-Shaher [42].	Deep RNN Model	• Dataset – COVID-19 Open Research Dataset Challenge (CORD-19). • Sentient classification on real-time data with several grammatical errors. • The deep RNN model achieved better accuracy than the CNN model.

continued on next page

Table 8.1 (*continued*)

Year	Author	Model	Proposed Contribution
2020	Shuja et al. [43].	NA	• Dataset – Open-source datasets on Covid-19 based on medical images, textual data, and speech data. • Comparative study of several datasets to identify features from them.
2020	Lamsal [44].	Deep LSTM Network	• Datasets – COV19Tweets Dataset (Lamsal 2020a) consists of 310 million tweets and GeoCOV19Tweets Dataset (Lamsal 2020b). • Topic modeling using frequent grams • Sentiment analysis on tweets.
2020	Serrano, Papakyriakopoulos, and Hegelich [45].	Bayesian Regression with Tf-Idf features	• Dataset – 32k misinformative and 119k factual comments collected from 113 and 67 YouTube videos. • The proposed model achieved better accuracy in sentiment classification compared to other ML models.

continued on next page

Table 8.1 (*continued*)

Year	Author	Model	Proposed Contribution
2020	Yang et al. [46].	Pre-Trained Models for different languages • XLNet for English • AraBert for Arabic • ERNIE for Chinese	• Dataset – 105 million collected multilingual tweets and Chinese Weibo messages. • Fine-grained sentiment classification. • ERNIE model outperforms other models and performs better on Chinese tweets.
2020	Li et al. [47].	Multilingual BERT Model	• Dataset – EmoCT (Emotion-COVID19–Tweet) dataset consists of 8.1 million collected tweets. • Pre-trained model was used for single-level and multi-level classification and achieved significant accuracy.

Table 8.2 Covid-19 data description.

Attributes	Datatype	Description
id	Number	Tweet Identification Number.
created_at	DateTime	Tweet creation Date and Time.
source	Text	Source URL of tweets.
original_text	Text	Original tweets.
favorite_count	Number	Favorite count of tweets.
retweet_count	Number	Retweet count of tweets.
original_author	Text	Name of the original author.
hashtags	Text	Hashtags are used in tweets.
user_mentions	Text	Mentioned usernames in tweets.
place	Text	Location of the tweets.

calculate the probability of recurrence of a sequence:

$$P(t_1, t_2, t_3, ...t_n) = P(t_1)P(t_2 \mid t_1)P(t_3 \mid t_1, t_2) ... P(t_n \mid t_1, t_2, t_3, ... t_{(n-1)})$$

(8.1)

$$= \prod_{i=1}^{n} P(t_i \mid t_1^{(i-1)})$$

(8.2)

In order to understand the mechanism, we can consider a piece of text as – "The Covid-19 wave is increasing". According to the probability chain rule, we can derive, P("The Covid19 wave is increasing") = P("The") × P("Covid19" | "The") × P("wave" | "The Covid19") × P("is" | "The Covid19 wave") × P("increasing" | "The Covid19 wave is"). After applying the probability chain rule, the probability of words in each sentence is:

$$P(E_1, E_2, E_3, ...E_n) = \prod_{j} P(E_j \mid E_1, E_2, E_3, ...E_{(j-1)})$$

(8.3)

$$= \prod_{j=1}^{n} P(E_j \mid E_1^{(j-1)})$$

(8.4)

The bigram model calculates the likelihood of occurrence for each word by using the conditional probability of one word ($P(E_i \mid E_{i-1})$) b ased on the known condition of all the preceding words ($P(E_i \mid E_1^{i-1})$) [6]

$$P(E_1, E_2) = \prod_{i=2} P(E_2 \mid E_1)$$

(8.5)

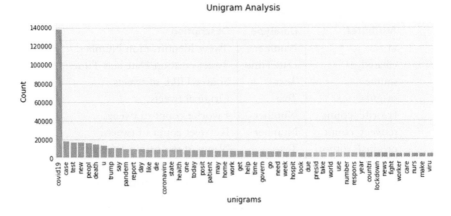

Figure 8.1 Popularity trend of most frequent unigrams.

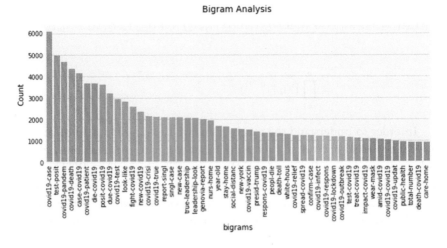

Figure 8.2 Popularity trend of most frequent bigrams.

The general equation for the conditional probability of one preceding word is

$$P(E_k \mid E_{(k-1)}) = \frac{\text{count}(E_{(k-1)}, E_k)}{\text{count}(E_{(k-1)})} \tag{8.6}$$

The most occurred unigrams, bigrams, and trigrams have been identified from the collected corpus based on the n-gram model. Figs. 8.1–8.3 graphically represent the popularity trend of the top 50 unigrams, bigrams, and trigrams, respectively.

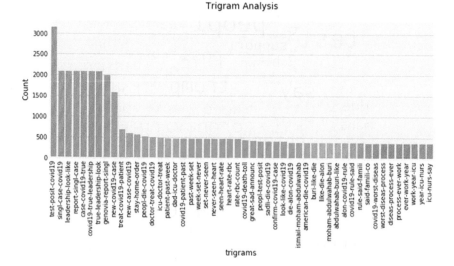

Figure 8.3 Popularity trend of most frequent trigrams.

According to the popularity trend of different grams identified by the n-gram model, it has been found that the unigrams have the highest popularity, while the popularity of bigrams is greater than that of trigrams.

8.4.4 Attribute II: Covid-19-specific word identification

Following the pre-processing phase, the Bag-of-Words (BOW) model has been constructed using commonly occurring words from the Covid-19 dataset. As a result, we compiled a list of the most frequent Covid-19 exclusive words. The word cloud is mainly used for a compact visual representation of the most frequent tokens from the text data. A dense word cloud is presented in Fig. 8.4 to visualize some of the most used words within the corpus. The more a specific word appears in the list, the bigger and bolder it appears in the word cloud.

Word Relevance and Occurrence

Considering different situations, we have noticed several words have occurred at different positions in the tweets. Identifying the most popular tokens from the dataset helps to analyze the impact of those tokens on the tweet. The frequency of each token has been found from the obtained list of most popular Covid-19 exclusive words. After finding the word relevance count, the probability of recurrence has been calculated as an occurrence score for each word based on the total of 521,891 words from the dataset.

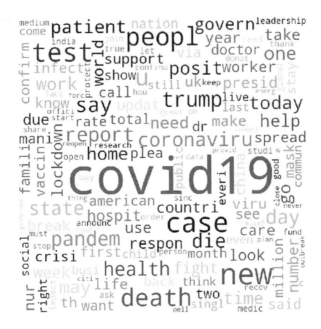

Figure 8.4 Some popular Covid-19-specific tokens from the Covid-19 dataset.

Table 8.3 Relevance and occurrence of most frequent Covid-19 exclusive words.

	Words	Relevance	Occurrence
1	covid19	137,911	0.264252
2	case	18,084	0.034651
3	test	16,645	0.031894
4	new	16,323	0.031277
5	people	15,913	0.030491

In Table 8.3 the relevance and occurrence of the most frequent Covid-19 specific words are presented,

$$P(W_i) = \frac{count(W_i)}{\sum_{i=0}^{n} count(W_{i=0}^n)} \tag{8.7}$$

8.4.5 Sentiment classification

In order to analyze the public opinions, Sentiment Analysis has been used. This contextual mining technique can use computational linguistics, Natural Language Processing (NLP), and text analysis. The social-media data can

Table 8.4 Sentiment-classification algorithm.

Sentiment-Classification Algorithm (compound_score, sentiment_score):	
1. for each id in TweetsDB.id:	
2. if tweet$_{id}$[compound_score] < 0:	
3. tweet$_{id}$[sentiment_score] = 0.0	# classified as Negative Tweets
4. if tweet$_{id}$[compound_score] > 0:	
5. tweet$_{id}$[sentiment_score] = 1.0	# classified as Positive Tweets
6. else:	
7. tweet$_{id}$[sentiment_score] = 0.5	# classified as Neutral Tweets
8. end	

be analyzed to retrieve subjective insights for classifying the text into *positive*, *neutral*, and *negative* classes. The sentiment polarity of each pre-processed tweet has been determined using the sentiment analyzer imported from the NLTK library.

In order to evaluate the *compound* sentiment polarity for each tweet, the polarity scores for the positive, neutral, and negative categories have been examined. On the basis of the compound sentiment polarities, the tweets have been classified into Positive, Neutral, and Negative. Furthermore, the sentiment ratings have been allocated for each tweet using the sentiment-classification algorithm presented in Table 8.4.

8.4.6 Sentiment modeling using bidirectional long short-term model

LSTM (Long Short-Term Model) networks have been seen to outperform similar neural-network models in classical textual sentiment analysis. In order to predict the sentiment ratings of Covid-19 tweets, we proposed a Bidirectional LSTM network based on the extracted features. The pre-processed tweets have been extracted along with their associated sentiment scores, i.e., 1.0 for *positive* and 0.0 for *negative* sentiments. Then, the X and y sets have been developed based on the pre-processed tweets along with the associated sentiment scores. The dataset has been divided in an 80:20 ratio, i.e., training sets (*X_train, y_train*) contain 80% of the total data and the remaining data are considered as the validation sets (*X_val, y_val*). The model generated a large number of Covid-19 specific tokens from the pre-processed corpus. We have used *word2vec* to convert these words into word vectors considering the vector length as 200 for each collected token from

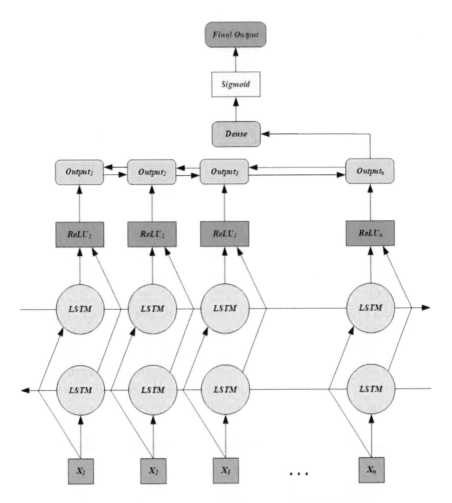

Figure 8.5 Graphical representation of Bidirectional LSTM model.

a sentence. The *X_train* and *X_val* sets have been scaled and restructured based on the evaluated word vectors. Finally, the proposed network takes the word vectors and the respective sentiment scores as the model input of the initial layer for training purpose. Fig. 8.5 shows the system architecture of the Bidirectional LSTM model.

The *Bidirectional* LSTM model along with the *Dense* layers has been developed based on the *TensorFlow* framework and *Keras* library. The five-layered model along with two outline activation functions has been trained for 30 epochs. The model has been associated with other training parameters, optimizer, accuracy, and loss. The *ReLU* (Rectified Linear Unit)

Table 8.5 Training and validation accuracy vs. loss using Bi-LSTM network.

Epochs	Train Loss	Train Accuracy	Val Loss	Val Accuracy
1st	57.48%	68.97%	51.97%	73.15%
5th	36.00%	83.38%	37.58%	82.62%
10th	27.76%	87.77%	34.46%	84.86%
15th	21.40%	90.85%	36.81%	86.13%
20th	16.69%	93.03%	41.97%	86.16%
25th	13.02%	94.74%	44.46%	87.06%
30th	10.39%	**95.87%**	50.84%	**87.08%**

Table 8.6 Confusion Matrix.

Predicted		Actual	
		Positive	*Negative*
	Positive	12,926 (TP)	1903 (FP)
	Negative	1932 (FN)	12,818 (TN)

activation function has been used for the first three *Dense* layers, which contain 128, 64, and 32 neurons, respectively. Finally, we have used the *Sigmoid* activation function for the final *Dense* layer, with 2 neurons. Throughout the training phase, we considered the batch size of the proposed deep network as 32 and verbose as 2. In order to analyze the model performance on the Covid-19 data, the accuracy vs. loss during training and validation phases are presented in Table 8.5 for some epochs.

The model has performed well on the respective dataset and achieved the training and validation accuracy of 95.87% and 87.08%, respectively. Fig. 8.6 represents the graphical plot based on the percentage of accuracy vs. loss during the execution of training and validation phases for the Bidirectional LSTM model.

Considering the performance of the model from the figure, we found that the major variance of loss is visible among the training and validation epochs. This represents relatively low model overfitting, which can be explained by the fact that the various tweet-collection parameters vary for the different times during the tweet-collection period. The confusion matrix and classification report in Tables 8.6 and 8.7 represent the differences between the actual and predicted tweets for the different sentiment categories.

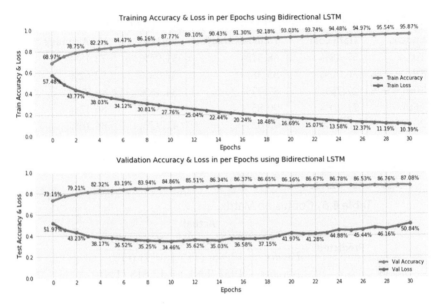

Figure 8.6 Performance analysis of the proposed Bidirectional LSTM model on the Covid-19 data.

Table 8.7 Classification Report.

	Precision	Recall	F1-Score	Support
Positive (1.0)	0.87	0.87	0.87	14829
Negative (0.0)	0.87	0.87	0.87	14750
Avg. / Total	0.87	0.87	0.87	29579

8.5 Benchmark comparison of recent NLP-based experiments on Covid-19

Here, we demonstrate performance comparisons with some recent experiments on Covid-19 using different machine-learning and deep neural-network models along with any baseline algorithm(s). Our main intention for this analysis is to identify the comparative accuracy measurements on sentiment prediction achieved by other models with similar large-scale textual data. In Table 8.8 we present some comparisons of prediction accuracy achieved by various models we identified throughout the survey.

From the analysis, we found that our proposed evolutionary classification-based Bidirectional LSTM neural-network model performs better than different State-of-the-Art machine-learning and deep neural-network models, but also achieved slightly lower accuracy on validation data than some

Table 8.8 Performance comparison between different ML or DNN models on large-scale Covid-19 data.

Machine-Learning or Deep Neural-Network Models	Overall Sentiment Prediction Accuracy
Deep RNN Model [42]	76.71%
LSTM on Chinese Weibo message [46]	78.00%
SVM w. Gaussian Membership-based Fuzzy logic [41]	79.00%
Logistic Regression w. trigrams + Tf-Idf [41]	81.00%
LDA + Deep LSTM [38]	81.15%
Random Forest [45]	82.20%
Bert on Chinese Weibo message [46]	83.00%
Bidirectional LSTM w. Evolutionary Classification (**Ours**)	**87.08%**
ERNIE on Chinese Weibo message [46]	88.00%
Bayesian Regression w. Tf-Idf [45]	89.40%
CNN w. *GloVe* Embeddings [35]	90.67%
Multilingual BERT on single-level classification [47]	95.62%

similar models. However, different datasets with several parameters have been used for many experiments selected for this comparative analysis. The performance of these ML or DNN models may vary due to different types of datasets with multiple parameters. ERNIE, a pre–trained model for sentiment prediction on the Chinese language [46] achieved 0.92% better accuracy than our proposed model. Our model achieved 2.32% and 3.59% lower accuracy than Bayesian Regression with Tf-Idf features [45] and Convolutional Neural Network with *GloVe* Embeddings [35]. The Multilingual BERT model on single-level classification achieved the highest sentiment prediction accuracy in our detailed comparative survey.

8.6 Discussion and future scope

The second wave of coronavirus infection is considered more dangerous than the first because it has already spread around the world. Almost two lakh new cases of Covid-19 were reported in India during April 2021.[4] Many countries have taken different strict measures to stop the spread of the new strain of coronavirus. Analyzing this situation, we hope that we will see much research work shortly as there has been tireless research based on Covid-19 over the last year and a half. We will also continue our relentless

[4] https://news.google.com/covid19/.

efforts to improve our research work. For our future work, we will try to implement the following to overcome certain limitations:

- A sentiment-relevance model will be developed strictly based on monolingual Covid-19 tweets using a classification algorithm. During the experiment, the extracted features will be used to develop the classification algorithm that will be further used to assign the sentiment scores to the tweets on the basis of the popularity of the Covid-19-specific words.
- As our large dataset consists of almost 235k tweets, if we classified all the tweets in *positive*, *negative*, and *neutral* sentiment classes then it would not have been a thorough observation of the dataset. To overcome this limitation in the future we want to perform fine-grained categorization of the tweets based on their refined sentiment scores.
- The dimension of daily transmission of Covid-19 worldwide has changed over time, and the variety of sensitive tweets from our dataset carries its message. We will take the initiative to identify the global sentiment trend regarding this pandemic by analyzing the daily average polarity rating.
- Although for handling local dependencies between neighboring words, the Bidirectional LSTM has proven powerful at the time of sentiment classification over large data it had to deal with excessive redundancy. Hence, instead of using the Bidirectional LSTM, we will try to develop a new deep hybrid model to achieve better accuracy in the sentiment evaluation.
- We will train our deep hybrid model using the tweets along with their updated sentiment scores for multimodal sentiment prediction to achieve better accuracy on the validation data.

8.7 Conclusion

In this chapter, we discussed in detail the various Covid-19-based NLP research works on different aspects that have taken place in recent times. We presented a detailed comparative study among several research studies distinguishing their approach, methodology, corpora, and primary contributions. We also propose experimentation keeping the focus primarily on finding the word attributes or features extracted from the Covid-19 tweets leading to the successful sentiment analysis of the same. The trend was analyzed for a group of most frequent words using the n-gram model and extracted the most relevant words as two main attributes of our dataset.

Then, using the sentiment analyzer, we calculated the sentiment ratings of the tweets collected during the period 19th April to 20th June 2020. Alongside, a model was developed to allocate the sentiment scores to the tweets considering their evaluated sentiment polarities and to classify all tweets into positive and negative classes based on their assigned sentiment ratings. The deep-learning-based Bidirectional LSTM model was trained using this categorized dataset consisting of vectorized tweets along with their corresponding sentiment ratings. We selected 80% of tweet samples randomly for the training phase and the remaining 20% of the data were used during the validation phase. After executing 30 epochs on 176,418 trainable parameters, the model achieved an accuracy of 87.08% on validation data. For the prospect, we want to extend this work for the enhanced semantics, fine-grained feature classifications, and sentiment trend shift concerning the time phase for training such tweets using a hybrid neural model for eradicating the overall local dependencies.

References

[1] S. Tuli, S. Tuli, R. Tuli, S.S. Gill, Predicting the growth and trend of COVID-19 pandemic using machine learning and cloud computing, Internet of Things (2020) 100222.
[2] A.D. Dubey, Twitter Sentiment Analysis during COVID19 Outbreak. Available at SSRN 3572023, 2020.
[3] S. Das, A.K. Kolya, G.S.T. Sense, Text mining & sentiment analysis of GST tweets by Naive Bayes algorithm, in: 2017 Third International Conference on Research in Computational Intelligence and Communication Networks (ICRCICN), IEEE, November 2017, pp. 239–244.
[4] P. Bhatia, Y. Ji, J. Eisenstein, Better document-level sentiment analysis from RST discourse parsing, arXiv preprint, arXiv:1509.01599, 2015.
[5] M. Araujo, J. Reis, A. Pereira, F. Benevenuto, An evaluation of machine translation for multilingual sentence-level sentiment analysis, in: Proceedings of the 31st Annual ACM Symposium on Applied Computing, April 2016, pp. 1140–1145.
[6] D. Jurafsky, Speech & Language Processing, Pearson Education India, 2000.
[7] R. Xia, F. Xu, J. Yu, Y. Qi, E. Cambria, Polarity shift detection, elimination and ensemble: a three-stage model for document-level sentiment analysis, Information Processing & Management 52 (1) (2016) 36–45.
[8] M.S. Mubarok, Adiwijaya, M.D. Aldhi, Aspect-based sentiment analysis to review products using Naïve Bayes, in: AIP Conference Proceedings, vol. 1867, AIP Publishing LLC, August 2017, p. 020060.
[9] B. Ma, H. Yuan, Y. Wu, Exploring performance of clustering methods on document sentiment analysis, Journal of Information Science 43 (1) (2017) 54–74.
[10] H. Peng, E. Cambria, X. Zou, Radical-based hierarchical embeddings for Chinese sentiment analysis at sentence level, in: The Thirtieth International Flairs Conference, May 2017.
[11] Y. Ma, H. Peng, T. Khan, E. Cambria, A. Hussain, Sentic LSTM: a hybrid network for targeted aspect-based sentiment analysis, Cognitive Computation 10 (4) (2018) 639–650.

[12] B.S. Rintyarna, R. Sarno, C. Fatichah, Evaluating the performance of sentence level features and domain sensitive features of product reviews on supervised sentiment analysis tasks, Journal of Big Data 6 (1) (2019) 1–19.

[13] X. Hu, L. Tang, J. Tang, H. Liu, Exploiting social relations for sentiment analysis in microblogging, in: Proceedings of the Sixth ACM International Conference on Web Search and Data Mining, February 2013, pp. 537–546.

[14] H. Lee, Y. Han, K. Kim, K. Kim, Sentiment analysis on online social network using probability model, in: Proceedings of the Sixth International Conference on Advances in Future Internet, November 2014, pp. 14–19.

[15] P. Fornacciari, M. Mordonini, M. Tomaiuolo, Social network and sentiment analysis on Twitter: towards a combined approach, in: KDWeb, September 2015, pp. 53–64.

[16] P. Zhou, Z. Qi, S. Zheng, J. Xu, H. Bao, B. Xu, Text classification improved by integrating bidirectional LSTM with two-dimensional max pooling, arXiv preprint, arXiv:1611.06639, 2016.

[17] C. Baecchi, T. Uricchio, M. Bertini, A. Del Bimbo, A multimodal feature learning approach for sentiment analysis of social network multimedia, Multimedia Tools and Applications 75 (5) (2016) 2507–2525.

[18] C. Baziotis, N. Pelekis, C. Doulkeridis, DataStories at SemeVal-2017 task 4: deep LSTM with attention for message-level and topic-based sentiment analysis, in: Proceedings of the 11th International Workshop on Semantic Evaluation (SemEval-2017), August 2017, pp. 747–754.

[19] Y. Yang, J. Eisenstein, Overcoming language variation in sentiment analysis with social attention, Transactions of the Association for Computational Linguistics 5 (2017) 295–307.

[20] B. Nakisa, M.N. Rastgoo, A. Rakotonirainy, F. Maire, V. Chandran, Long short term memory hyperparameter optimization for a neural network based emotion recognition framework, IEEE Access 6 (2018) 49325–49338.

[21] L. Gong, H. Wang, When sentiment analysis meets social network: a holistic user behavior modeling in opinionated data, in: Proceedings of the 24th ACM SIGKDD International Conference on Knowledge Discovery & Data Mining, July 2018, pp. 1455–1464.

[22] B. Dahal, S.A. Kumar, Z. Li, Topic modeling and sentiment analysis of global climate change tweets, Social Network Analysis and Mining 9 (1) (2019) 1–20.

[23] N.C. Dang, M.N. Moreno-García, F. De la Prieta, Sentiment analysis based on deep learning: a comparative study, Electronics 9 (3) (2020) 483.

[24] P. Chauhan, N. Sharma, G. Sikka, The emergence of social media data and sentiment analysis in election prediction, Journal of Ambient Intelligence and Humanized Computing (2020) 1–27.

[25] X. Ji, S.A. Chun, J. Geller, Monitoring public health concerns using Twitter sentiment classifications, in: 2013 IEEE International Conference on Healthcare Informatics, IEEE, September 2013, pp. 335–344.

[26] G. Coppersmith, M. Dredze, C. Harman, Quantifying mental health signals in Twitter, in: Proceedings of the Workshop on Computational Linguistics and Clinical Psychology: From Linguistic Signal to Clinical Reality, June 2014, pp. 51–60.

[27] D. Georgiou, A. MacFarlane, T. Russell-Rose, Extracting sentiment from healthcare survey data: an evaluation of sentiment analysis tools, in: 2015 Science and Information Conference (SAI), IEEE, July 2015, pp. 352–361.

[28] D.L. Mowery, Y.A. Park, C. Bryan, M. Conway, Towards automatically classifying depressive symptoms from Twitter data for population health, in: Proceedings of the Workshop on Computational Modeling of People's Opinions, Personality, and Emotions in Social Media (PEOPLES), December 2016, pp. 182–191.

[29] Y. Zhang, M. Chen, D. Huang, D. Wu, Y. Li, iDoctor: personalized and professionalized medical recommendations based on hybrid matrix factorization, Future Generation Computer Systems 66 (2017) 30–35.

[30] A. Vij, J. Pruthi, An automated psychometric analyzer based on sentiment analysis and emotion recognition for healthcare, Procedia Computer Science 132 (2018) 1184–1191.

[31] J. Lee, J. Kim, Y.J. Hong, M. Piao, A. Byun, H. Song, H.S. Lee, Health information technology trends in social media: using Twitter data, Healthcare Informatics Research 25 (2) (2019) 99.

[32] L. Abualigah, H.E. Alfar, M. Shehab, A.M.A. Hussein, Sentiment analysis in healthcare: a brief review, in: Recent Advances in NLP: The Case of Arabic Language, 2020, pp. 129–141.

[33] P. Arora, H. Kumar, B.K. Panigrahi, Prediction and analysis of COVID-19 positive cases using deep learning models: a descriptive case study of India, Chaos, Solitons and Fractals 139 (2020) 110017.

[34] I. Arpaci, S. Alshehabi, M. Al-Emran, M. Khasawneh, I. Mahariq, T. Abdeljawad, A.E. Hassanien, Analysis of Twitter data using evolutionary clustering during the COVID-19 pandemic, Computers, Materials & Continua 65 (1) (2020) 193–204.

[35] S. Das, A.K. Kolya, Predicting the pandemic: sentiment evaluation and predictive analysis from large-scale tweets on Covid-19 by deep convolutional neural network, Evolutionary Intelligence (2021) 1–22.

[36] M. Kabir, S. Madria, CoronaVis: a real-time Covid-19 tweets analyzer, arXiv preprint, arXiv:2004.13932, 2020.

[37] J. Samuel, G.G. Ali, M. Rahman, E. Esawi, Y. Samuel, Covid-19 public sentiment insights and machine learning for tweets classification, Information 11 (6) (2020) 314.

[38] H. Jelodar, Y. Wang, R. Orji, S. Huang, Deep sentiment classification and topic discovery on novel coronavirus or COVID-19 online discussions: NLP using LSTM recurrent neural network approach, IEEE Journal of Biomedical and Health Informatics 24 (10) (2020) 2733–2742.

[39] V.K.R. Chimmula, L. Zhang, Time series forecasting of COVID-19 transmission in Canada using LSTM networks, Chaos, Solitons and Fractals 135 (2020) 109864.

[40] N. Zheng, S. Du, J. Wang, H. Zhang, W. Cui, Z. Kang, T. Yang, B. Lou, Y. Chi, H. Long, M. Ma, Predicting COVID-19 in China using hybrid AI model, IEEE Transactions on Cybernetics 50 (7) (2020) 2891–2904.

[41] K. Chakraborty, S. Bhatia, S. Bhattacharyya, J. Platos, R. Bag, A.E. Hassanien, Sentiment Analysis of COVID-19 tweets by Deep Learning Classifiers—A study to show how popularity is affecting accuracy in social media, Applied Soft Computing 97 (2020) 106754.

[42] M.A. Al-Shaher, A hybrid deep learning and NLP based system to predict the spread of Covid-19 and unexpected side effects on people, Periodicals of Engineering and Natural Sciences (PEN) 8 (4) (2020) 2232–2241.

[43] J. Shuja, E. Alanazi, W. Alasmary, A. Alashaikh, Covid-19 open source data sets: a comprehensive survey, Applied Intelligence (2020) 1–30.

[44] R. Lamsal, Design and analysis of a large-scale COVID-19 tweets dataset, Applied Intelligence (2020) 1–15.

[45] J.C.M. Serrano, O. Papakyriakopoulos, S. Hegelich, NLP-based feature extraction for the detection of COVID-19 misinformation videos on Youtube, in: Proceedings of the 1st Workshop on NLP for COVID-19 at ACL 2020, July 2020.

[46] Q. Yang, H. Alamro, S. Albaradei, A. Salhi, X. Lv, C. Ma, M. Alshehri, I. Jaber, F. Tifratene, W. Wang, T. Gojobori, SenWave: monitoring the global sentiments under the Covid-19 pandemic, arXiv preprint, arXiv:2006.10842, 2020.

[47] I. Li, Y. Li, T. Li, S. Alvarez-Napagao, D. Garcia-Gasulla, T. Suzumura, What are we depressed about when we talk about COVID-19: mental health analysis on tweets using natural language processing, in: International Conference on Innovative Techniques and Applications of Artificial Intelligence, Springer, Cham, December 2020, pp. 358–370.

CHAPTER 9

Sentiment-aware design of human–computer interactions

How research in human–computer interaction and sentiment analysis can lead to more user-centered systems?

Souvick Ghosh
School of Information, San José State University, San José, CA, United States

Indeed, any interface that ignores a user's emotional state or fails to manifest the appropriate emotion can dramatically impede performance and risks being perceived as cold, socially inept, untrustworthy, and incompetent.

Brave & Nass, 2009, p. 54

9.1 Introduction and definitions

Human–computer Interaction (HCI) explores the design of interfaces that allow human users to interact with computational systems and applications. By investigating the user behavior and modes of interaction, research in HCI attempts to develop an understanding of system features and characteristics that provide maximum user satisfaction. User satisfaction could result from a number of factors including but not limited to efficiency, effectiveness, ease of use, helpfulness, and novelty of the system.

Sentiment Analysis, on the other hand, is the process of determining the mood, emotion, or sentiment of an individual. While literature in sentiment analysis uses the above terms interchangeably, prior research [32] has suggested that the three terms could be differentiated based on the duration and direction of manifestation. Moods are long term and could last for hours or days, while emotions are more transcendental and may only last for seconds. Emotions are circumstantial and could result from personal experience, interactions, or situations. Moods may be a culmination of several emotions directed at different subjects or originating from multiple instances. Sentiments, however, are more directional. A person may develop a feeling towards an object or another person and these feelings

Computational Intelligence Applications for Text and Sentiment Data Analysis
https://doi.org/10.1016/B978-0-32-390535-0.00014-8

could develop over long periods of time and may persist throughout the lifetime of the user. Automatic sentiment analysis – which computer scientists are interested in – attempts to compute this feeling (also called opinion or attitude) that a person has towards another person, entity, topic, or object. These feelings explain why we love certain products and individuals and hate some others.

In the next section, we will look at the symbiotic relationship between HCI and sentiment analysis, and for the rest of this chapter, we will look at different ways in which we can develop more sentiment-aware systems by combining research in both of these areas.

9.2 Relationship between HCI and sentiment analysis

Humans are emotional beings. Any interaction between the user and the environment is not devoid of emotion. Computing interfaces are artifacts that are present in the environment and allow users to accomplish specific tasks (or goals). The social and cultural aspects of the interaction influence how the users feel, how they behave, and how they perceive the interface. In the early years of Human–Computer Interaction (HCI) design, the focus was on system efficiency, task completion, and cost effectiveness. The end-users were often forgotten or pushed to the background. The users – who are emotional beings – were expected to "discard their emotional selves to work efficiently and rationally with computers" [3, p. 54]. The limitations of computing and the inability to collect user feedback on a large scale contributed to human–system interactions being reduced to cognitively simple and devoid of emotions.

The advancement of machine learning has also provided an added impetus to research in sentiment analysis. However, most new and emerging technologies relying on sentiment analysis also have a steep learning curve. While effective interface design could mitigate some usability complexities, machine-learning research has traditionally lacked innovation in designing interfaces [39]. The end-user often rejects new technology with a poor interface design. To overcome this, we need to sensitize the user to the affordances and complexities of the newer technology. The process may include collecting feedback from the users, testing out design prototypes, and creating a dialog between the designers, developers, and the end-users.

Over the last few decades, the expectations from computers have changed, and user satisfaction has become an essential aspect of system design. The ubiquity of mobile devices and high-speed wireless connectivity has created a seamless integration of computing devices in everyday life. Applications support users in finding information on the Web, making dinner reservations, or making travel arrangements. Conversational agents are being used in healthcare, banking, and schools. In other words, the role of systems evolved, and the need for effective human–computer interaction has become more critical than ever. A recent study by Yang et al. [39] reported that a broad overlap of HCI and sentiment-analysis research could be found in intelligent user interfaces, user modeling, recommender systems, social networks, and affective computing.

As HCI strives to match the advanced computing systems, there is a growing awareness that human emotions can play an active role in how such interactions are implemented. Some of these changes came from a better understanding of how emotions work. However, designers also realized that if an interface – voice-based or graphical – ignores the emotional state of the user and reacts in a cold, socially inept way, the user may be unsatisfied and reject the interface. Therefore, there is a strong correlation between how the system behaves and the user's perception of the system's performance and effectiveness. However, the wheels do not need to be reinvented on all sides. By recognizing the interdisciplinary nature of the problem and leveraging the findings in Machine Learning, Human–computer Interaction, Psychology, Cognitive Science, we could fast track the development of socio-affective computing. The advances in sentiment analysis and HCI can reinforce each other and create a symbiotic relationship between them, thereby creating more user-friendly system interfaces.

As HCI designers became aware of the importance of emotion in their design, they also began to distinguish the differences between users' emotions and sentiments. "While emotions and moods are fleeting—emotions last only seconds and moods last for hours or even days—sentiments can persist indefinitely and are thus responsible for guiding our propensities to seek out or avoid particular objects and situations. In this sense, sentiments are of critical importance for HCI because they motivate users to return to particular software products or Websites" [3]. This newly understood relationship between good design and sentiment led to a need for a greater understanding of how to measure and analyze sentiment in ways that could support HCI. In the following sections, we discuss emotional intelligence and the possible ways of developing sentiment-aware interfaces. We will look at theoretical underpinnings and algorithmic developments and highlight the challenges and directions of research.

9.3 Emotional intelligence

When users interact with most computing systems, they do not expect any emotion from the systems. The system-level interaction is without empathy, consideration, thoughtfulness, or remorse. Let us look at some examples.

1. Example 1:

   Tim composed a text or email message on his phone. Right before he hit send, the application crashed without sending the message or saving it. Once the application restarts, it does not give Tim any feedback or option to resume. Instead, it expects Tim to accept the glitch as if nothing wrong has happened.

   (Lack of remorse)

2. Example 2:

   Susanne's grandmother died, and she is looking for funeral dresses. The chatbot asks her the occasion, which Susanne clarifies. The next thing the chatbot does is suggest clothing ideas from bridesmaid collections.

   (Lack of empathy)

3. Example 3:

   John starts talking to his voice-based personal assistant about his health condition. The assistant fails to return relevant information. John decides to explain his situation in more detail, but the system cuts him off midway and starts providing irrelevant information.

   (Lack of communication etiquette)

The above examples may be hypothetical, but how many times have we encountered interfaces that are emotionless, and our encounter with the system leaves such a bad impression that we never go back to the system again. In the words of Soleymani et al. [32], "automatic sentiment analysis is the computational understanding of one's position, attitude or opinion towards an entity, person or topic." Research has also revealed that people experience at least one emotion 90% of the time [34]. Since sentiment can be used to influence user's interactions with others and their surroundings, sentiment analysis has great potential to improve the interaction between the user and any system.

Another important aspect of human interactions with computers is the task-based or goal-oriented nature of it. The user may be searching for information, operating smart devices, taking notes, writing documents, or composing music. Even casual chitchats, which may not have any specific goals, are motivated by loneliness, a desire for companionship, or novelty. As such, the user expects the computer to help him achieve those goals. The role of the interface is critical, as it can account for the success or failure of the interaction. By evaluating the user's emotions at different stages of the interaction, the interface could modify its behavior accordingly and communicate to pacify (in the case of a system-level error), encourage (if the user is struggling), or empathize (if the user is in a state of grief or stress) with the user. The assistance offered by the interface need not be targeted only toward the goal. It could be psychological too, where the user perceives the system as a friend and values it enough to use it in the future [3,14,28].

Although we argue how emotional intelligence is important while designing interactive systems, displaying the nuances of human emotion is a difficult task for an artificially intelligent system. However, research in sentiment analysis suggests that a system can display "emotion" (or what a human user would perceive as emotion) in two steps. First, the system should be able to accurately identify the emotion (Emotion Detection) being displayed by the user. The emotion-detection process can be done gradually as the interaction progresses. Once the system is sufficiently confident about user sentiment, the second step would be to modify its responses, take the user sentiment into account, and adjust the response to provide maximum satisfaction to the user (Emotion Expressiveness).

9.4 Sentiment-aware conversational systems

In the previous section, we argued how emotional intelligence has become important while designing interactive systems. This came in two forms – emotion detection and emotion expressiveness. For a system to connect to the users on an emotional level, it has to recognize the user's mood, the user's emotional state, and the sentiment expressed during each interaction (which could be speech utterances, text responses, or facial expressions). This section will focus on conversational interfaces, which allow the user to talk to (e.g., personal assistants) or text (e.g., chatbots) the system. These interactions happen over multiple turns, in natural language, and, therefore, are called conversational. The user can perform simple tasks by talking, find out relevant information about a topic, or engage in casual chit-chats.

Research [9] has shown that if the users are not satisfied with the performance of a conversational agent, they use more negative words to display their frustration and anger. This is common for any natural language interaction – even for human–human – where emotions play an integral part in the communication experience. For a sentiment-aware system, this would involve processing the human-emotional symbols in real-time and responding with empathy and discretion to create a more engaging and effective conversation and improve the user experience. The analysis need not be based on text alone but could include multimodal signals like voice (modulation and acoustic features) and video (gaze detection and facial expression).

One of the more recent developments in conversational systems has happened in the form of embodied conversational agents (ECA). An ECA is a conversational agent that is not limited to voice or text but comes with an artificially generated face and body (or in the form of an avatar). What sets an ECA apart is its ability to display human-like facial expressions, gestures, and body language while interacting with the user. Human–human conversations involve both verbal and non-verbal cues [20] – along with copresence – therefore, an ECA can engage in more realistic conversations with human users.

In a human–human interaction, the participants nod their heads to indicate listening and use eye-gaze variations and brow behavior to display emotions. Humans also use hand gestures and intonations to assert importance and assign sentiment to different parts of the dialog [10]. The multimodal nature of ECA makes it possible to exploit backchanneling [4,8,19] and turn taking, which are two important aspects of human conversations.

Fig. 9.1 presents Maslow's five-tiered hierarchy of needs, which suggests that basic human needs must be satisfied before we attend to higher-order needs [11,12]. An emotionally intelligent system must be able to detect when the user is facing a threat to his physiological needs (which could be as severe as looking for food stamps or homeless shelters or searching for the nearest restaurant) and safety needs (requesting an ambulance, emergency care, or law enforcement). These are low fault-tolerance services that the system should prioritize over everything else. However, the user may feel lonely and need the system to be the listener and provide company (psychological needs). In such cases, the goal of the system would be to display empathy and prolong the conversation. Users also love the feeling of accomplishment (esteem needs) and are offended when the system actions make the user look incompetent or inefficient. Any threat to these needs makes the user assess the system negatively.

Next, I would like to highlight some of the properties that a sentiment-aware conversational agent should have. The properties are presented as follows:

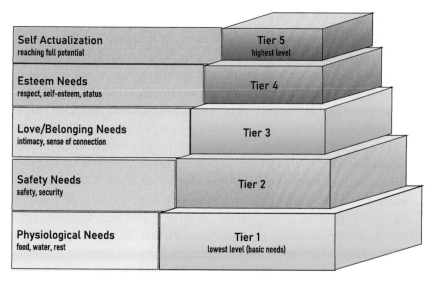

Maslow's Hierarchy of Needs

Figure 9.1 Maslow's Hierarchy of Needs [11].

- **Personality**:

  The system should have a personality of its own. HCI designers use the concept of persona, a hypothetical end-user of the product being designed. This concept could be extended to conversational agents too. Ideally, the agent should have multiple personalities for the user to choose from. The different personalities would result in richer dialogs suited to the current mood of the user. The personality becomes more important for embodied conversational agents who come with a face or avatar. The user can choose the face, the voice, and the personality type.

- **Mixed Initiative**:

  While the agent should be proactive and assist the users with their tasks, users prefer control over the task. For an information system, it could be selecting the query keywords or the source of information. Brave and Nass [3] pointed out that system helpfulness and ease-of-use are more important for new users of a system. Experienced users, on the other hand, prefer the system to be more efficient and aesthetically appealing.

- **Empathy**:
  According to Nickerson et al. [23], empathy is the capability to project our feelings onto someone else. While modeling empathy is a challenging task, some simple strategies should help the agent be perceived as an empathetic being. Empathy increases user engagement and makes the agent more likable. Yalçın [38] proposed a hierarchical model of empathy with three levels – communication competence, affect regulation, and cognitive mechanisms. Looije et al. [17] proposed three dimensions of empathy: complimentary, attentive, and compassionate. Any conversational agent should perfect the lower levels before attempting higher-order empathetic responses. The simplest form of empathy function is to listen to the speaker attentively. The next stage is to mirror the sentiment of the conversational partner. More complex forms of empathy would be to display concern, counter negative emotions with positive or motivational responses, and manipulate the sentiment in the best interests of the conversational partner [6,35].

- **Attentive**:
  Like any real-time system, conversational agents should be attentive to the changes in user sentiments and should pick up cues proactively. For example, if the users are bored or inattentive, they may perceive the system negatively. The agent should alter the prosodic features to capture the attention of the user. It could also change the topic – focusing on trending news items or those from the user's list of interests – during chit-chats to make the conversation more interesting.

- **Feedback**:
  Norman [24] highlighted that the users prefer feedback from any interface, which makes them aware that the system received their command (or input) and is processing it. Feedback could be visual (e.g., clicking a button on the chat interface turns it green, thinking face for an embodied conversational agent) or audio (e.g., the system tells the user that it is looking for the information). An ideal interface should never leave the user in a state of uncertainty or make them think (more cognitive load) more than necessary [15].

- **Reinforce Positive Emotions**:
  When the users are happy or excited about the system, they ignore the flaws and focus on the positive aspects of the system performance. A conversational agent should reinforce these positive emotions whenever possible (e.g., show excitement when the user does and be happy when the user feels happy). For negative emotions, the agent should

empathize with or calm down the user. Light attempts at humor [22] or narrating relatable stories could also be helpful in certain situations.

- **Performance Assessment and Reporting**:
  The system should break a task into smaller sub-tasks and assess if it has fulfilled all of them. This would allow the system to acknowledge failure and allow the user to suggest alternate strategies. A more advanced system would dynamically adapt to changing sub-goals and recommend actions to the user.

9.5 Methodological approaches

For a user, his context is built around his idea of self (opinion of oneself) and the world around him. This may depend on the social and cultural background of the user. For an agent to determine the context, it needs to identify the topic of conversation and personalize it based on the user's background. It depends on the context of use, which could be the time and location of the interaction, the device being used, and the environment. Since user–agent interactions are often goal oriented, negative emotions affect the user's perception of system performance and reduce user satisfaction. Based on appraisal theory, the overall interaction should enable the user to achieve his goals, and for each interaction, the user's emotion should guide the agent's actions.

Before we look into the various ways of detecting and expressing sentiment, we must understand the complexities of human emotions and the language we use to express them. For humans, language is a way of communicating and expressing ourselves. Our words have underlying emotions that are abstract and often hedged. We do not display what we feel and do not say what we think. Also, we do not express emotions only through words or in writing. It could be facial expressions, nodding of the head, sweating, stammering, or shaking. Fear is hard to differentiate from anger, and happiness is similar to love. While binary (positive and negative) or tertiary (positive, negative, and neutral) classification of sentiment polarity is more straightforward, it is challenging to develop a nuanced understanding of human emotions. Emotions help us to bond, and it is a part of who we are. Our entire persona and social character are built around how we express our emotions.

Therefore, to build sentiment-aware conversational agents, we have to consider multiple modalities and different categories of data (see Fig. 9.2).

Imagine your professor speaking from the podium or an actor delivering his lines. A human speaker monitors his listeners to detect cues of boredom, excitement, or any other affective state. Likewise, when interacting with a conversational agent, a user looks for a similar experience, even if unconsciously. For an agent to be perceived as helpful, as a friend, or an engaging conversational partner, the agent must detect and express emotions. Research in this domain has been continuously evolving to make agents more effective and sentiment detection more accurate. For sentiment detection, the choice of algorithm and method will depend on the following factors:

1. The type of data collected for analysis.

   The agent has to use multiple modalities of data, which could include audio (or voice dialogs), video (facial expressions of the user), and text (dialog or chat transcripts). Different categories of data may also be available, for example, brain signals captured using an electroencephalograph (EEG) device, physiological signals like blood pressure, heart rate, or muscle tension (using an electromyography device) [3], and facial data captured using brow, lip, or nose movements, eye gaze, or pupil dilation. The physiological and facial features are crucial discriminators for sentiments like anger, fear, and happiness. To personalize the responses to the user, the agent may also consider social media or other publicly available data to develop a short- and long-term understanding of the user and the context of interaction. This is similar to a human–human conversation, where our knowledge of the conversational partner contextualizes the discussion.

2. How the raw data is processed and features are extracted.

   Although different modalities of raw data may be available, it is also important to determine how the data is processed and more advanced features. When audio is transcribed to text, it is important to note how utterances are identified and separated. Also, acoustic features like pitch and amplitude are indicators of the expressed sentiment [2,3,31]. The audio or video data could also be analyzed to identify paralinguistic cues like laughter, sarcasm, pauses, or disfluencies.

3. The quality of the annotations for the gold-standard data.

   Any supervised learning algorithm depends on the quality of the gold-standard training data. This, in turn, depends on the number of annotators used, their familiarity with the subject matter, and the inter-annotator agreement.

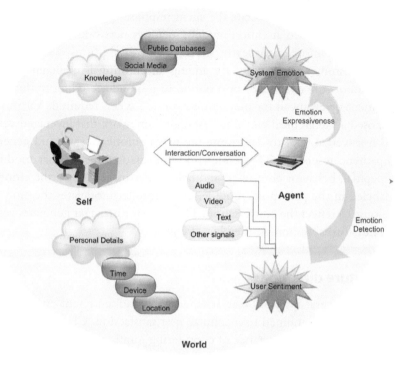

Figure 9.2 Sentiment-Aware Agent–User Interaction.

4. The categories of sentiment used.

Binary classification of sentiment is easier than tertiary, which in turn is an easier task when compared to the fine-grained classification of sentiments (e.g., anger, fear, sadness, joy, surprise, disgust).

The automatic analysis of sentiment could be based on lexicons (presence of positive or negative words), sentiment cues (hashtags, emojis), or underlying word meanings (embeddings) [25]. The keyword-based approaches construct dictionaries (or polarity lexicons) like SentiWordNet [1], WordNet Affect [33], or LIWC [26]. On the other hand, learning models using word embeddings – like GloVe [27], Word2Vec [21], or BERT [7] – aim to capture the sentiment by training on large corpora. Traditional supervised models like Support Vector Machines, Naive Bayes, and Random Forest have been used extensively for sentiment-detection purposes. Recently, end-to-end models and multi-head transformer architectures have shown commendable performance while detecting sentiment [16,29,37]. Fine-tuned BERT models have also been used to predict the users' personality and generate the agent responses [13]. Some of the other research studies used attention models, memory networks, adversarial networks, and reinforcement learning [18]. Feine et al. [9] used chat texts to predict customer satisfaction. By adding an emotional-intelligence module, chatbots can adapt the conversation to respond according to the user's sentiment or even call for human intervention when required. Yalçın [38] proposed a hierarchical empathy-response framework that leveraged verbal and non-verbal cues to determine the user's emotional state and generate empathetic responses. The framework consists of three distinct modules: perceptual, behavior controller, and behavior manager. Once the emotion is labeled in the perceptual module, the controller modulates the empathy response to reflect the conversation. The behavior manager generates verbal and non-verbal responses. (See Fig. 9.2.)

9.6 Future directions

There are several application areas where HCI and sentiment-analysis techniques can be combined to maximize user satisfaction. Clavel and Callejas [5] highlight "the importance of considering jointly sentiment analysis and dialog modeling" [5, p. 87] through their museum conversational agent. As the visitors view the different pieces of art in the museum, the agent gauges the interest of the visitors. It identifies the art pieces that the visitor appreciates and starts a conversation around that artifact. In this scenario, the agent is not only determining the visitor's sentiment (likes and dislikes expressed towards artistic objects) but generating dialogs to keep the user engaged (and entertained!). The authors also suggested using a conversational agent to train job seekers for interviews. Another application area is customer service, where the customer rarely completes the satisfaction surveys. Such surveys are biased and mundane and fail to elicit user feedback. Feine et al. [9] developed customer-service chatbots that detect the happiness or the frustration of the customer through analysis of the chat text. Since humans express their sentiments while talking and writing, processing the text (or transcripts) allows the system to determine the customer's emotional state and satisfaction level. Similarly, sentiments could be assessed for various human–computer interfaces – determining voter inclinations, stock-market predictions, and movie reviews. Sentiment-aware interfaces could also be useful in education where the system can assess the students' engagement and participation levels. Such systems should help with student success and course design, delivery, and evaluation. Similarly, consumer brands could monitor customer satisfaction and brand perception by analyzing social-media conversations about the brand.

The next step would be to advance research on embodied conversational agents (ECA). Since embodied agents use a face and voice, the need for emotion awareness becomes exponentially greater. ECAs can be used for mental-health services where the risk and rewards are both high. Emotion expressiveness becomes crucial for user satisfaction and engagement, and a mismatch of emotion could trigger an immediate rejection of a service by the user. For example, consider Nora and ECA who can identify stress, anxiety, and depression in children who have suffered trauma [36]. Since Nora is used for trauma-informed care, it needs to identify signs of trauma and de-escalate the situation through emotion-regulation techniques. An ECA can help reduce the bottleneck in mental-health professions by acting as the first step in evaluation and emergency healthcare. ECAs could also be used to provide companionship to active adults [5,30] and help them deal with isolation.

9.7 Ethical considerations

However, future developments are not without challenges, both methodological and ethical. First, the users must be aware at all times of the categories of data that are being collected. Additionally, they should be informed about how the data will be processed and what possible insights could be generated. Emotions are very private feelings that the user may not want to disclose. Therefore, the users should have the option of opting out of any sentiment analysis. If an artificially intelligent system can access the hidden states of the user's emotion, then the user may feel vulnerable and betrayed. Such an invasion of privacy will violate the norms of trust and render the system unattractive. Similarly, should the agent manipulate the sentiment of the user? While it makes sense to cheer up the user who is feeling upset, how can the agent determine if the user would prefer being left alone? Also, users may exercise their right to be forgotten where the agent removes all collected data at the end of the user–system interaction. Finally, the system should be able to differentiate between right and wrong (is not that subjective?), legal and illegal (varies from one country to another), moral and immoral (subjective again). For example, if the user asks the agent about ways to kill himself, the agent should abstain from answering. Instead, it should evaluate the user for stress and call for help if required.

Methodologically, researchers should explore how to implement turn taking in user–system interaction. There is also the question of data sufficiency, or should I say feature sufficiency. How much data is enough? What are the features that should help us differentiate between the range of sentiments that human users display? Also, what should be the training data. A supervised learning model trained on social-media data may only represent extroverted users or those active on the social networks. Models trained on chat transcripts could pose threats to user privacy. Also, data tends to be biased towards the majority. Unfiltered human–human chats are also racist, sexist, and inappropriate for training. How can we remove offensive content and yet preserve the usefulness of the data? Finally, how could we preserve long-term context, and how can we encrypt the data to ensure maximum privacy and security of the stored data?

While these are some of the questions that will need to be debated and discussed by a multidisciplinary audience, the convergence of HCI and sentiment-analysis techniques opens up new research and development directions. The accelerated use of machine learning and other AI techniques in modern applications may make it possible for greater use of sentiment analysis in the designs of everyday computing interfaces. The relationship between HCI and sentiment analysis is likely to become stronger in the years to come. Sentiment analysis has evolved algorithmically over the last decade, but it is time to bring back the human in the loop for a better user experience.

References

[1] S. Baccianella, A. Esuli, F. Sebastiani, SentiWordNet 3.0: an enhanced lexical resource for sentiment analysis and opinion mining, in: LREC, 2010, pp. 2200–2204.

[2] G. Ball, J. Breeze, Emotion and personality in a conversational agent, in: J. Cassel, J. Sullivan, S. Prevost, E. Churchill (Eds.), Embodied Conversational Agents, 2000, pp. 189–219.

[3] S. Brave, C. Nass, Emotion in human–computer interaction, in: Human–Computer Interaction Fundamentals, vol. 20094635, CRC Press, Boca Raton, FL, USA, 2009, pp. 53–68.

[4] C. Goodwin, Conversational Organization: Interaction Between Speakers and Hearers, Academic Press, London, 1981.

[5] C. Clavel, Z. Callejas, Sentiment analysis: from opinion mining to human-agent interaction, IEEE Transactions on Affective Computing 7 (2015) 74–93.

[6] A. Coplan, P. Goldie, Empathy: Philosophical and Psychological Perspectives, Oxford University Press, 2011.

[7] J. Devlin, M.W. Chang, K. Lee, K. Toutanova, BERT: pre-training of deep bidirectional transformers for language understanding, arXiv preprint, arXiv:1810.04805, 2018.

[8] S. Duncan, Some signals and rules for taking speaking turns in conversations, Journal of Personality and Social Psychology 23 (1972) 283.

[9] J. Feine, S. Morana, U. Gnewuch, Measuring service encounter satisfaction with customer service chatbots using sentiment analysis, in: 14th Internationale Tagung Wirtschaftsinformatik (WI2019), 2019, p. 1115.

[10] J. Gratch, J. Rickel, E. André, J. Cassell, E. Petajan, N. Badler, Creating interactive virtual humans: some assembly required, IEEE Intelligent Systems 17 (2002) 54–63.

[11] S. Ghosh, Designing human-computer conversational systems using needs hierarchy, School of Information Student Research Journal 11 (2021) 3.

[12] S. Ghosh, S. Ghosh, "Do users need human-like conversational agents?" - Exploring conversational system design using framework of human needs, in: DESIRES, 2021, pp. 117–127.

[13] S.S. Keh, I. Cheng, et al., Myers-Briggs personality classification and personality-specific language generation using pre-trained language models, arXiv preprint, arXiv: 1907.06333, 2019.

[14] J. Klein, Y. Moon, R.W. Picard, This computer responds to user frustration: Theory, design, and results, Interacting with Computers 14 (2) (Feb. 2002) 119–140, https:// doi.org/10.1016/S0953-5438(01)00053-4.

[15] S. Krug, Don't Make Me Think!: Web & Mobile Usability: Das Intuitive Web, MITP-Verlags GmbH & Co. KG, 2018.

[16] Z. Lin, P. Xu, G.I. Winata, F.B. Siddique, Z. Liu, J. Shin, P. Fung, CAiRE: an end-to-end empathetic chatbot, in: Proceedings of the AAAI Conference on Artificial Intelligence, 2020, pp. 13622–13623.

[17] R. Looije, M.A. Neerincx, F. Cnossen, Persuasive robotic assistant for health self-management of older adults: design and evaluation of social behaviors, International Journal of Human-Computer Studies 68 (2010) 386–397.

[18] Y. Ma, K.L. Nguyen, F.Z. Xing, E. Cambria, A survey on empathetic dialogue systems, Information Fusion 64 (2020) 50–70.

[19] R. Maatman, J. Gratch, S. Marsella, Natural behavior of a listening agent, in: International Workshop on Intelligent Virtual Agents, Springer, 2005, pp. 25–36.

[20] D. McNeill, Hand and Mind, De Gruyter Mouton, 2011.

[21] T. Mikolov, K. Chen, G. Corrado, J. Dean, Efficient estimation of word representations in vector space, arXiv preprint, arXiv:1301.3781, 2013.

[22] J. Morkes, H.K. Kernal, C. Nass, Effects of humor in task-oriented human-computer interaction and computer-mediated communication: a direct test of SRCT theory, Human-Computer Interaction 14 (1999) 395–435.

[23] R.S. Nickerson, S.F. Butler, M. Carlin, Empathy and knowledge projection, in: The Social Neuroscience of Empathy, 2009, pp. 43–56.

[24] D. Norman, The Design of Everyday Things, revised and expanded edition, Basic Books, 2013.

[25] A. Ortigosa, J.M. Martín, R.M. Carro, Sentiment analysis in Facebook and its application to e-learning, Computers in Human Behavior 31 (2014) 527–541.

[26] J.W. Pennebaker, M.E. Francis, R.J. Booth, Linguistic inquiry and word count: LIWC 2001, Mahway: Lawrence Erlbaum Associates 71 (2001) (2001) 2001.

[27] J. Pennington, R. Socher, C.D. Manning, GloVe: global vectors for word representation, in: Proceedings of the 2014 Conference on Empirical Methods in Natural Language Processing (EMNLP), 2014, pp. 1532–1543.

[28] R. Picard, Affective Computing, Massachusetts Institute of Technology, Cambridge, 1997.

[29] A. Radford, K. Narasimhan, T. Salimans, I. Sutskever, et al., Improving Language Understanding by Generative Pre-Training, OpenAI, 2018.

[30] L. Ring, B. Barry, K. Totzke, T. Bickmore, Addressing loneliness and isolation in older adults: proactive affective agents provide better support, in: 2013 Humaine Association Conference on Affective Computing and Intelligent Interaction, IEEE, 2013, pp. 61–66.

[31] K.R. Scherer, Vocal measurement of emotion, in: The Measurement of Emotions, Elsevier, 1989, pp. 233–259.

[32] M. Soleymani, D. Garcia, B. Jou, B. Schuller, S.F. Chang, M. Pantic, A survey of multimodal sentiment analysis, Image and Vision Computing 65 (2017) 3–14.

[33] C. Strapparava, A. Valitutti, et al., WordNet affect: an affective extension of WordNet, in: LREC, Citeseer, 2004, p. 40.

[34] D. Trampe, J. Quoidbach, M. Taquet, Emotions in everyday life, PLoS ONE 10 (12) (2015) e0145450.

[35] F.B. de Waal, S.D. Preston, Mammalian empathy: behavioural manifestations and neural basis, Nature Reviews. Neuroscience 18 (2017) 498.

[36] G.I. Winata, O. Kampman, Y. Yang, A. Dey, P. Fung, Nora the empathetic psychologist, in: Interspeech, 2017, pp. 3437–3438.

[37] T. Wolf, V. Sanh, J. Chaumond, C. Delangue, TransferTransfo: a transfer learning approach for neural network based conversational agents, arXiv preprint, arXiv:1901. 08149, 2019.

[38] Ö.N. Yalçın, Empathy framework for embodied conversational agents, Cognitive Systems Research 59 (2020) 123–132.

[39] Q. Yang, N. Banovic, J. Zimmerman, Mapping machine learning advances from HCI research to reveal starting places for design innovation, in: Proceedings of the 2018 CHI Conference on Human Factors in Computing Systems, 2018, pp. 1–11.

CHAPTER 10

Towards the analyzing of social-media data to assess the impact of long lockdowns on human psychology due to the Covid-19 pandemic

A. Chatterjee[a], B. Das[a], and A. Das[b]
[a]Techno College Hooghly, Kolkata, West Bengal, India
[b]RCCIIT, Kolkata, West Bengal, India

10.1 Introduction

Artificial Intelligence and Machine Learning are very useful in analyzing the mental frame of mind of a human being. Many research studies have been performed on this aspect and it has become one of the popular fields of research over time. Sentiment analysis and Emotion analysis are two very important tools that are using to understand the complex human mind and its nature currently.

Sentiment analysis is the computational treatment of human opinions, thinking, etc., whereas emotion analysis is more intense sentiment analysis, like happiness, sadness, anger, disgust, fear, surprise as per Ekman's Six basic emotions. A few of these sentiments can lead to depression sometimes. According to the WHO, depression is a common mental disorder. Globally, more than 264 million people of all ages suffer from depression. Depression is a leading cause of disability worldwide and is a major contributor to the overall global burden of disease. More women are affected by depression than men. The worst effects of depression can lead to suicide. There are effective psychological and pharmacological treatments for moderate and severe depression. Close to 800 000 people die due to suicide every year. According to the WHO official website, suicide is the second leading cause of death in 15–29-year olds. In our work, we will try to determine the various psychological effects on human beings that can lead to depression during lockdowns due to COVID19.

Computational Intelligence Applications for Text and Sentiment Data Analysis
https://doi.org/10.1016/B978-0-32-390535-0.00015-X

225

10.1.1 Major contribution of the chapter

This chapter helps to identify the different psychological disorders of a person and tries to determine the solution of the problem. It also tries to derive some kind of suggestive system for different segments of people like daily hawkers, businessmen and service holders, bloggers, social-media enthusiasts, students, teachers, celebrities, etc. It further subsegments the analysis based on gender, economic conditions, government or private employees, and final-year or pre-final-year students. Finally, it advises the counseling requirement to the person who is depressed or stressed or going through some psychological disorder due to these long lockdowns. In this way, this chapter helps to reduce the number of suicides due to various psychological disorders in this pandemic period.

10.1.2 Organization of the chapter

This chapter is divided into five major sections. In the first section we discuss the previous related studies. In the next section we depict how the data has been obtained from the social-media platform Twitter. The approach of our work is explained in the next section. The Algorithm of our work is presented and discussed in the following section. The final section presents the conclusion and future scope where we have tried to determine the probable future uplift on our work.

10.2 Related work

Depression analysis is a very common research area in recent years. In [1] the authors performed depression analysis of Bangla Social media. The authors used the LSTM-RNN model for their work and prepared a large dataset for this. Their results shows that high accuracy can be achieved for small datasets on complex psychological tasks like depression analysis by tuning a Deep Recurrent model. Real-time Tweeter-data analysis is performed in different research papers [2–6] to analyze the sentiments of the people to detect the cyberbullies in different languages, like French, Arabic, etc. In [7] the authors focused on mining tweets written in English to determine the people's thinking and interest about McDonalds or KFC in terms of good/bad reviews. In this work they used R language. In [8] real-time twitter data is categorized according to the sentiments. The work has been done in several stages and the processed tweets are matched with the existing bag of words (BoW) and are ranked as positive, negative, and neutral. In [9] opinion mining has been done on the 2019 Election in India by real-time twitter-data analysis. In [10] an automatic sentiment–extraction mechanism from twitter and news feeds was shown. In this paper, a Latent Semantic Analyzer extracted the most discussed topics and visualized them using a word-cloud method. The text data for classification of tweets that determines the state of the person according to the sentiments that is positive, negative, and neutral has been shown in [11]. Here, the authors have proposed the text representation, Term Frequency Inverse Document Frequency (tfidf), Keras embedding along with the machine-learning and deep-learning algorithms for classification of the sentiments. In our chapter we have used Word Clouds and TF-IDF (Term Frequency-Inverse Document Frequency) models by using the Python Language. Word Clouds (also known as wordle, word collage or tag cloud) are visual representations of words that give greater prominence to words that appear more frequently. On the other hand, the TF indicates the count of a word(t) in a corpus. As the corpus consists of several documents, each document and its words will have its own TF count (Eq. (10.1)). The IDF indicates the number of times a word(t) appears within a document (Eq. (10.2)). TF-IDF is performed for the word (t) in Eqs. (10.1) and (10.2). As per this technique the rarest word will contain the highest count/weight. In this chapter we have identified and analyzed the tweets related to depression, anxiety, suicidal thoughts due to long lockdowns and other related issues.

10.3 Data layout

Tweets done by users are accumulated on the basis of inputs identified by us in the formation of hashtags. The categorization of the tweets is completed by accumulating the tweets first. The accumulation process is done using twitter API and the API is accessed by using several key identifiers, like Consumer Key, Consumer Secret, Access Token, and Access Token Secret key to collect the tweets from different twitter accounts based on matched key words specified by us. Fig. 10.1 shows some of the raw tweets collected against different search key words by using twitter API. The tweets are presented with usernames and indicates whether it is a tweet or a retweeted tweet. The data is then used to compute the sentiments of the tweets. We have only considered the tweets with negative-sentiment polarity in our work.

Search Keyword= 'Pandemic'

RT @pmsariya007: Floods,earthquakes,economic crisis,people losing their jobs, taking down businesses,pandemic getting worse, bubonic plague...
RT @asap_locky: I hate this pandemic if I wanted to waste my early 20's I would have gotten married out of high school and never left my ho...
RT @_rahkiah_: I hate this pandemic, If I wanted to waste my early 20s I would of joined the military
RT @MiaFarrow: @realDonaldTrump Other than golfing, demolishing the bulwarks of our country, insulting fellow citizens, debasing the presi...
RT @SaraCarterDC: You should be ashamed. @JaniceDean is an amazing woman. She lost family due to this horrible pandemic. I follow her posts...
#2800gradepay_mphw_fhw_health_gujarat
MPHW/FHW of Gujarat haven't got any single holiday since this COVID Pandemic,... https://t.co/Sfj48jhNox
There are two COVID Americas. One hopes for an extension of federal unemployment and stimulus. The other is saving... https://t.co/VSqaGo2Twc
5/ Obviously I just left & waited, assuming the speaker would be fixed or other arrangements would be made to keep... https://t.co/ArizLCDEpi
RT @TedKessler1: I have some bad news about @QMagazine. The issue that comes out on July 28 will be our last. The pandemic did for us and t...
RT @GovLarryHogan: Nearly half of new cases belong to Marylanders in their 20s and 30s, and the positivity rate for Marylanders under 35 is...

Search Keyword= 'Suicide due to job loss'

RT @Prakash_mavchi: #ExamsincovidAsucide
In MP's Khandwa, 27 people committed suicide in one month due to #examsstress, financial crisis an...
#ExamsincovidAsucide
In MP's Khandwa, 27 people committed suicide in one month due to #examsstress, financial crisi... https://t.co/WkeOrmkY0Q
@dougducey Avoided the topic of mental health & addiction. You contributed to the stigma that costs lives. Relapse... https://t.co/sljGJ8oX1X
@bobsnee Duck and cover didn't lead to about 30,000 deaths due to delaying medical care, massive job loss, and an a... https://t.co/S0Syn96KpA
@archdelux1 @YangGanger @NPR_junky @CNN Victimhood at its finest. She fails to acknowledge the uptick in deaths fro...
https://t.co/ixijReGW9p

Search Keyword= 'Street hawkers'

@OlamideAdedeji Just drive around Lagos for 2hrs & pay attention to how we interact with each other. From drivers i...
https://t.co/Vq3weiSVxA
RT @KenMuokatene: Yesterday afternoon i left my office to walk around town past kimathi street, moi aven. Tom mboya street, river road , n...
Yesterday afternoon i left my office to walk around town past kimathi street, moi aven. Tom mboya street, river ro... https://t.co/9CtfjUw5qa
Extended lockdown make them again cut off payments.Who will compensate?Shopkeepers r not able to pay rent months.... https://t.co/JpB1H5XtPy

Figure 10.1 Sample Tweets.

$$TF(t) = \frac{\text{Number of times } t \text{ appears in a document}}{\text{Total number of terms in the document}} \qquad (10.1)$$

$$IDF(t) = \log_e\left(\frac{\text{Total number of documents}}{\text{Number of Documents with } t \text{ in it}}\right). \qquad (10.2)$$

10.4 Our approach

We show our approach in Fig. 10.2. First, the connection is established with the Twitter API. In the next step, lockdown-related Twitter data is extracted for a specific period by using different key words like suicide, anxiety, stress, job loss, Covid19, pandemic, lockdown, etc. (See Figs. 10.3 and 10.4.) Then, polarity classification is performed on the extracted data. Cleaning and preprocessing of the tweets are executed next. Cleaning of the unwanted characters such as HTML tags, punctuation marks, special characters, white spaces, etc., is performed. This step is known as Noise removal. Some words do not contribute much to the machine-learning model and are removed. The method is known as Stopword removal. Feature extraction using the TF-IDF algorithm has been done in the next step (Fig. 10.7). In this step we have segregated the corpora on the basis of search keywords. With this Term Frequency (TF) method we have computed the importance of each word. The approach is to count the

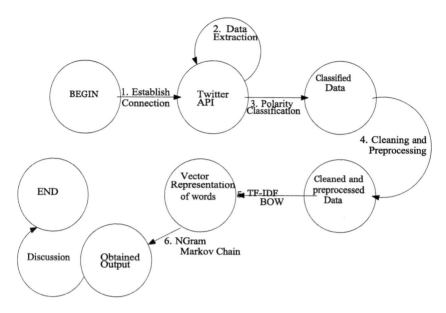

Figure 10.2 Our Methodology.

number of times a word appears in a document. Hence, the word's importance is directly proportional to its frequency. However, we also want to take into consideration how unique the words are, this method is called Inverse Document Frequency (IDF). Concurrently, we have applied the Bag of Words model to construct the vector. Hence, we have two vector representations for the same set of words belongs to a tweet. This method has resulted in the Word2Count Vector (Tables 10.1 and 10.2). The Bag of Words (BOW) model is used to preprocess the text. This keeps a count of the total occurrences of the most frequently used words. The same set of tweets has been considered in Tables 10.1 and 10.2 as in Fig. 10.7. On the other hand, the Ngram approach is conducted in this chapter to predict the related words in a corpus. This indicates the probability of having the word W_n after the sequence of words $W_1 ... W_{(n-1)}$. It can be written as $P(W_n|W_1 ... W_{(n-1)} = P(W_1 ... W_n)/P(W_1 ... W_{(n-1)}))$. From here, we have used the Markov Chain Assumption. A Markov chain is a sequence of random variables with the Markov property. The Markov assumption says the probability of a word depends only on the previous word. A first-order Markov chain considers the probability of a word following another one. A more realistic approach is to compute higher-order n-gram models. Here, we have used the higher-order Ngram Approach (Fig. 10.8) in this

TF-IDF Method
Search Key Word: suicide due to lockdown
Sample Tweets
0)Deaths from suicides and drug overdoses currently exceed deaths due to the COVID-19 virus
1)In Gandhinagar, capital of gujarat young man commit suicide yesterday due to job lost during lockdown
{'of', 'capital', 'suicide', 'yesterday', 'job', 'Deaths', 'virus', 'lockdown', 'deaths', 'during', 'currently', 'the', 'lost', 'man', 'and', 'gujarat', 'commit', 'overdoses', 'due', 'from'
'Gandhinagar,', 'suicides', 'young', 'drug', 'In', 'to'}
Output (TF)

	COVID-19	Deaths	Gandhinagar,	...	virus	yesterday	young
0	0.071429	0.071429	0.0000	...	0.071429	0.0000	0.0000
1	0.000000	0.000000	0.0625	...	0.000000	0.0625	0.0625

Output(IDF)

	COVID-19	Deaths	Gandhinagar,	...	virus	yesterday	young
0	0.021502	0.021502	0.000000	...	0.021502	0.000000	0.000000
1	0.000000	0.000000	0.018814	...	0.000000	0.018814	0.018814

TFXIDF

(0, 25)	0.2499024950406278
(0, 0)	0.2499024950406278
(0, 4)	0.2499024950406278
(0, 23)	0.2499024950406278
(0, 24)	0.1778076834486106
(0, 8)	0.1778076834486106
(0, 10)	0.2499024950406278
(0, 5)	0.2499024950406278
(0, 20)	0.2499024950406278
(0, 7)	0.2499024950406278
(0, 1)	0.2499024950406278
(0, 22)	0.2499024950406278
(0, 11)	0.2499024950406278
(0, 6)	0.4998049900813256
(1, 16)	0.2580914777342982 5
(1, 9)	0.2580914777342982 5
(1, 17)	0.2580914777342982 5
(1, 15)	0.2580914777342982 5
(1, 26)	0.2580914777342982 5
(1, 21)	0.2580914777342982 5
(1, 3)	0.2580914777342982 5
(1, 18)	0.2580914777342982 5
(1, 27)	0.2580914777342982 5
(1, 13)	0.2580914777342982 5
(1, 19)	0.2580914777342982 5
(1, 2)	0.2580914777342982 5
(1, 12)	0.2580914777342982 5
(1, 14)	0.2580914777342982 5
(1, 24)	0.1836342120806570 6
(1, 8)	0.1836342120806570 6

Figure 10.3 Feature Extraction using TF-IDF.

N gram Approach
Search Keyword: anxiety due to lockdown
Sample Tweet
Yesterday I was due to go to a do (without Teddy and wife) with some mates. I suffered an anxiety episode leading up to it, and couldn't force myself to go. I've not seen my friends socially for 5 months. Yeah. Lockdown is a piece of cake.

Out Put (Tri Gram):
('Yesterday', 'I', 'was') ('I', 'was', 'due') ('was', 'due', 'to') ('due', 'to', 'go') ('to', 'go', 'to') ('go', 'to', 'a') ('to', 'a', 'do') ('a', 'do', '(without') ('do', '(without', 'Teddy') ('(without', 'Teddy', 'and') ('Teddy', 'and', 'wife)') ('and', 'wife)', 'with') ('wife)', 'with', 'some') ('with', 'some', 'mates.') ('some', 'mates.', 'I') ('mates.', 'I', 'suffered') ('I', 'suffered', 'an') ('suffered', 'an', 'anxiety') ('an', 'anxiety', 'episode') ('anxiety', 'episode', 'leading') ('episode', 'leading', 'up') ('leading', 'up', 'to') ('up', 'to', 'it,') ('to', 'it,', 'and') ('it,', 'and', 'could') ('and', 'could', 'not') ('could', 'not', 'force') ('not', 'force', 'myself') ('force', 'myself', 'to') ('myself', 'to', 'go.') ('to', 'go.', 'I') ('go.', 'I', 'have') ('I', 'have', 'not') ('have', 'not', 'seen') ('not', 'seen', 'my') ('seen', 'my', 'friends') ('my', 'friends', 'socially') ('friends', 'socially', 'for') ('socially', 'for', '5') ('for', '5', 'months.') ('5', 'months.', 'Yeah.') ('months.', 'Yeah.', 'Lockdown') ('Yeah.', 'Lockdown', 'is') ('Lockdown', 'is', 'a') ('is', 'a', 'piece') ('a', 'piece', 'of') ('piece', 'of', 'cake')

Figure 10.4 Sample output of Ngram Approach.

chapter. The Markov Assumption is applied in this chapter to determine the intensity of the psychological problems of a person and to justify the need for counseling of that person. Finally, some of the most important key words found from different tweets have been presented by Construction of Word Clouds (Figs. 10.5 and 10.6) methods.

Table 10.1 Sample output 1-
Word2Count (BOW).

Key Word	W2C
and	1
covid	1
currently	1
deaths	2
drug	1
due	1
exceed	1
from	1
overdoses	1
suicides	1
the	1
to	1
virus	1

Table 10.2 Sample output 2-
Word2Count (BOW).

Key Word	W2C
capital	1
commit	1
down	1
due	2
gandhinagar	1
gujrat	1
in	1
job	1
lock	1
lost	1
man	1
of	1
suicide	1
to	2
yesterday	1
young	1

Figure 10.5 Word-Cloud Representations 1.

Figure 10.6 Word-Cloud Representations 2.

10.5 Algorithm

10.5.1 Algorithm for analyzing the impact of long lockdowns on human psychology

INPUT: *i*) Tweets (s_{tw}) of Negative Polarity (N_{pol}), *ii*) α = Set of Negative Polarity Key word N_{kw}

OUTPUT: User (U_{id}) need to take care

$S_{Tw} = s_{tw} \in N_{pol}$ and $\alpha = N_{kw}$

Compute, $W2C(S_{Tw})$ And $TFIDF(S_{Tw})$

if $W2C(T_{kw}) > \wedge TFIDF(T_{kw}) \geq f_{avg}$ **then**

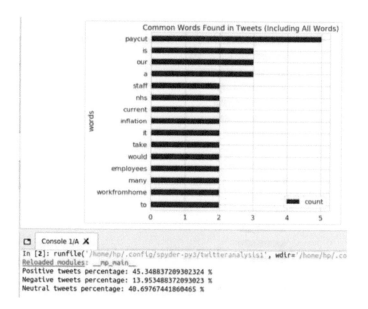

Figure 10.7 Sample Tweets with key word "paycut".

if $T_{kw} \in \alpha$ **then**

The U_{id} need to take care

else

Compute $MC(S_{Tw})$ and include Key word with N_{pol} into α

10.5.2 Discussion

In this chapter, we have gathered the tweets from different Twitter Handles by using different Python tools based on key words supplied by us. We have gathered the tweets based on different sections of people, like students, hawkers, businessmen, etc. We have considered the tweets only with negative polarity for our work. Hence, in this way we have been able to segregate those who are not negatively affected. We have created a set(α) of negative key words (N_{kw}) for our initial reference. We have computed BOW and TF-IDF on the selected tweet (S_{Tw}). Consider the Key word (T_{kw}) where the number of occurrences > 1 and the frequency of a Key word (f_k) ≥ average frequency (f_{avg}). The higher the number of occurrences and frequency indicates the importance of the words. Then, we check whether the word (T_{kw}) belongs to α or not. If it is found to be in

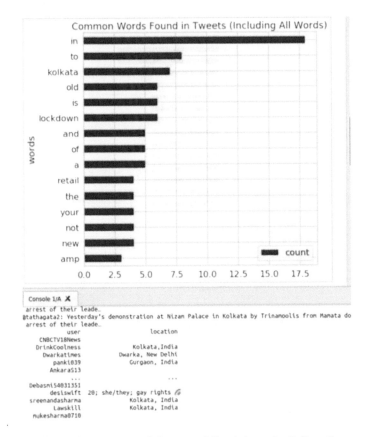

Figure 10.8 Sample Tweets with key word "Lockdown in Kolkata".

α then it indicates the User (U_{id}) of the tweet needs to take care and may need counseling also. If any of the above conditions were found to be false then we compute the Markov Chain (MC) on the tweet S_{Tw} to determine the next probable key word that may be entered by the user. If that word is found with negative polarity then we include that key word into set α. In this way the set α becomes a dynamic set of negative key words.

10.5.3 Performance analysis

Our method deals with different sections of people. We have tried to determine the emotional status of the people belonging to the different genders and professions. We have used several methods like TF–IDF, BOW, Ngram, Markov Chain, etc., for more accuracy.

Figure 10.9 Sample Tweets with Polarity.

10.5.4 A few findings

In Fig. 10.7 we have explored 5000 tweets with the key word "PAYCUT" and the results show that it is the most mentioned key word among all other words in the tweets. In Fig. 10.8 we have shown the location of the tweets along with the user names that has helped us to analyze the impact of lockdowns location-wise. In Fig. 10.9 we have shown the sentiment polarity of the key word "Lockdown in Kolkata" and found that 56% of the tweets are showing negative polarity. Here, we want to mention that all tweets have been collected during the period of 14th May, 2021 and 24th May, 2021 to emphasize the most current situation. We have found that people are not happy with the lockdown situation due to several reasons. The probable reasons that we found in our study are paycuts, job loss, price hikes, insecurity of jobs, financial instability, depression, etc. In Fig. 10.10 we have

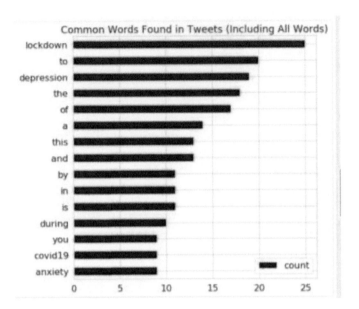

Figure 10.10 Correlation between Lockdown and Depression.

shown the correlation between the key words Lockdown and Depression, anxiety, etc., to focus on the negative effect of lockdowns.

10.6 Conclusion and future scope

In this work we have tried to determine the twitter handles with negative psychological thinking due to the long lockdowns. We have also determined some methods to identify the intensity of people's problems so that proper counseling measurement can be indicated. Here, we have also tried to identify the person according to their profession, gender, etc. This classification is performed based on the key word search from the twitter. However, in future we will try to classify the segments of the people based on some other factors, like on the degree of Social-Media usage time by a user, the number of followers of a user, etc. In this chapter we have only tried to measure the psychological effect of long lockdowns on human beings, but the methodology can be applied to identify other psychological problems due to any other issues in future apart from these lockdowns. In this work, we have not specified any particular age group also and that can be another effective approach of this work in the future. In this chapter we have not considered tweets written in other languages apart from English.

In the future we can try to identify the tweets written in other languages also to cover more users by our system. We can also try to extract automatic sentiment from news feeds along with the other social media also.

References

[1] A.H. Uddin, D. Bapery, A.S.M. Arif, Depression analysis from social media data in Bangla language using long short term memory (LSTM) recurrent neural network technique, in: 2019 International Conference on Computer, Communication, Chemical, Materials and Electronic Engineering (IC4ME2), Rajshahi, Bangladesh, 2019, pp. 1–4, https://doi.org/10.1109/IC4ME247184.2019.9036528.

[2] H. Kaur, M. Talluri, J.S. He, Get Twitter information: a collaborative Android application for big data analysis, in: 2015 International Conference on Collaboration Technologies and Systems (CTS), Atlanta, GA, 2015, pp. 483–484, https://doi.org/10.1109/CTS.2015.7210475.

[3] D. Cenni, P. Nesi, G. Pantaleo, I. Zaza, Twitter vigilance: a multi-user platform for cross-domain Twitter data analytics, NLP and sentiment analysis, in: 2017 IEEE SmartWorld, Ubiquitous Intelligence Computing, Advanced Trusted Computed, Scalable Computing Communications, Cloud Big Data Computing, Internet of People and Smart City Innovation (SmartWorld/SCALCOM/UIC/ATC/CBD-Com/IOP/SCI), San Francisco, CA, 2017, pp. 1–8, https://doi.org/10.1109/UIC-ATC.2017.8397589.

[4] H. Nurrahmi, D. Nurjanah, Indonesian Twitter cyberbullying detection using text classification and user credibility, in: 2018 International Conference on Information and Communications Technology (ICOIACT), Yogyakarta, 2018, pp. 543–548, https://doi.org/10.1109/ICOIACT.2018.8350758.

[5] A. Mangaonkar, A. Hayrapetian, R. Raje, Collaborative detection of cyberbullying behavior in Twitter data, in: 2015 IEEE International Conference on Electro/Information Technology (EIT), Dekalb, IL, 2015, pp. 611–616, https://doi.org/10.1109/EIT.2015.7293405.

[6] A.H. Alduailej, M.D. Khan, The challenge of cyberbullying and its automatic detection in Arabic text, in: 2017 International Conference on Computer and Applications (ICCA), Doha, 2017, pp. 389–394, https://doi.org/10.1109/COMAPP.2017.8079791.

[7] S.A. El Rahman, F.A. AlOtaibi, W.A. AlShehri, Sentiment analysis of Twitter data, in: 2019 International Conference on Computer and Information Sciences (ICCIS), Sakaka, Saudi Arabia, 2019, pp. 1–4, https://doi.org/10.1109/ICCISci.2019.8716464.

[8] R.J.R. Raj, P. Das, P. Sahu, Emotion classification on Twitter data using word embedding and lexicon based approach, in: 2020 IEEE 9th International Conference on Communication Systems and Network Technologies (CSNT), Gwalior, India, 2020, pp. 150–154, https://doi.org/10.1109/CSNT48778.2020.9115750.

[9] B.R. Naiknaware, S.S. Kawathekar, Prediction of 2019 Indian election using sentiment analysis, in: 2018 2nd International Conference on I-SMAC (IoT in Social, Mobile, Analytics and Cloud) (I-SMAC), Palladam, India, 2018, pp. 660–665, https://doi.org/10.1109/I-SMAC.2018.8653602.

[10] K. Bharathan, P. Deepasree Varma, Polarity detection using digital media, in: 2019 9th International Conference on Advances in Computing and Communication (ICACC), Kochi, India, 2019, pp. 181–187, https://doi.org/10.1109/ICACC48162.2019.8986172.

[11] K.S. Naveenkumar, R. Vinayakumar, K.P. Soman, Amrita-CEN–SentiDB: Twitter dataset for sentimental analysis and application of classical machine learning and deep learning, in: 2019 International Conference on Intelligent Computing and Control Systems (ICCS), Madurai, India, 2019, pp. 1522–1527, https://doi.org/10.1109/ICCS45141.2019.9065337.

CHAPTER 11

Conclusion

Dipankar Das[a], Anup Kumar Kolya[b], Soham Sarkar[b], and
Abhishek Basu[b]

[a]Dept. of Computer Science & Engineering, Jadavpur University, Kolkata, India
[b]Department of Computer Science & Engineering, RCC Institute of Information Technology, Kolkata, India

11.1 Introduction

This book aims to discuss the various applications, approaches, and classifiers for sentiment analysis by applying the techniques of computational intelligence. The versatile contributory chapters address the issues and challenges being faced in the time of Machine learning, Artificial Intelligence, Deep learning, along with embedded systems, OSI models, and advanced computing techniques in HCI are employed in a multimodal manner on text, image, and dataset from social media, the medical domain, Covid, and various Healthcare datasets.

11.2 Discussion

A model is developed in Chapter 2 based on a deep multitask learning algorithm to detect the emotion of a suicide attempter in a multitask environment. The authors have collected suicide notes from various reputed sources as a dataset. Suicide notes serve as an appropriate source of emotionally charged content for convenient study on the mental health of a suicide attempter. The authors have framed the popular emotion model to analyze the mental health of suicide attempters from emotionally charged content. The authors have used three attention-based deep-learning architectures Convolution Neural Networks (CNN), Bidirectional Gated Recurrent Units (Bi-GRU), and Bidirectional Long Short-Term Memory (Bi-LSTM) each for the single-task and the multitask problem. The CEASE Corpus is used as an experimental setup and has achieved 60.76% precision.

Deep-learning techniques are applied in Chapter 3 to address the challenges of a different area of NLP application. The authors used a benchmark dataset that is created over the decades. The authors have raised various important challenging areas in NLP to deal with the 'What', 'Why', and 'How' applications of SA. However, they are facing difficulties in the growth of research for data scarcity in their computational domain.

Chapter 4 reports on the detection of negative streaks existing in the human mind. The authors mainly surveyed the chat dataset of students. ML technology has been used to study their sentiments from their day-to-day communications and practices. The authors developed a system that is able to identify those who are facing alarmingly stressed conditions. The system is showing an encouraging result on a limited dataset.

An OSN model is developed that is used to identify the behavioral pattern of groups and individuals both directly over the periods of time on the textual and multimedia data in Chapter 5. The model consists of three parts; i.e., i) Network-Structure Analysis, ii) Text Analysis, and iii) Smartphone Sensing. Network-Structure Analysis finds the key structural properties and variance on a social network that highlights the entire growth and community behavior. Both network-communicative and community-formative behavior detects the context and polarity of textual content shared throughout online social networks. In Smartphone Sensing, the intensity and degree of addiction of an individual are identified using online social-network activity.

An outline of word embedding (Chapter 6) was presented to determine the performance of a supervised model by choosing the right set of word embeddings on a sentiment analysis task. For the evaluation of sentiment analysis, Word2Vec, GloVe, ELMo, and BERT models are used. The entire task is divided into two steps, i.e., in the 1st step the MoCE model is used for the sentiment classification and in the 2nd step, gcForest is used for polarity identification.

A medical-annotated system (Chapter 7) is developed to prepare a structured corpus from the unstructured corpus. These authors have used MedicineNet and WordNet of medical data to identify the lexicon from the medical domain. Then, they applied a machine-learning classifier to identify the medical domain and sentiment, respectively. Medical concepts have been identified in the form of uni-gram, bi-gram, tri-gram, and more than trigrams. Thereafter, they used sentiment-based ranking for summarization. Finally, the system is evaluated in the presence of a group of medical practitioners.

The summarization (Chapter 8) of various top-quality research studies, e.g., sentiment analysis, knowledge discovery, predictive analysis, topic classification, learning models, etc., have been studied in detail. The authors prepared the Covid-19 dataset to obtain better quality of work in the sentiment domain using web data. It is shown how to develop a corpus from Covid-19 tweets based on two popular feature sets; namely word-trend detection and relevant-word identification. Then, they converted such attributes into corresponding word-vector trains. The authors applied a simple Bidirectional Long Short-Term network and achieved 87.08% validation accuracy. Finally, they compared their system with existing benchmark models and datasets.

As HCI designers (Chapter 9) have understood the importance of emotion in their design, they are researching how to determine the difference between mood, emotion, and sentiment. HCI is attempting to apply the advanced computing system to experiment on how emotion can play an important role in such interactions. Hence, they wanted to develop a socio-affective computing system after identifying the interdisciplinary pattern of the problem and leveraging the findings in Cognitive Science, Human–Computer Interaction, Psychology, and Machine Learning. They firmly highlighted certain areas of interaction between HCI and emotion or sentiment such as Applications that support users in finding information on the Web, making dinner reservations, or making travel arrangements. Conversational agents are being used in healthcare, banking, and schools, which is a broad overlap of HCI and sentiment-analysis research. Furthermore, it could be found in intelligent user interfaces, user modeling, recommender systems, social networks, and affective computing.

The research work described in Chapter 10 is used to determine the effect of the Covid-19 Lockdowns on human psychology based on emotion and intense analysis. Here, Twitter is considered as the main source of data. Some traditional algorithms such as TF-IDF, Bag of Words, and Markov Chain are applied to detect various psychological effects, like Anxiety, Stress, Depression, Insecurity, Fear, Panic, etc., of these long lockdowns. Some counseling course is introduced to overcome various psychological problems.

11.3 Concluding remarks

We hope that the next generation of machines will gain more intelligence in a lucid manner to predict emotions, feelings, and all types of effects. The ongoing technologies in terms of deep learning will pave the way for the development of more nature-inspired approaches to the design of computationally intelligent sentiment-data-analysis systems that will be capable of handling semantic knowledge and act as a platform to investigate concepts not only from linguistic patterns but also from audio, video, and social signals.

Hopefully, the versatile chapters and their multifarious objectives will serve the purpose of readers of different ages and professions and help their understanding in assessing the developments of the recent trends.

Index